The U.S. Anti-Apartheid
Movement

The U.S. Anti-Apartheid Movement

Local Activism in Global Politics

Janice Love

PRAEGER SPECIAL STUDIES • PRAEGER SCIENTIFIC

New York • Philadelphia • Eastbourne, UK
Toronto • Hong Kong • Tokyo • Sydney

Library of Congress Cataloging in Publication Data

Love, Janice
  The U.S. anti-apartheid movement.

  Bibliography: p.
  Includes index.
  1. South Africa—Race Relations. 2. Civil rights—
South Africa. 3. South Africa—Relations—United States.
4. United States—Relations—South Africa. I. Title.
II. Title: U.S. anti-apartheid movement.
DT763.L66 1985   305.8′00968   85-3564
ISBN 0-03-001328-3

DT
763
.L66
1985

Published in 1985 by Praeger Publishers
CBS Educational and Professional Publishing
a Division of CBS Inc.
521 Fifth Avenue, New York, New York 10175, U.S.A.

© 1985 by Praeger Publishers

All rights reserved

56789 052 987654321
Printed in the United States of America on acid-free paper

INTERNATIONAL OFFICES
Orders from outside the United States should be sent to the appropriate address listed below. Orders
from areas not listed below should be placed through CBS International Publishing, 383 Madison Ave.,
New York, NY 10175 USA

Australia, New Zealand
Holt Saunders, Pty, Ltd., 9 Waltham St., Artarmon, N.S.W. 2064, Sydney, Australia

Canada
Holt, Rinehart & Winston of Canada, 55 Horner Ave., Toronto, Ontario, Canada M8Z 4X6

Europe, the Middle East, & Africa
Holt Saunders, Ltd., 1 St. Anne's Road, Eastbourne, East Sussex, England BN21 3UN

Japan
Holt Saunders, Ltd., Ichibancho Central Building, 22-1 Ichibancho, 3rd Floor, Chiyodaku, Tokyo, Japan

Hong Kong, Southeast Asia
Holt-Saunders Asia, Ltd., 10 Fl, Intercontinental Plaza, 94 Granville Road, Tsim Sha Tsui East, Kowloon,
Hong Kong
**Manuscript submissions should be sent to the Editorial Director, Praeger Publishers, 521 Fifth
Avenue, New York, NY 10175 USA**

To my mother, Joan B. Love,
and to my father, James N. Love

Contents

List of Tables

List of Acronyms

AACP	All African Council of Churches
ACOA	American Committee on Africa
ANC	African National Congress
CAAC	Connecticut Anti-Apartheid Committee
EMU	Eastern Michigan University
FNLA	National Front for the Liberation of Angola
ICCR	Interfaith Center on Corporate Responsibility
IDAF	International Defense and Aid Fund
IGO	International Governmental Organizations
INGOs	International Nongovernmental Organizations
IUEF	International University Exchange Fund
IRRC	Investment Responsibility Research Center
MPLA	Popular Movement for the Liberation of Angola
MSU	Michigan State University
NAACP	National Association for the Advancement of Colored People
OAU	Organization of African Unity
PAC	Pan Africanist Congress
SALC	Southern African Liberation Committee
SEC	Securities and Exchange Commission
SMO	Social Movement Organization
SWAPO	South West African People's Organization
UM	University of Michigan
UN	United Nations
UNITA	National Union for the Total Independence of Angola
WCCAA	Washtenaw County Coalition Against Apartheid
WMU	Western Michigan University
ZANU	Zimbabwe African National Union
ZAPO	Zimbabwe African People's Union

Preface

This book portrays the work of people and organizations in the United States who address a persistent global problem designated by the world community as a crime against humanity and a threat to international peace and security. The problem is apartheid.

Apartheid is the system of racial segregation and domination in South Africa. It became official policy with the National Party electoral victory in 1948, but the system has its foundations much earlier in South Africa's history (Carter 1958; Marquard 1973; Magubane 1979; O'Meara 1983; Wilson and Thompson 1983). For its architects, apartheid means "separate development," a scheme in which each of various ethnic groups has a right to its own national existence and self-fulfillment in substantial isolation from the others. In practice, however, "separate development" means that 16 percent of the country's population, the whites, live and work in 87 percent of the land, whereas the Africans, 72 percent of the population, are assigned to 13 percent of the land in fragmented areas called *bantustans.* Africans may not purchase land in white areas and may not remain there without permits. The other two population groups in the country, the Indians and Coloureds, live in segregated areas in white territories.

As of 1983, about 54 percent of the approximately 21 million Africans lived in the bantustans, and the other 46 percent, at times referred to by the government as "tempory sojourners," resided in the white areas. Over 3.5 million blacks (the term used for Africans, Coloureds, and Indians as a combined group) have been removed from white areas since 1960, and over a million more Africans have been forcibly relocated within the bantustans. Another 1.7 million blacks are under threat of removal (Africa Fund 1984).

Africans are considered to be citizens of their assigned bantustan, and thus are deemed by the government not to be citizens of South Africa. As foreigners, they are completely excluded from participation in national governmental bodies and are expected instead to exercise political participation in the governance of their homeland. Under the new constitution of South Africa adopted in 1983, Coloureds and Indians will participate with whites in a tricameral parliament with separate chambers for each racial group, but whites will retain control of effective governmental power through several constitutional provisions that accentuate their authority to the detriment of the other two groups.

South Africa is a wealthy country, but its wealth, like its political authority, is unevenly distributed. In 1975, whites earned 66.3 percent of personal disposable income; Africans accounted for 15.3 percent, Coloureds 12.8 percent, and Asians 5.6 percent (Thompson and Prior 1982, 3). These disparities also recur in other areas such as education, housing, and health care. Outside of these socio-economic indicators of apartheid's brutality, one of the greatest difficulties experienced by Africans is the separation of families. Many husbands work in and reside near the cities while their wives and children must remain in the bantustans. These families are often reunited only once or twice a year across great distances.

In recent years, both internal and external challenges to apartheid have increased. Since the mid-1970s, newly independent black regimes in Angola, Mozambique, and Zimbabwe virtually surround South Africa with neighbors antagonistic to apartheid. The Nambibian people continue to be at war with the apartheid regime because of its illegal occupation of their country. At the same time, internal unrest, defiance, and resistance have grown inside South Africa, and a number of successful acts of guerrilla sabotage have occurred. Tensions and cleavages among whites themselves have risen as a result of differences over how to respond to these challenges.

One regime response has been to modernize apartheid through the new constitution, more efficient control over the pass system and movement of labor, and certain amenities allowed to a small number of blacks. Another response has been a dramatic rise in military expenditures, an increased militarization of the society, and repeated attacks on black neighboring states. Accompanying this external military aggression has been an increase in internal repression and control through the use of detention, bannings of people and organizations, imprisonment, torture, and other officially sanctioned coercion and violence. In South Africa, the percentage of the population in prison is the highest in the world, and in the first eight months of 1983 alone, 306 people were detained without communication to family or friends. Since 1963, at least 59 people have died while in custody of the security police (Africa Fund 1983).

Apartheid is unique in the modern world since its

primary purpose is racial subjugation constitutionally enforced by a minority of whites over a majority of blacks.
Because of the system's reprehensibility, people and organizations all over the world have tried for several decades to
eliminate it.

This study examines some of these efforts. One of its
purposes is to describe systematically the anti-apartheid
movement in the United States as an arena of activism in
which people attempt to address the problem using institutions locally available. Another purpose is to evaluate the
effectiveness of this activism. Do the activists have any
impact? If so, what is it and how do they make it? Do
their efforts matter at all either to those they are trying to
help or to the forces they oppose?

For some time international relations scholars have been
concerned with the question of whether or not citizens
groups or nongovernmental organizations (NGOs) play any
important role in international affairs (Angell 1969; Feld
1972; Keohane and Nye 1972; and Rosenau 1969). This
study attempts to provide some insight on the issue by
examining the role that U.S. nongovernmental groups play
within a larger worldwide anti-apartheid movement that
includes both governments and NGOs.

The book begins by briefly describing the international
movement and then analyzing the U.S. component in greater
detail. Particular attention is paid to sanctions activities,
especially those pressuring state and local governments to
sever their financial ties to South Africa. This latest trend
has brought new participants and renewed enthusiasm to
the movement, but it has also alarmed many in business and
government. The second chapter examines the potential
impact of economic sanctions on South Africa, one of the
principal goals of the movement, and the responses by
businesses, governments, and others to this thrust of the
activists' efforts.

Chapter 3 presents a framework for analyzing and
evaluating specific movement campaigns that are detailed in
Chapters 4 and 5. These chapters provide in-depth examination of sanctions campaigns conducted in Connecticut and
Michigan as cases of recent movement activities targeting
state and local governments. Campaign processes are
analyzed to discover the factors that contributed to the
outcomes they achieved. Then, using a goals-based technique, the impact of the campaigns is evaluated. Chapter 6
compares the cases and their effectiveness.

The approach of comparing case studies of campaigns
within the context of the whole movement will provide the
reader with insights into the nature of social movements and

activism generally, anti-apartheid work specifically, and the potential impact of citizens who from their various locales attempt to contribute to international problem solving.

Acknowledgments

There are many persons who made vital contributions to this project through their aid in conducting the research itself and/or through their personal support of me.

This book developed from my doctoral thesis. My dissertation committee helped with their active involvement in formulating ideas, gathering information, reading and commenting on drafts, and giving me periodic boosts in morale. Chad Alger, chair of the committee, was particularly enthusiastic about my pursuing this topic, and he translated that enthusiasm into important, concrete support such as financial aid, contacts for interviews, letters of introduction, and numerous discussions about how to resolve specific problems. I am appreciative not only of his support for this specific project but also of him personally and professionally as a model for how to conscientiously and responsibly wed concerns for academic integrity and activism. To another member of the committee, Chuck Hermann, I am grateful for his thoughtful reflections and concentrated attention on this research in its various stages of development, his generous provision of access to the facilities of the Mershon Center at the Ohio State University, and his good humor. His active interest in and support for the totality of my well-being have been a source of strength for me throughout my graduate career, and I am privileged to have had the opportunity of such fruitful encounters with him. Don Sylvan and Bill Liddle, the other two members of the committee, helped enormously with their probing questions and attentive assistance.

Other academics who have read and commented on various portions of this thesis are Gary Marx, Bill Minter, Barry Thorne, James L. Wood, and Mayer Zald. Although I did not always heed their advice, I found it useful, and I appreciate the feedback.

Several people who have been particularly helpful in the logistics of carrying out this research are Harriet Bradham, Carla Burton, Pat Coate, Sheila Elliott, Lori Joye, and Betty Morrison. I owe them thanks for typing, careful attention to detail, and cheerful correction of my mistakes in writing letters and meeting deadlines. I am grateful to several sources of travel or office support: the Department of Government and International Studies at the University of South Carolina, the Department of Political Science at Denison University, and the PEO Educational Fund.

A number of people aided me in getting access to documentation and in interviewing respondents. Without their endorsements, letters of introduction, or phone calls, this study would have been impossible. This help came from Mia Adjali, Peggy Buchanan, Barbara Eldersveld, Christy Hoffman, Gail Hovey, Bill Howard, Bill Minter, Prexy Nesbitt, Melba Smith, Tim Smith, and David Wiley. Among these people, Gail Hovey especially spent a great deal of time securing access for me and encouraging my work. Prexy Nesbitt deserves special thanks for many thoughtful reactions to the research. In addition, I am very appreciative that the American Committee on Africa, the Interfaith Center on Corporate Responsibility, and *Africa News* let me use their files and archives to collect information.

At the heart of this investigation have been the interviews conducted with persons involved with the anti-apartheid movement. All of them are busy people with little time to respond to inquiries such as mine. I am indebted to them for their willingness to see me, to answer my questions, and to provide documents for use in the research. I am particularly grateful to the activists in Connecticut and Michigan who extended their hospitality to me and took the risk of exposing the inner workings of their organizations.

I am fortunate to have a strong support system of friends and family who always lovingly carry me through difficult periods and who joyously celebrate my little and big accomplishments. They, too, have been crucial to the successful completion of this thesis. Much love and deeply felt thanks are due to my mother, Jean Love, and my father, Jim Love, who nurtured in me a passion for racial justice and who first initiated me in activism; to Joncker Biandudi, Bill Dixon, and Beverly Purrington who provided love, humor, camaraderie, and confidence during various stages of this work; to Peter Sederberg whose love and sensitive attention have been a wonderful discovery, and without whose help in both mundance and momentous matters this book would not have been finished; and to Molly Howes whose depth of devotion and constancy of care are the source of great joy, inspiration, and sustenance in my life.

For their enormous personal and professional assistance, I am grateful to all these people and institutions.

1

An Overview of
the Anti-Apartheid
Movement

The anti-apartheid movement is a multiracial, worldwide movement consisting of governmental and nongovernmental actors operating at international, national, and subnational levels in an attempt to end racial oppression in southern Africa. At the heart of the movement are the efforts of both black and white people from the region itself. Africans in southern Africa have actively opposed white domination since they first encountered colonialism (Gerhart 1978; Karis and Carter 1972; Roux 1964), but in the last three decades they have had considerable support from outside the region. Although these activities from outside southern Africa have varied in number and intensity across time, they have consistently focused attention on the issues of racism and apartheid since the early 1950s when several organizations were founded in Britain and the United States with anti-apartheid work as their principal purpose (Shepherd 1977, 116–39). Among the events that precipitated the beginnings of persistent and organized international anti-apartheid efforts were the founding of the UN at the end of World War II, the push for self-determination and independence on the part of colonial territories, and the 1948 electoral success in South Africa of the Afrikaner's National Party, the party that instituted apartheid as official policy.

Because the activities have stretched across three decades and because they involve a wide array of organizations working in a number of different campaigns, the

1

boundaries of the movement are difficult to discern. Even the label "anti-apartheid" is somewhat misleading because movement efforts have almost always focused on white minority rule and racial oppression in all of southern Africa—including the former Portuguese territories of Mozambique, Angola, and Guinea-Bissau (West Africa), as well as Zimbabwe (formerly Rhodesia) and Namibia (South West Africa). For the purpose of this study we will define the anti-apartheid movement as consisting of those organizations and persons who endeavor to support the struggles of black people from the region in their attempts to end white minority rule. This definition excludes some who maintain that they are attempting to help end apartheid but who do not follow the initiatives or suggested action guidelines of those who have lived under racial domination. The people or organizations left out of this definition may be well intentioned and perhaps effective in their programs, or they may be fraudulent. Whichever is the case, however, they are not considered to be part of the movement because they distinguish themselves from a mainstream assertion among activists who seek to end racial oppression—that those who have experienced the oppression ultimately have the best understanding of how to end it. This assertion brings to the movement some degree of shared values and group identity, two attributes important to social movements in general. The definition is problematic in that blacks from the region are themselves not always agreed on what should be done to rid the world of apartheid. But, as will be discussed later, a great deal of consensus does exist about principal emphases for the movement.

The international character of the movement will be examined first and then will follow a more in-depth discussion of its component in the United States.

THE INTERNATIONAL ANTI-APARTHEID MOVEMENT

Outside the region of southern Africa where blacks combat racial oppression directly, the anti-apartheid movement has consisted of four principal thrusts of activity that will be examined briefly. These thrusts are: efforts to achieve sanctions; direct aid to resistance movements or the victims of white minority rule; research and publication; and educational work. Within these efforts, governmental anti-apartheid activities frequently occur in intergovernmental organizations (IGOs) such as the UN or the Organization of African Unity (OAU), but unilateral actions or collaboration with international nongovernmental organizations (INGOs) is not uncommon for a few governments. There have been impressive examples of international coordination among INGOs but the bulk of their activity has been on the national or subnational levels. Churches, students, trade unions, women's and general civil rights organizations have been prominent among the INGOs most persistent in anti-apartheid work. Several sources document the activities of the international movement (for instance, Minty 1978; Shepherd 1977; Sjollema 1982; numerous UN Center Against Apartheid publications). The discussion here will be limited, however, to a few illustrations of the major thrusts listed above. More detail will be given in a later protrayal of the U.S. anti-apartheid movement.

Sanctions Activities

Sanctions activities within the movement have been of a very broad character. This discussion will focus primarily on the efforts targeted at South Africa rather than the whole of southern Africa. Attempts have been made to isolate South Africa militarily, economically, politically, and culturally. For the most part activists have wanted to prevent any contacts with South Africans that would in any way aid or affirm apartheid. At the same time, however, they do not seek to cut off much needed assistance to the victims of racial oppression.

A significant amount of the governmental sanctions activities have been centered in the United Nations. The General Assembly first called for sanctions against South Africa in 1962. Then in 1963, the UN Security Council adopted a resolution for a voluntary embargo on military sales to South Africa. The embargo was made mandatory in 1977 following the political unrest in South Africa in 1976, the death in detention of Black Consciousness leader Steve Biko, and the extensive repressive measures taken by the South African government against dissidents.

Other actions at the UN included numerous General Assembly resolutions urging the Security Council to take effective measures against South Africa such as an oil embargo, a cessation of trade and investment, no further credits from the International Monetary Fund, comprehensive economic sanctions as well as the total isolation of the country in diplomatic, military, nuclear, cultural, academic, sports, and other relations. The year 1982 was declared the International Year of Mobilization for Sanctions against South Africa. The Security Council has so far been con-

strained from acting to isolate South Africa further because
of the veto power of its permanent members, especially the
United States and Britain. On its own, however, the
General Assembly in 1973 declared apartheid to be a "crime
against humanity," and has prevented South Africa from
taking part in plenary sessions since 1974. Instead, the
African National Congress (ANC) and the Pan Africanist
Congress (PAC), two guerrilla groups fighting apartheid,
have been given observer status in plenaries and in the
Special Committee on Apartheid (Thompson and Prior 1982,
230).

Outside the UN, governments have taken concrete
measures toward sanctions. The OAU has endorsed a trade
boycott of South Africa since 1963, and at its request, the
Arab states in OPEC placed an embargo on all oil sales to
South Africa in November 1973. From that time until 1979,
South Africa relied on Iran, an oil producer not observing
the boycott, for a reported 87 percent of its oil imports
(Myers et al. 1980, 127). The Swedish government in 1979
passed legislation prohibiting Swedish business from owning
companies in South Africa or Namibia or from owning interest in South African or Namibian companies. It further
stipulated that businesses currently investing in these
countries cannot expand their operations (Sjollema 1982,
125–27). In 1976 Norway stopped granting export credit
guarantees for trade with South Africa. Canada removed
its commercial consuls from South Africa and ended access
to its Export Development Corporation facilities for sales to
the apartheid regime in 1977. Denmark and the Netherlands
have made similar restrictions on commercial relations. The
U.S. Congress passed legislation in 1978 limiting the
Export-Import Bank's credit to South African purchasers,
and the Carter administration adopted policies curbing sales
of computers to the South African government and sales of
many other items to its police and military. Denmark's
parliament took further sanctions measures in May 1984 by
passing a resolution that bans Danish tankers from trans-
porting oil to South Africa, orders an end to all Danish
investment in South Africa, and requires the country's
power companies to prove they are reducing coal imports
from the apartheid nation. However, these governments
have shown varying degrees of enthusiasm about enforcing
these measures (Christenson 1981, 62; Myers et al. 1980,
127; Sjollema 1982; Stoltenberg 1978; *Wall Street Journal*, 29
May 1984).

Nongovernmental organizations have been at the forefront of pressing governments and businesses alike for the
severance of economic and military links with South Africa.

Such activities in the United States will be discussed in some detail in a later section of this chapter, but a few illustrations from other parts of the world will serve to demonstrate the international character of these pressures. Campaigns to end bank loans to South Africa have been prominent among groups in several countries including Belgium, Britain, Canada, Federal Republic of Germany, France, the Netherlands, Switzerland, and the United Stated. More coordination has occurred across national boundaries in bank campaigns than in most others (Baker 1979; Haslam 1981; Shepherd 1977; Sjollema 1982; von Bothmer 1981). Two well-known Christian international nongovernmental organizations (INGOs), the World Council of Churches (WCC) and the All Africa Council of Churches (AACC), have withdrawn their monies from banks making loans to South Africa, as have many organizations and individuals within countries where bank campaigns have been conducted (Sjollema 1982; UN Centre, March 1978).

NGO efforts to end trade with and investment in South Africa have occurred in all the countries mentioned above as well as in Australia, New Zealand, and Sweden. Much of the governmental action to curb economic relations with South Africa illustrated earlier, especially in the West, has come after intense activist campaigns to achieve such measures or more. INGOs that have gone on record as favoring some form of economic sanctions against South Africa are: the World Council of Churches, the World Peace Council, the All Africa Council of Churches, the International Confederation of Free Trade Unions, the World Confederation of Labor, the World Federation of Trade Unions, the Women's International League for Peace and Freedom, The Organization of African Trade Union Unity, the International League for Human Rights, and the Nordic Trade Union Council (UN Commission on Human Rights 1978). There is a great deal of cooperation between the UN and INGO sanctions efforts in international as well as domestic campaigns. For example, the Center Against Apartheid monitors and encourages sanctions activities by providing activists with publications, research, publicity, and cosponsorship of conferences and receptions.

In attempting to limit or end economic relations with South Africa these various organizations have responded to the wishes of a number of prominent black leaders who have indicated their support for the economic isolation of South Africa. To oppose foreign investment in South Africa is a crime under the Terrorism Act punishable by penalties ranging from five years imprisonment to the death sentence. Therefore, resistance leaders in South Africa must be cautious about advocating the cessation of trade and investment. Despite the danger they face, significant voices favoring sanctions have been heard within the country. Table 1-1 lists South Africans who have made known their support for economic disengagement from South Africa. To get around the legal problems, their statements have often come in the form of the following illustration

> I firmly believe if disinvestment could start it could bring a hastened end to apartheid. Perhaps an exodus of American companies from South Africa could bring change. (Tomazile Botha, Africa Fund 1980)

Such advocates fully realize that if South Africa suffers economic hardship, blacks within the country will suffer disproportionately. Nevertheless they seek sanctions because they believe that economic pressures can contribute to the demise of the apartheid regime. This argument was made by the South African Black People's Convention Congress statement in 1972:

> Advocates of the continued investment claim that if foreign investors withdraw this would result in large scale unemployment of Blacks. Withdrawal can only mean the downfall of the Vorster regime. . . . Black people in general are prepared to suffer any consequences if this means ultimate Black freedom. . . . Foreign investors claim their presence in this country contributes toward the development of Black community. This claim is disputed by the reality of the Black experience in this country. We resolve therefore. . . . To call upon foreign investors to disengage themselves from this white-controlled exploitative system. (Africa Fund 1980)

Although the prevailing opinion among resistance leaders inside and outside the country appears to favor trade and investment embargos, there are black leaders in the country who oppose sanctions. Four notable ones are: Lucy Mvubelo, Secretary General of the National Union of Clothing Workers and Vice President of the Trade Union Council of South Africa; Chief Gatsha Buthelezi, head of the largely Zulu-based Inkatha movement and head of the KwaZulu homeland; David Thebehali, the mayor of Soweto; and Percy Qoboza, former editor of the *World*, the news-

TABLE 1-1. South African Advocates for Economic Sanctions Against South Africa

---

1. The African National Congress; banned in 1960
2. Steve Biko, Black Consciousness Movement leader; killed in police custody in 1977.
3. Black People's Convention; banned in 1977.
4. Thozamile Botha, leader of the 1979 strike at the Port Elizabeth Ford Motor Company; detained and banned in 1980, subsequently escaped into exile.
5. Christian Institute in South Africa; banned in 1976.
6. Chief Albert J. Luthuli, former president of the African National Congress and Nobel Prize winner in 1964; deceased.
7. The Pan-Africanist Congress; banned in 1960.
8. Oliver Tambo, Acting President General of the African National Congress; in exile.
9. Bishop Desmond Tutu, General Secretary of the South African Council of Churches.
10. Donald Woods, former editor of the East London (South Africa) Daily Dispatch; banned in 1977, now in exile.

Sources: Africa Fund 1980, ICCR 1979, and Schmidt 1980.

paper with the largest circulation among blacks in South Africa; Mr. Qoboza was also a member of the Soweto Committee of Ten and was detained by the police in 1977. The *World* was banned in 1977 as well (Myers et al. 1980, 51–52).

Despite the opposition of sanctions by some blacks, there is wide recognition of a consensus in favor of an economic embargo developing among most black leaders. In a March 1978 diplomatic cable, U.S. Ambassador William Bowdler reported:

. . . that blacks who reflect on foreign investment as an issue are now roughly divided between those favoring disinvestment and those who would like to see it remain in instances where it contributes to black aspirations directly and in the near term. A smaller segment continues to favor investment on any basis. . . . With radicalization of black attitudes, [the] tendency to call for disinvestment grows stronger, . . . [the] role of American firms here will become increasingly controversial and [the] rationale for continued presence will seem less

> and less persuasive to growing numbers of blacks. (Myers et al. 1980, 52)

The economic sanctions debate has been a controversial aspect of the anti-apartheid movement. The potential for sanctions to aid in bringing about an end to apartheid will be evaluated in the next chapter. The foregoing discussion demonstrates, however, that calls for sanctions have been made repeatedly over the last 20 years and proposals for punitive economic measures against apartheid have gained legitimacy in many quarters.

Economic or military sanctions are not the only kind of international isolation sought for South Africa. Activists attempted with mixed outcomes to persuade entertainers and tourists from visiting the white dominated country, and South African sports interactions worldwide have been the focus of major anti-apartheid campaigns in several countries. Believing that sports are an important channel through which South Africa can win friends and supporters around the world, governments, NGOs, and IGOs have actively sought, with a high degree of success, to keep South Africa from participating in a wide range of sports events and to persuade athletes of other countries from visiting South Africa. For example, due to international pressures, especially from African governments, South Africa was excluded from the 1968 Olympic games and was expelled from the Olympic Movement itself in 1972. And, in a three-year campaign with demonstrations that at one point brought out more than 50,000 people, British anti-apartheid activists achieved the cancellation of the 1970 South African cricket tour in Britain (Lapchick 1977, 9–14).

In other acts of isolating apartheid, the World Alliance of Reformed Churches, having declared apartheid a theological heresy, suspended the white Dutch Reformed Churches of South Africa from membership in 1982. The Lutheran World Federation took similar action in 1984 against two small white southern African Lutheran churches for failing to unite with predominantly black Lutheran churches in the region.

These illustrations serve to demonstrate that a central component of the international movement has been efforts to cut the apartheid regime off from any support or affirmation it may receive from around the world. While working for sanctions of various kinds against white minority rule, however, many organizations in the movement also have endeavored to give direct aid to the victims of racial oppression. We turn now to a discussion of that important thrust in the movement.

Direct Aid

Direct aid has come in several forms, the bulk of it being
military and nonmilitary assistance to the movements that
are or have been engaged in guerrilla war against the white
minority regimes. The oldest and strongest of the groups
fighting apartheid is the African National Congress (ANC),
founded in 1912 within the country and outlawed by the
government in 1960, at which point it began operating
underground and from outside the country. Among its
leaders have been Chief Albert Luthuli, Nobel Peace Prize
winner in 1961, Nelson Mandela, serving (since 1964) a life
sentence, and Oliver Tambo, presently the head of the
organization. Apparently in some disarray at this point,
the second group claiming to be engaged in warfare against
the apartheid regime is the Pan-Africanist Congress (PAC),
founded in 1959 from a dissident group within the ANC.
Its first and most renowned campaign was a nonviolent
demonstration at Sharpeville to protest pass laws in 1960.
Police responded to the demonstrators with gun fire and 67
Africans were killed; 186 were wounded. The Sharpeville
incident was the turning point for both groups in their
decisions to begin guerrilla actions against the regime.
Robert Sobukwe was the most famous of PAC leaders and he
remained in detention or under ban until his death in 1978.

There are or have been numerous other guerrilla movements from other southern African countries. The South
West People's Organizations (SWAPO) is the group fighting
the South African government for control over Namibia. In
the conflict over Zimbabwe both the Zimbabwe African
National Union (ZANU) and the Zimbabwe African People's
Union (ZAPU) received aid from abroad. In a coalition in
the last years of the war, these groups together formed the
Patriotic Front. In the wars in the former Portuguese
colonies of Mozambique, Angola, and Guinea Bissau, the
major groups were: Mozambique—FRELIMO (Front for the
Liberation of Mozambique); Angola—MPLA (Popular Movement for the Liberation of Angola), FNLA (National Front
for the Liberation of Angola), and UNITA (National Union
for the the Total Independence of Angola); and Guinea
Bissau—PAIGC (African Independence Party of Guinea and
Cape Verde). These movements, some of which are now
governments, received assistance from both governmental
and nongovernmental sources.

Direct aid from the international anti-apartheid movement has had other targets as well. For example, aid has
been granted for scholarships for black students (refugee
and nonrefugee); legal defense or other aid for prisoners,

detainees, exiles, or refugees; financial support for the families of these persons; and refuge and relocation for deserters from the regimes' armed forces.

African governments and especially the frontline states—those countries bordering the white minority controlled territories—have made some of the most important contributions to those resisting racial domination. The governments of Tanzania and Zambia, for example, have harbored refugees, accepted exiles, and given some of the guerrilla groups a base from which to operate. The newly independent countries of Angola and Mozambique joined the ranks of the frontline states once the Portuguese colonial rule ended in the mid-1970s. More recently Zimbabwe joined the group. The governments in these countries have suffered frequent retaliation by the South African military for the physical support they provide to those who are in resistance to apartheid. The South African government appears determined to disrupt their political and economic stability so they cannot provide a great deal of assistance to the guerrilla movements. After enduring repeated attacks on their territory and enormous economic hardship, Angola and Mozambique have made agreements with South Africa to lessen their support for SWAPO and the ANC (respectively) in exchange for a cessation of South Africa's aggression. These accords have caused some friction among the frontline states and the guerrilla groups, and the full implication of their implementation is not yet known.

The OAU and nonfrontline African states have also given material aid to the guerrillas. Nigeria and Algeria recently gave $1 million each to the ANC. Egypt, Gabon, the Ivory Coast, and Senegal have also extended assistance (Karis 1983/84, 398).

The governments of the Soviet Union and the People's Republic of China have been responsible for major amounts of military assistance to the liberation movements in southern Africa. As is typical of the rivalry between these two powers, when one supports a particular group, the other will support a rival group. The Soviet Union has had close ties to the ANC in the South Africa conflict, SWAPO in Namibia, ZAPU in Zimbabwe, and the MPLA in Angola. China has at various times been most allied with the PAC in South Africa, ZANU in Zimbabwe, UNITA in Angola,[1] and FRELIMO in Mozambique.

Western governments have also given funds to guerrilla movements or other victims of white minority rule, and they often channel such monies through national and international NGOs. The Scandinavian governments are the largest contributors. For example, in 1982 Sweden provided $4.2

million and Norway provided $1.65 million to the ANC (Karis 1983/84, 398). Other Western governments, such as the Netherlands, Austria, Australia, Italy, West Germany, Canada, and the United States have also provided assistance in varying amounts to various organizations (Shepherd 1977, 130–34).

The UN has been an important source of funds and other aid for guerrilla movements and others from southern Africa through several programs established in the 1960s as a result of African and Asian governments' pressures. Three of these programs are the Trust Fund for South Africa, the Educational Programe for Southern Africa, and the Fund for Namibia. From 1965 to 1980, the Trust Fund for South Africa disbursed 95 grants totaling $10.47 million (United Nations 1981, 1). The UN also has a Special Committee on Apartheid, a committee of the General Assembly, and its staff counterpart in the Secretariat, the Center Against Apartheid. Through these structures the UN stays in close touch with persons in resistance to white minority rule.

NGO and INGO direct aid has also been noteworthy. The International University Exchange Fund (IUEF), founded by European student movements in the 1960s, existed primarily for providing scholarship aid and training for Africans in southern Africa to remain and work with resistance movements. It also granted funds to southern Africa student movements for research, publication, and financial aid. The Black People's Convention, and Black Allied Workers' Union and political detainees were also recipients of IUEF aid. With an annual budget over $300,000, its funds came primarily from Scandinavia, the Netherlands, and Canada (Shepherd 1977, 127). This organization was infiltrated by South African government agents in the 1970s, and since then the World University Service has sponsored a similar scholarship program but not on the scale of the IUEF.

Legal aid and support for the families of prisoners and detainees is provided by the International Defense and Aid Fund (IDAF) begun in 1956 and now with branches in over a dozen countries. A great deal of the IDAF budget comes from Scandinavian governments and from the UN trust funds for southern Africa. In this way the organization is an important conduit for governmental aid. Shepherd asserts that IDAF has shown remarkable ingenuity in getting assistance to families of imprisoned Africans and in hiring counsel for their defense (1977, 124–25). The International Commission of Jurist, Amnesty International, and the International League for Human Rights have also been significant contributors to the defense of the rights of prisoners in southern Africa.

Church-related INGOs such as the World Council of Churches, the Lutheran World Federation, and the All Africa Council of Churches have provided assistance to refugees and scholarships for students. In addition, in 1970 the WCC founded a Programe to Combat Racism with one of its purposes being to give grants to guerrilla movements for educational, medical, publication, or other humanitarian purposes. From 1970 to 1980, the WCC gave over $2 million to movements from all of the southern Africa countries (Sjollema 1982, 130–31). The AACC has a similar program, too.

Trade union INGOs also have provided direct aid to victims of white minority rule. Among these have been the International Confederation of Free Trade Unions, the World Federation of Trade Unions (Shepherd 1977, 128). and the Organization of African Trade Union Unity (UN Center Against Apartheid, March 1980). Other INGOs making financial or material contributions to southern Africans are: Afro-Asian People's Solidarity Organization; All-Africa Students Union, International Union of Students; World Federation of Democratic Youth; and World University Service (UN Center Against Apartheid, March 1978).

NGOs in many countries have participated in direct aid programs through the INGOs discussed above or through more localized organizations. Much of this aid comes from relief organizations, churches, students, and local or national anti-apartheid organizations in western countries, but significant numbers of NGOs from non-Western countries, such as Eastern Europe, give assistance as well (UN Center Against Apartheid, March 1978).

Often many of the organizations involved in direct aid are the same ones attempting to achieve sanctions against South Africa, but this is not always the case. The other two major components of movements activities, research/publication and educational work, also are carried out frequently by the organizations already mentioned.

Research/Publication and Education

In order to raise money for direct aid or to convince people and organizations to join the efforts to isolate South Africa, organizations in the anti-apartheid movement do a great deal of educational work about southern Africa, racism, and the international support apartheid receives. To back up these educational and other activities, there is a vast amount of research and publication, including film-making, being conducted in a relatively few organizations, both governmental and nongovernmental. In addition, organizations and individuals who are hesitant to campaign actively for sanctions or direct aid (for example, academic associations), sometimes make important contributions through research or educational work.

These components of the movement, however, are rarely ends in and of themselves. More often they are support services for activism, and in this respect they play a vital role in the movement. As will be demonstrated later in this study, the movement's credibility, legitimacy, and success depend in part on the depth and accuracy of its members' understanding of those forces they want to oppose.

THE U.S. ANTI-APARTHEID MOVEMENT

The anti-apartheid movement in the United States is composed primarily of nongovernmental groups whose activities signify a rejection of institutional cooperation with apartheid and thus a rejection of the major thrusts of U.S. government and business policies toward southern Africa. U.S. governmental policy makers did not pay much attention to southern Africa until the early 1960s. Since then U.S. foreign policy has fluctuated between virtually embracing white minority regimes and applying fairly mild punitive measures against them. The closest embrace between the U.S. government and apartheid has come under the Reagan administration's policy of constructive engagement. The Nixon administration, however, also cultivated close ties to Portugal at a time when that colonial power refused to allow independence in Angola, Mozambique, and Guinea Bissau. The most punitive measures were achieved under Carter with his administration's support for the 1977 UN mandatory arms embargo and the continuation of economic sanctions against Rhodesia even after some blacks had joined that government. These latter sanctions had been instituted in 1968 under the Johnson administration at the request of Britain in the Security Council. Even though on occasion the U.S. government has issued verbal condemnations of apartheid or applied some negative pressure, never has it used repeated or consistent strong measures against the white minority regimes while at the same time building close ties to or identification with the guerrilla movements and newly independent black states in southern Africa. It is this last option that is most appealing to anti-apartheid groups in the United States.

U.S. businesses operate in an environment in which officially the U.S. government neither encourages nor discourages commerce with or in South Africa. Despite this official stance, several arms of the government, such as the Export-Import Bank, the Department of Agriculture, and the Commerce Department, have facilitated business relations between the two countries. However, the business climate in South Africa has been on the whole so attractive that companies need no prodding from the government to help them see that a lot of money can be made there. Especially in the last two decades, U.S. banks and corporations have become increasingly important business partners for South Africa. The extent and nature of U.S. trade and investment in South Africa will be discussed in the next section of this chapter, but important to note here is that the anti-apartheid movement in the United States has generally opposed U.S. business involvement in the white minority controlled nations.

Going against the flow of governmental and business relations in southern Africa, anti-apartheid sentiment and activities have been evident in the United States at least since 1912 when the National Association of Colored People (NAACP) played a part in helping to organize the African National Congress (Hauck et al. 1983, 8). The Council on African Affairs, a radical, black-led, and interracial organization, was also devoted to the liberation of Africans in these early years (Lynch 1978). Then the American Committee on Africa (ACOA) was founded in 1953 out of a group concerned with supporting black South African pass law resisters. Thus, some organizational groundwork had already been laid when apartheid became a prominent item on the agenda of others concerned about human rights and racial justice.

The catalyst for more widespread and sustained attention to white minority rule were incidents like those at Sharpeville when South African police opened fire on a group of unarmed protesters. As is the case in other countries, every time there is a major crisis or important event in southern Africa that dominates world news, the U.S. anti-apartheid movement is renewed and gains new adherents. There are persons in leadership in the movement who have been active since the 1950s when the previously mentioned efforts to support the Defiance Campaigns against pass laws within South Africa began. New leaders and participants were infused in the early 1960s in response to Sharpeville and then again in the early 1970s in response to the escalating warfare in Angola, Mozambique, and Guinea Bissau. More adherents got involved in the late

1970s after a series of explosive events: The 1976 riots triggered by the protests of school children in Soweto, an African township, in which at least 1,000 people died, most of them shot by police; the 1977 police murder of Steve Biko, a leader of the Black Consciousness movement; and the 1977 attempt by the government to silence its critics through a series of detentions of individuals and bannings of people and organizations.

During these several decades of fairly concentrated anti-apartheid work, many of the activists were simultaneously involved in or concerned about the anti-war, civil rights, black power, or corporate responsibility movements that were gaining strength in the country. Thus as anti-apartheid efforts gained momentum, its participants interacted with, drew insights from, and influenced other social movements while at the same time having their own strong organizational basis. Shepherd (1977) documents much of the movement's early history and Hauck et al. (1983) also lend insights into its activities.

Within the United States, the movement has embodied the same four major thrusts of activity—sanctions, direct aid, education, and research/publication—that characterize the international movement. Table 1-2 outlines these four types of activity as manifested in the United States, their targets, their strategies and tactics, and the types of groups involved. Table 1-3 lists the national organizations that lead the U.S. movement. Although not specifically mentioned in this list, major U.S. Christian organizations, especially ones in Protestant denominations, have frequently provided the bulk of human and material resources to sustain both the movement and many of these national organizations.

This study will focus primarily on economic sanctions activities, but first will come some illustrations of the other thrusts of activities. Shepherd (1977) gives further description of specific U.S. campaigns (prior to 1977).

• In May 1972, 20,000 black people marched in Washington to express solidarity with southern Africa liberation movements.

• In the summer of 1976, the Women's Division, Board of Global Ministries, United Methodist Church sponsored courses on southern Africa in various "Schools of Mission" held across the country in which approximately 28,000 people (mostly women) spent three days to a week (depending on the particular program in their area) involved in intensive study on southern Africa.

TABLE 1-2. Major Thrusts of Activity in the U.S. Anti-Apartheid Movement

Type of Activity	Primary Targets of the Activity	Activists' Strategy/Tactic	Type of Group Involved
Sanctions	Governmental organizations--mainly legislatures National State Local	Lobbying Letters and calls to decision makers Negotiations with decision makers Extended discussions between groups of activists and groups of decision makers	Churches Local Regional National
	Businesses--as direct and indirect targets Financial corporations Nonfinancial corporations	Provision of testimony, research, and expertise to decision makers Press conferences, public statements, and other media work Victory celebrations	University groups Students Faculty/staff
	Nongovernmental institutional investors Universities Churches Labor Unions Private Individual Trusts	Gaining access to and publicly releasing secret documents Attendance at important events, such as shareholder meetings Demonstrations, picketing, and other direct action: shareholder resolutions; (re businesses, sports, and entertainers) boycotts; (re businesses, esp. banks) withdrawing funds	Labor unions Local National Black organizations Local Regional National
	Sports organizations and individual athletes Entertainers and artists		Other community groups (such as women's groups)

16

Academic associations and scholars

Groups organized spe-
cifically for
anti-apartheid work
Local
National

Direct Aid

Governmental organizations
International
National (executive and
legislative)

Nongovernmental groups
and individuals
Blacks
Churches
Students
Neighborhoods/communities

Lobbying
Letters and calls to decision makers
Demonstrations
Fund raising benefits (such as
concerts)
Direct solicitation of funds
Harboring and relocating refugees
Sponsoring teams of observers for
trails, other proceedings in
southern Africa

Groups organized spe-
cifically for
anti-apartheid work
Local
National

Education

Those being mobilized into anti-
apartheid campaigns

Leaders of campaigns

Decision makers in some of the
targeted organizations

Show films
Provide speakers (from local,
community, or national
organizations, or southern
Africa)
Teach-ins
Seminars
Leaflets
Demonstrations
Distribution of publications

Groups organized spe-
cifically for
anti-apartheid work
Local
National

17

TABLE 1-2. Continued

Type of Activity	Primary Targets of the Activity	Activists' Strategy/Tactic	Type of Group Involved
Research/Publi-cation/Media	Those being mobilized into anti-apartheid campaigns	Publication of pamphlets, newsletter, magazines, books Production of firms and records	Groups organized spe-cifically for anti-apartheid work
	Leaders of campaigns	Research on economic, military, polit-ical, and social conditions in southern Africa; business relations between southern Africa and the West; other kinds of relations between southern Africa and the West; anti-apartheid strategies and tactics	
	Decision makers in some of the targeted organizations		

18

TABLE 1-3. U.S. National Anti-Apartheid Organizations

Those with anti-apartheid work as their <u>primary focus</u>:

1. American Committee on Africa (ACOA), New York City
2. American Coordinating Committee for Equality in Sports and Society, (ACCESS), New York City
3. International Defense and Aid Fund for Southern Africa--U.S. Committee (IDAF), Cambridge, MA
4. South African War Resisters (SAMRAF), New York City
5. TransAfrica, Washington, D.C.*
6. Washington Office on Africa (WOA), Washington, D.C.

Those with anti-apartheid work as a <u>major program</u> focus (partial list):

7. American Friends Service Committee--Southern Africa Program (AFSC), Philadelphia
8. Association of Concerned Africa Scholars, East Lansing, MI
9. Congressional Black Caucus, Washington, D.C.*
10. Interfaith Center on Corporate Responsibility (ICCR), New York City
11. Lawyers' Committee for Civil Rights Under Law--Southern Africa Project, Washington, D.C.
12. National Black United Front, New York City*

---

*Predominately black organization.

• In 1983 the on-going aid programs of the Africa Fund contributed about $75,000 to aid for Namibian refugees in Angola and provided a number of small grants totaling over $20,000 to aid African refugees in the United States; in 1981 the Fund shipped over a half ton of penicillin to Namibian refugee centers; in 1977 it sent more than $80,000 worth of donated medicines and sterilizer and boiler parts to the Mozambique Health Ministry (Africa Fund 1977, 1981 and 1983).

• The Namibian Medical Refugee Aid Drive in Minnesota, in cooperation with the Africa Fund, sent $50,000 worth of medicines, equipment and books to Namibian refugees in 1981 (Africa Fund 1981).

• The Southern Africa Project of the Lawyer's Committee for Civil Rights Under Law aided, in full or in part, over 26 legal cases regarding South Africa or Namibia in 1983. The Project paid lawyers' fees and other litigation costs, supplied legal memoranda, and sent legal observers to trials in South Africa. Among the cases were issues such as the right of Africans to remain residents in their traditional villages rather than being forcedly relocated by the government, the right of residents in the African homeland of Ciskei to remain free from state harassment, and the right of peaceful black political and trade union organizations and their leaders to exist (Southern Africa Project 1983).

• In 1980, a broad-based coalition of over one hundred civil rights, anti-apartheid, political, religious, and sports groups was formed to mobilize protest and direct action against a 1981 tour of a South African rugby team, the Springboks. The group, Stop the Apartheid Rugby Tour (SART), organized protests in New York, Chicago, Los Angeles, Rochester, N.Y., Washington, D.C., and Racine, Wisconsin. Upwards of two thousand people gathered in the rain for a demonstration in Albany, N.Y. against a game that attracted three hundred spectators. After these protests and demonstrations, New York City Mayor Koch and the Chicago City Council withdrew permission for the use of facilities in their cities for the Springboks. Two hundred members of Congress voted for a Sense of the Congress Resolution calling for the tour to be cancelled. Top officials in Rochester, Los Angeles, Newark, New York State, and Illinois spoke out against the tour. There were three national television shows on the protest over the tour. In the end, the tour experienced five cancellations and two secret matches. A major leader of the SART protests received numerous threats (tied to his SART activities) by phone, had a car destroyed, his home broken into, and for a month was forced to hire bodyguards for constant protection for himself and his family (Lapchick 1981).

• In 1979, the Institute for International Education, financed by private donations, began a program of scholarships for black South African students (not exiles or refugees) to study in colleges and universities in the United States. In 1980, the U.S. Congress passed legislation that provided $8 million over two years for this program (*New York Times,* 31 December 1982).

• TransAfrica has given the press confidential documents from the Reagan administration made available from sources inside the government. One such leak came in 1981 in State Department papers summarizing formal meetings between administration and South African officials. Another exposure came in 1982 from a secret CIA document analyzing recent acts of sabotage by the ANC and its growing popularity (*Africa News,* 1 November 1982; Leonard 1983, 223–26).

• As a part of the cultural and entertainment boycott,

Ben Vereen, Gladys Knight and the Pips, Tony Bennett, The Floaters, Phyllis Hyman, The Jacksons, Elton John, Roberta Flack, Stevie Wonder, Kool and the Gang, Dionne Warwick, and Quincy Jones among others have declared that they will not perform in South Africa or the homelands.

· In 1982, as a part of a world-wide campaign involving mayors from 54 countries, 33 mayors across the United States signed an appeal to the South African government for the immediate and unconditional release of Nelson Mandela, president of the ANC who has been imprisoned since 1962 (UN Center Against Apartheid, August 1982).

These illustrations are not a comprehensive cataloguing of anti-apartheid events in recent years, but they do serve to give some glimpses on the wide variety of activities and groups working on research and publication, education, direct aid, and non-economic sanctions. Economic sanctions efforts, however, have been the dominant thrust in the movement in the United States and we now turn to a discussion of this work.

Economic Sanctions Activities

Most anti-apartheid activists and sympathizers agree gener-ally that U.S. corporate involvement serves to buttress racial domination by whites in South Africa, Namibia and formerly in Angola, Mozambique, and Zimbabwe. Most would advocate some form of economic pressure against South Africa, that is, an end to new investments or loans, an end to trade with the military or police, no economic cooperation with the government, or total sanctions, a cessation of all trade, investment, and/or bank loans.

Activists have attempted to influence U.S. business to end their dealings with South Africa through methods that target the business directly and those that target them indirectly. With the latter, the activists try to convince a third party to help the movement achieve corporate economic disengagement. The third party is usually an institution with significant holdings or investments but has on occasion also been the U.S. government. The institutional investors targeted have included churches, labor unions, universi-ties, student associations, foundations, insurance compa-nies, and state and local governments. Sometimes these institutions themselves become important movement partici-pants, creating a new constituency within the movement. This has been the case most often with churches. Histori-cally some of the most active groups have been in the

Episcopal Church, the United Church of Christ, and the United Methodist Church.

Various strategies and tactics used to influence all of these targets on the sanctions question are listed in Table 1-2. The choice of strategy has been a contentious issue in this thrust of the movement. The dispute is basically between the use of shareholder resolutions or other methods that involve influencing business policies "from the inside" versus a withdrawal of investments or other tactics that end connections to business that have operations in South Africa. The first strategy is often labeled the shareholder activism approach and the second is called the divestment approach.

Shareholder activism has been used in a wide range of issues in addition to apartheid and in many respects is peculiar to the United States. As Vogel (1978) points out, advocates of this method of achieving corporate responsibility maintain that those who are affected by the business should help to shape its policies; that is, business decisions should be made more public by having greater citizen participation in their formulation whether the policy is about consumer product safety, the manufacture of weapons, the hiring of women and ethnic minorities, or involvement in South Africa. The use of shareholder resolutions to confront corporations in their in annual meetings became popular in the early 1970s. An individual, group, or institution that holds stock in the corporations submits a policy resolution for vote by all the stockholders. These resolutions rarely receive more than 5 percent of the votes, but for many years a Securities and Exchange Commission (SEC) ruling required only 3 percent to allow a resolution to be reintroduced in subsequent years. Beginning in 1983, however, the SEC ruled that a resolution must get 5 percent of the votes in the first year to be reintroduced in the second year, 8 percent in the second year, and 10 percent in the third year. As a consequence, activists have celebrated victories when they receive more than 5 percent approval for their resolutions.

Despite its backing away from earlier rulings more supportive of shareholder activism, Vogel (1978) maintains that the SEC has been of great help in asserting the rights of stockholders to participate in setting corporate policy. This is why the strategy is most popular in the United States; unlike government standards in other countries, the SEC has in some respects forced U.S. corporations to take these activists' efforts seriously.

Church organizations were the first actively and persistently to pursue corporate responsibility issues regarding

South Africa, and the Interfaith Center on Corporate Responsibility (ICCR, formerly the Corporate Information Center) coordinates and organizes most of these church activities. Since 1971, ICCR has constructed social profiles on corporations, explored alternative investment opportunities, and guided particular churches in filing resolutions. The resolutions filed do not always request that the corporation or bank withdraw its operations. Sometimes they ask for policies such as a ban on new investment, no sales to the government, police or military, an end to joint investment with the government, or adherence to particular labor practices. Sometimes they simply ask for disclosures of information that activists have been unable to acquire elsewhere.

In recent years churches have been joined by other institutional investors such as universities or state pension funds. For example, in early 1982, the American Lutheran Church and eight other organizations, including the California Public Employee Retirement System and the California Teachers Retirement System, sponsored a resolution to prevent Xerox corporation from expanding its operations in South Africa or selling its products to the police and military. With the combined support of these eight sponsors the resolution received an unusually high vote of 10 percent representing about 1.5 million shares (*Africa News* 31 May 1982). Hauck et al. (1983) point out the growth of shareholder activity among foundations and insurance companies, too.

Frequently a part of shareholder activism has been dialogue sessions between activists and/or their sympathizers and corporate executives in order that activists can express concerns, negotiate some acceptable policy, or get better information about business behavior. In some rare cases (and not on South Africa-related issues), shareholder suits have been filed against corporations as a means to achieve activists goals.

Although on the whole corporate executives reacted very defensively to shareholder challenges in the early years of this approach, many now take them more in stride and even initiate dialogue sessions themselves. Many stay in close touch with organizations like the Investor Responsibility Research Center in Washington, D.C. (IRRC) to find out the latest trends in institutional investors' corporate responsibility activities. In his analysis of the corporate responsibility movement generally, Vogel (1978) suggests that on the whole shareholder resolutions have been quite modest in their demands and that corporations typically have responded in one of four ways: on rare occasion management has endorsed the activist resolution; they have negotiated compromises with activists to have the resolution withdrawn voluntarily; they have successfully opposed the resolution and then declared a policy change that essentially does what the resolution requires; and they have simply and steadfastly refused any compromise (Vogel 1978, 198).

In summarizing the effects of shareholder pressures, Vogel asserts that the most important impact has been, along with other significant pressures, in setting the agenda in governmental processes. "The extent to which demands addressed to the corporation anticipate the substance of subsequent government regulations of business is indeed striking," including the southern Africa cases of corporate compliance with the embargo against Rhodesia, the decision of the Department of Commerce (under Carter) to restrict the sale of technology to the South African government, and the role of the United States in Angola during Portuguese rule (Vogel 1978, 31). Other than the unintended indirect impact on business through subsequent governmental regulation, Vogel maintains that the challenges have had mostly procedural rather than substantive effects on the corporations in question.

One of the effects of the shareholder approach frequently criticized by those engaged in divestment efforts is the offering of a more palatable policy option to institutional investors who are the targets of divestment campaigns. The divestment approach seeks to have investors or consumers disengage from all businesses that refuse to end their ties to South Africa, and any policy short of complete withdrawal is considered too compromising. Divestment activists have attempted to get churches, universities, states, and other institutions to sell their shares or withdraw their patronage from banks and corporations that do business in or with South Africa. Sometimes the institutional investor's response to pressures has been not to disengage from the business but to pledge to join in shareholder resolutions against management. Divestment advocates assert that shareholder resolutions and dialogue sessions may have some limited utility in the movement, especially for purposes such as disclosure of corporate practices, but they resent that such tactics have diverted activist energies away from a drive towards total disengagement and that corporate responsibility actions have taken the wind out of the sails of some divestment campaigns, especially among church and university investors. Many shareholder activists are uncomfortable and even dismayed that institutional investors sometimes take shareholder resolutions as a means for getting out from under pressure or, even worse, as an excuse for virtual inaction. From the point of view of these activists, such response is completely inadequate. Nonetheless, if institutions are resolute about not withdrawing investments from corporations involved in South Africa, they should have other policy options, these activists contend. Under such conditions, they believe shareholder resolutions and similar efforts are credible and reasonable. When this dispute is pushed to its sharpest or perhaps most extreme form, however, divestment advocate often disagree fundamentally with shareholder activists about the long-term prospects for reforming private profit-making organizations into "good citizens" accountable to the public interest.

Despite the dispute among activists regarding the divestment and corporate responsibility approaches, there is a great deal of cooperation among individuals and leaders in the anti-apartheid movement across this division. For example, ICCR has played an important role in supplying research and information to divestment proponents and in securing church cooperation in campaigns to withdraw accounts from banks making loans to South Africa. And, despite the opportunity to opt for the corporate responsibility approach, many institutional investors were convinced to take divestment policy positions instead. Tables 1–4 through 1–6 list the South Africa sanctions-related activities (including divestment) of U.S. churches; Tables 1–7 and 1–8 show the results of campus divestment activities; and Tables 1–9 and 1–10 display labor unions and black organizations' actions as being total or partial. Total means that the action affects all monies or investments. Partial means that some of the funds are affected while others are not. Further discussion of the impact of this activity is in the next chapter.

Churches were the earliest targets of divestment activists and quickly became involved as participants in the movement. Shepherd (1977) and Vogel (1978) both discuss in some detail the first major bank campaign in the United States in 1966, led primarily by students. Protestant denominations withdrew an estimated $23 million in deposits from ten banks, including First National City Bank (now Citibank), to protest the banks' policies of making loans to South Africa. After a great deal of publicity surrounding these protests, the banks did not renew the loan arrangements with South Africa on the pretext that South Africa no longer needed the money. In fact, however, the banks began to make secret agreements for loans. The secret loans were uncovered in 1973 when activists learned through the "Frankfurt Documents" sent to ICCR that

TABLE 1-4. National Church Organizations' Divestment Actions

Church (Year)	Bank Accounts Closed		Bank Investments Withdrawn		Corporate Investments Withdrawn		Divestment Policy Partial/Total
	Banks	Amount	Banks	Amount	Companies	Amount	
American Baptist Church Pension Board	1	?					P
American Friends Service Committee (1978)					?	$1,300,000	T
American Luthern Church (1980)			2	$2,000,000	27 (in process)	$29,750,000	T
Christian Church (Disciples of Christ) (1976)	1	?	1	?	The General Assembly in 1983 urged all its agencies and congregations to establish by 1985 a process of divestment from corporations doing substantial business in Africa and asked church groups to use banks that do not make loans to South Africa		
Episcopal Church (1981)	1	?	1	?			P

Organization		Amount	Notes	Type
National Council of Churches (1980)	1	$4,700,000		P
Presbyterian Church (1981)			Began a policy of divestment from financial institutions "insofar as practicable"; entered into a study process; other specific actions unknown	P
Reformed Church in America--General Synod (1980)			Began a policy of complete divestment from corporations and banks involved in South Africa; specific actions taken unknown at this point	T
United Church of Christ-- Board for World Ministries (1979)	1	?		P
United Methodist Church-- Council on Finance and Administration (1980)			Established a policy that UMC agencies should not do business with or invest in banks making loans to South Africa	P
World Division, Board of Global Ministries (1981)	1	$20,000,000 (management of investment portfolio removed)		P
Women's Division, Board of Global Ministries (1980)	3	$515,000+		P

TABLE 1-4. Continued

Church (Year)	Bank Accounts Closed		Bank Investments Withdrawn		Corporate Investments Withdrawn		Divestment Policy
	Banks	Amount	Banks	Amount	Companies	Amount	Partial/Total
Board of Global Ministries (1980)	1	$57,000,000					P
Board of Church and Society (1980)	1		?				P
Unitarian Universalist Association (1980)			1			$292,119	P

Sources: Africa Fund, March 1983; Howard and Smith 1981.

TABLE 1-5. Other Sanctions-Related Activities by National Church
Organizations with Partial Divestment Policies

---

1. American Baptist Church National Ministries: its position requests
    corporations to cease further investment in South Africa and to termi-
    nate present operations as expeditiously as possible.

2. Episcopal Church: its position urges banks and corporations to cease
    business with the South African government, not to expand their busi-
    ness in South Africa, and to cease any business in the country that
    does not assist "in the struggle for human dignity and freedom. . . ."

3. United Church of Christ: its position is that investments of any unit
    of the church should be examined with respect to their possible in-
    volvement in any business whose operations are supportive of apartheid.

4. United Presbyterian Church: its position urges businesses and
    financial institutions to discontinue operations, investments, and
    loans in South Africa.

Source: Taken from Howard and Smith 1981.

American banks were lending funds to South Africa through
the European-American Banking Corporation. The bank
campaign was renewed and some of the results can be seen
in Tables 1–4, 1–5, and 1–6. Banks' responses will be
discussed in more detail in the next chapter.

One of the places where divestment campaigns were
most evident was on college and university campuses.
Students and sometimes faculty pressured their institutions'
boards of trustees to sell the South African related securities in the investment portfolios of endowment funds. Not
only did these activists achieve some measure of success in
a number of universities, as can be seen in Tables 1–7 and
1–8, but this new wave of activity also brought an influx of
fresh leaders into the national movement. Many of these
university-based campaigns spilled over into other arenas
when their leaders began targeting still another set of
institutions, state and local governments.

Anti-Apartheid Campaigns in State and Local Governments

State and local governments were targeted by activists in
the early 1970s but just in the last few years has there

TABLE 1-6. Divestment Actions by Other Church Organizations

1. The Connecticut Province of the Sisters of Notre Dame de Namur divested stock in South Africa-related companies in 1979.
2. The Lutheran School of Theology withdrew investments from Illinois Continental Bank in 1981 because of the bank's policy of doing business with South Africa.
3. The New Brunswick Theological Seminary announced in 1982 that it would divest from companies doing business in South Africa.
4. Davis Community Church (California) withdrew its accounts from Security Pacific National Bank of Davis in 1980 because of the bank's South Africa policies.
5. The Adrian Dominican Sisters (Adrian, Michigan) divested 6,000 shares of common stock from Citibank in 1981.
6. The American Baptist Church regions of Cleveland and New York closed their Citibank accounts. The ABC of Metropolitan New York withdrew a $1.5 million investment portfolio from Citibank in 1981.
7. The Catholic Archdiocese of Milwaukee sold $300,000 worth of Citicorp bonds in 1981.
8. The Holy Name Province of Franciscans has withdrawn seven checking and savings accounts from Citibank.
9. The Sisters of the Immaculate Heart of Mary of Monroe (Michigan) divested 1,100 shares of Citibank stock.
10. The Riverside Church (New York City) withdrew all operating accounts (or about $6 million) from Citibank in 1981.
11. The Sisters of Saint Joseph (Rochester, New York) sold 1,000 shares of Citicorp stock in 1981.
12. The Union Theological Seminary (New York City) withdrew accounts from Citibank worth about $4 million in 1980.
13. The Joint Strategies and Action Committee (JSAC) withdrew their payroll account of $80,000 from Citibank in 1982.
14. The U.S. Office of the World Council of Churches divested from Citibank in 1980.

The following Roman Catholic Orders and Protestant denominations announced a pledge to own no investments in Citibank because of its South Africa policies.

Protestant and Orthodox Agencies

American Baptist Church National Ministries
American Friends Service Committee
American Lutheran Church
Church Women United
Episcopal Church Publishing Company
National Council of Churches
Reformed Church in America
Unitarian Universalist Association

30

TABLE 1-6. Continued

Protestant and Orthodox Agencies (continued)

United Christian Missionary Society of the Christian Church
    (Disciples of Christ)
United Church Board for World Ministries
United Methodist Board of Global Ministries
United Presbyterian Church Foundation
World Council of Churches

Roman Catholic Orders and Dioceses

Adrian Dominican Sisters, Michigan
Congregation of Sisters of St. Joseph, Buffalo, New York
Dominican Fathers and Brothers, Province of St. Albert, Illinois
Marianist Society, New York Province
National Catholic Rural Life Conference
Order of St. Augustine, Pennsylvania
Roman Catholic Archdiocese of Milwaukee
Servants of the Immaculate Heart of Mary, Monroe, Michigan
Sisters of Charity, Nazareth, Kentucky
Sisters of the Good Shepard
Sisters of Loretto
Sisters of Mercy, Buffalo, New York
Sisters of Mercy, New York Province
Sisters of Notre Dame de Namur, Connecticut Province
Sisters of St. Francis of Assisi, Milwaukee, Wisconsin
Sisters of St. Francis, Clinton, Iowa
Sisters of St. Francis, Wisconsin
Sisters of St. Francis, Stella Niagra, New York
Sisters of St. Francis, Allegheny, New York
Sisters of St. Joseph, Rochester, New York
Sisters of St. Mary, Buffalo, New York
Mount Saint Mary Academy
Our Lady of Mercy Generlates

Sources: Africa Fund, March 1983; Howard and Smith 1981.

been a major emphasis on getting these institutions to withdraw funds from businesses operating in South Africa. Tables 1–11 and 1–12 show the states and cities where anti-apartheid legislation has been introduced. This segment of the U.S. anti-apartheid movement was chosen for greater examination and evaluation as an arena in which we might

TABLE 1-7. University/College Divestment Actions

University/College (Year)*	Total Amount Divested ($ millions)	No. of Businesses	Partial/ Total
Amherst (1978)	1.3	4 corporations	P
Antioch (1978)	?	?	T
Boston Univ. (1979)	6.6	?	P
Brandeis (1979)	0.35	1 corporation	P
Brown (1984)	?	?	P
Carlton (1979)	0.295	1 bank	P
Colby 1980	0.9	2 corps., 1 bank	P
Columbia (1979)	2.7	3 banks	P
Hampshire (1976)	(initial) 0.04	?	P
Harvard (1981)	50.9	1 bank	
Haverford (1982)	?	1 corp., 2 banks	P
Howard (1978)	1.8	?	P
Univ. of Maine (1982)	3.0	?	?
Univ. of Massachusetts (1977)	0.6	3 corporations	T
Eastern Michigan Univ. (1980)	2.5	1 corporation	P
Michigan State (1979)	8.3	15 corps. and banks	T
Univ. of Michigan (1979)	0.306	1 corporation	P
Western Michigan Univ. (1982)	?	?	P
Mt. Holyoke (1981)	0.459	1 corporation	P
State Univ. of New York, Oneonte (1978)	0.08	1 bank	P
Oberlin (1980)	?	1 corporation	P
Ohio State (1978)	0.25	1 corporation	P
Ohio Univ. (1978)	0.06	4 corporations	T
Oregon State Schools	The Board of Higher Education established a policy of total divestment that is now being challenged in court.		T
Rutgers (1980)	?	?	P
Smith (1977)	0.697	1 corporation	P
Swarthmore (1981)	2.2	3 corporations	P
Tufts (1979)	0.1	2 corps., 1 bank	P
Vassar (1978)	6.5	6 banks	P
Wesleyan (1980)	0.367	1 corporation	P
Williams (1980)	0.7	1 corp., 6 banks	P
Univ. of Wisconsin (1978)	11.0	25 corporations	T
Yale 1979)	1.6	2 banks	P

*Year the policy was established.
Sources: Africa Fund, March 1983; New York Times, 15 April 1984.

TABLE 1-8.   Student Organizations' Divestment Actions

---

1. The Association of Students of the University of California at Los
    Angeles: The association withdrew its funds from the Bank of America
    and Security Pacific Bank in 1980. The action represented a total
    divestment and amounted to $25 million.

2. The Co-op system at the University of California at Berkeley: withdrew
    accounts totaling $4 million from Bank of America in 1979 to protest
    their participation in loans to South Africa.

3. The Student Council for the entire University of California system in
    1978 called on all students to withdraw their accounts from the Bank of
    America to protest the bank's loans to South Africa.

4. The New York University Law School Student Bar Association: withdrew
    its $11,000 account from the La Guardia Place Branch of Citibank in
    1978.

5. The Yale Class of 1984 voted (90 percent majority) to keep investments
    of a special class fund out of corporations operating in South Africa.
    The money will be turned over to Yale at the class's 25th reunion at
    which time the fund is estimated to be worth $2-3 million.

6. Princeton and Harvard students set up alternative alumni contribution
    funds that will not hold South Africa related securities.

Sources: Africa Fund, March 1983; New York Times, 15 December 1983; and
Soriano 1984.

begin to understand further the impact of the whole movement.   Chapters 4 and 5 will be devoted entirely to an
analysis and impact assessment of campaigns in Connecticut
and Michigan.
     State governments have responsibility for regulating
large investments for state employees' pension funds and
state university endowments.   They also have sizable deposits in banks and purchase goods and services the state
uses.   Cities also have bank deposits and purchasing
agreements, and some have financial holdings for pension
funds.   Seeing the potential for bringing greater pressure
to bear on companies operating in South Africa, activists
try to convince state legislatures and city councils to join
the divestment efforts.   This potential was brought to their
attention in part by alternative investments advocates who

TABLE 1-9. Labor Unions' Divestment Activities

The Joint Furriers Council withdrew an $8 million payroll account and a $16 million welfare and pension account from Manufacturers Hanover Trust in 1977.

The United Radio, Electrical and Machine Workers Union withdrew a $4 million payroll account from Chase Manhattan bank because of the bank's loan to South Africa.

The following unions have taken positions against economic involvement in South Africa; those with asterisks (*) have withdrawn funds from banks that make loans to South Africa.

AFL-CIO
Amalgamated Meat Cutters' and Butcherworkers' Union
International Longshoremen's and Warehousemen's Union
Service Employees' International Union
*United Electrical, Radio and Machine Workers of America
*United Automobile, Aerospace and Agricultural Implements Workers of
    America (UAW)
AFSCME Local 1716 of Hartford, AFL-CIO
*Joint Board Fur, Leather and Machine Workers' Union of the United Food
    and Commercial Workers International Union, AFL-CIO
Illinois State AFL-CIO
*International Longshoremen's and Warehousemen's Union, Local 6
District 1199 National Union of Hospital and Health Care Employees
*Retail, Wholesale and Department Store Workers Union, AFL-CIO
*District 31 United Steel Workers of America, AFL-CIO

Sources: Africa Fund, February 1980 and October 1979; Houser 1979; Myers, et al. 1980; and Nesbitt 1977.

promote the use of pension fund monies for revitalization of cities and communities experiencing capital flight.

Anti-apartheid divestment campaigns targeting state and city governments are important for several reasons: state and city financial holdings are considerably larger than those of universities or churches; policy makers across the country are forced into the debate about South Africa and divestment; that is, discussions about how Americans can help end apartheid are no longer confined to idealistic religious communities or the ivory towers of university campuses, but local lawmakers and governmental bureaucrats are now involved in the issue as well. As they get involved in the debate, these decision makers demonstrate

TABLE 1-10.   Black Organizations' Divestment Policies

1. The Coalition of Black Trade Unionists in 1980 called upon the "American trade union movement to withdraw their bank accounts including
   pension funds from banks that make loans to South Africa and also from
   banks that loan money to companies that invest in South Africa."

2. The NAACP in 1966 asked the U.S. government to prevent any further
   investment by American companies in minority-dominated governments; in
   1980 the organization called on U.S. corporations to withdraw their
   investments in South Africa and reaffirmed its call for economic
   sanctions against South Africa.

3. The National Black Agenda for the 80s (a meeting in Richmond, VA in
   1980 of 1,000 black leaders representing over 300 organizations) passed
   a resolution requesting the U.S. government "to sever all economic,
   diplomatic, political, and cultural relations with South Africa."

4. The National Black Caucus of State Legislators passed a resolution in
   1981 calling on their members in 42 states to introduce divestment
   legislation.

5. The Summit Conference of Black Religious Leaders on Apartheid (a 1979
   meeting of religious leaders from 38 states and 52 cities) demanded
   immediate economic disengagement of U.S. corporations from South
   Africa.

6. TransAfrica, a national black lobby on African affairs, actively works
   to break all U.S. economic and political connections to South Africa.

7. Martin Luther King, Jr., called for sanctions against South Africa in a
   statement made jointly with Chief Albert J. Lutuli of the African
   National Congress on Human Rights Day, 10 December 1962.

Sources: Africa Fund, February 1980 and January 1982; Shepherd 1977; UN
Center Against Apartheid 1982.

that foreign policy issues can be of vital concern to governmental bodies outside Washington, D.C.; and when they
pass laws requiring partial or total divestment, they are
making policies that directly oppose U.S. national foreign
policy. At this point, legislation has been introduced into
at least 23 state legislatures, 25 city councils, and three
county councils. Legislation has passed only in seven
states although other governmental actions have been taken

TABLE 1-11. State Anti-Apartheid Legislation

| | | | Type of Legislation (in one or more measures) | | | | | | |
| | Year First Introduced | Repeated or Multiple Introductions | Pension Fund Divestment | | Operating Fund Divestment | | Bank Deposits Withheld | | Other |
State			Partial	Total	Partial	Total	Partial	Total	
Alabama	1983			X					
California	1973	yes		X		X		X	X
Colorado	1983			X		X			
Connecticut	1979	yes	X+	X+1					
Florida	1982			X		X			
Illinois	1979	yes						X	
Indiana	1983			X		X	X		X
Iowa	1983		X		X		X		
Kansas	1983	yes		X+*					
Maryland	1980	yes	X*	X			X+		
Massachusetts	1977	yes	X+	X+					X

36

State	Year							
Michigan	1978	yes	X	X	X+	X+	X	X+
Minnesota	1979	yes	X+1	X	X+1			X
Nebraska	1980	yes	X+	X+*	X+1	X		
Nevada	1981	yes	X*	X*	X+	X*		X
New Jersey	1983		X*	X*				
New York	1977	yes	X*	X			X	X
Ohio	1979	yes	X	X		X	X	X
Oregon	1979	yes	X	X	X	X	X	X
Pennsylvania	1981	yes		X				X
Rhode Island	1983			X				
Texas	1981	yes	X	X		X	X	X
Wisconsin	1977	yes	X	X	X	X	X	X*

+ The measure passed; * One or more of this type of legislation were nonbinding resolutions; 1 vetoed by governor

Partial means either (1) all funds are prohibited from certain (but not all) transactions with South Africa-related companies; or (2) some (but not all) funds are prohibited from all transactions with South Africa-related companies; or (3) some funds are prohibited from some transactions with South Africa-related companies.

The year designated is not necessarily the year in which the legislation passed or became law.

37

TABLE 1-12. City Anti-Apartheid Legislation

City or County	Year First Introduced	Selective Purchasing	Pension Fund Divestment		Operating Fund Divestment		Bank Deposits Withheld		Other
			Partial	Total	Partial	Total	Partial	Total	
California									
Berkeley	1979					X			
Cotati	1978					X1			
Davis	1978					X2			
Sacramento	1979			X+					
Santa Cruz	1983							X3	
Connecticut									
Hartford	1980		X						
Delaware									
Wilmington	1982			X					
Dist. of Columbia									
Washington	1975	X*		X		X			X*
Georgia									
Atlanta	1982			X*					
Illinois									
Chicago	1977								X+
Indiana									
Gary	1975	X*							X
Maryland									
Baltimore	1981								X
Massachusetts									
Boston	1984			X4		X4		X4	

Location	Year						
Cambridge	1979		X	X5	X5		X5
Michigan							
East Lansing	1977	X					
Grand Rapids	1982					X	X X
Minnesota							
Duluth	1980						
Minneapolis	1977		X6				
New Jersey							
Atlantic City	1983			X*			
Newark	1984		X				
New York							
New York City	1977	X*	X	X+	X+		X+
Ohio							
Cuyahoga Co.	1984						X
Oregon							
Multnomah Co.	1982			X*			
Portland	1983			X*			
Pennsylvania							
Philadelphia	1982		X				
Texas							
Dallas	1982	X+					X+
Wisconsin							
Dane Co.	1977	X					
Madison	1976	X					

+ Measure failed to pass; * Measure is nonbinding; 1 Measure was rescinded in 1983; 2 A nonbinding referendum passed the measure in 1978, and the city council took binding action in 1980; 3 A binding referendum; 4 Measure includes a prohibition against transactions with banks or corporations related to Namibia; 5 Nonbinding referendum; 6 Pending.

In most cities there have been repeated or multiple introductions of legislation; the year designated is not necessarily the year in which the legislation passed.

39

in five additional states. Connecticut, Kansas, Maryland, Massachusetts, Michigan, Minnesota, and Nebraska have had legislation pass with different outcomes in each case. These cases will be discussed briefly.

Comprehensive divestment bills affecting all state investments were passed in Connecticut in 1980 and 1981. The 1980 bill called for the withdrawal of funds from corporations that have not adopted the Sullivan Principles. (The Sullivan Principles were designed by executives from businesses investing in South Africa and are an attempt to apply fair employment practices to corporations' operations in South Africa. These principles are discussed in detail in the next chapter.) Believing that the inclusion of the Sullivan Principles in the 1980 bill compromised the goal of divestment, in 1981 activists from the Connecticut Anti-Apartheid Committee pushed for comprehensive legislation requiring withdrawal of state funds from all banks, corporations, and their affiliates and subsidiaries doing business in South Africa regardless of their position on the Sullivan Principles. The legislation involving approximately $186 million in investments passed with an almost three-quarters majority in both houses, but the governor vetoed the bill after intense lobbying by businesses affected by the legislation. The veto was sustained when both houses voted a second time on the bill, but in 1982 a compromise bill was passed requiring divestment from corporations not conforming to a list of standards regarding their operations in South Africa. Further details about the Connecticut case can be found in Chapter 4.

Anti-apartheid legislative activities began in 1978 in Michigan when students and faculty at the University of Michigan asked their state representative to introduce a measure requiring all state universities to divest their holdings in business with ties to South Africa. After having exerted pressure for several months, students were frustrated by the unwillingness of the University of Michigan Board of Regents to pursue a divestment policy, and they sought a remedy through legislation that would affect all state universities. The legislation did not pass.

With encouragement from a number of groups in the state, the next year the sponsor of the bill decided to seek total divestment of all state funds. The sponsor reintroduced the university divestment bill and introduced two other measures: one requiring state pension funds to divest and one prohibiting the deposit of any state funds in banks that lend to the government of South Africa or any of its parastatals. In 1980, the banking bill passed and has been implemented by banks in the state agreeing not to make loans to South Africa. In 1982, the university bill passed and became law after a long and arduous process in the legislature, but it is now being contested in court by the University of Michigan. The pension bill has met a great deal of opposition, and up until recently its backers gave it lower priority as they pursued the passage of the other legislation. The Michigan case is also the subject of a thorough evaluation, which can be found in Chapter 5.

After passing a budget amendment in 1979 that prohibited any *further* South Africa-related investments, in 1983 the Massachusetts legislature became the first state legislature to pass and override the governor's veto of legislation that would require divestment of all holdings in companies doing business in South Africa. This bill was the only one in the 1982 session that was passed over Governor King's veto, and it is the most comprehensive pension divestment bill to become law so far. It includes a provision that divested funds be reinvested as much as possible in businesses that have substantial operations in Massachusetts. Two legislators from the Boston area, one black and one white, introduced and persistently fought for passage of the legislation. Supporters from across the state were organized into a coalition called Mass Divest. Significant support came from churches, labor, and community groups including the Black Ecumenical Commission, the Catholic Archdiocese of Boston, and the public employees' and teachers' unions. The day-to-day work was carried out by a core group of activists, most of whom were from the Boston Coalition for the Liberation of Southern Africa, organized in the mid-1970s, and the TransAfrica Boston Support Group. Affected by the 1983 bill are about $91 million in stocks and bonds in 27 major banks and corporations that were acquired prior to the time that the 1979 legislation went into effect. A copy of the 1983 bill is in Appendix B.

The activists in Minnesota were not so successful when they faced gubernatorial opposition. In 1982 the governor there vetoed a bill preventing any future investments of state funds in South Africa-related companies, and the legislature failed to override the veto. Sponsors there plan to reintroduce similar legislation. Maryland became the first southern state to pass legislation when in 1984 it made a law to prohibit deposit of state funds in banks loaning money to the South African government or its parastatals. Non-binding resolutions were passed unanimously by the Nebraska state legislature in 1980 and by the Kansas legislature in 1982. These resolutions urged the divestment of state monies, but Nebraska went further in 1984 to prohibit investments in corporations not adhering to the Sullivan Principles.

In Wisconsin legislation is awaiting action, but other state anti-apartheid measures have been taken. In 1978, the University of Wisconsin Board of Regents divested itself of stock in all businesses with investments in South Africa. This action came as a result of a ruling by the state Attorney General that investments by the university in such businesses violated a statute establishing a "no discrimination" standard required of the Regents' investments. The standard provided that "no such investment shall knowingly be made in any company, corporation, subsidiary or affiliate which practices or condones through its actions discrimination on the basis of race, religion, color, creed or sex. . . ." (Wisconsin Office of the Attorney General 1978). A total evaluation of investment policies resulted from this ruling, and even though over $11 million was involved, the investment advisors concluded that the portfolio had been reconstructed with no ill effects.

Actions in other states are varied. In 1980 in California, after many years of pressure on the state legislation about the issue of corporate responsibility in southern Africa and on other issues, Governor Jerry Brown established a Public Investment Task Force to develop guidelines to assure that state investment practices conform to socially responsible criteria and public interest goals. In Oregon a court case resulted from a challenge to the Board of Higher Education regarding its right to pursue a divestment policy. The challenge came from the state Attorney General who said that such investment decisions should be the jurisdiction of the Oregon Investment Council. In 1978, People for Southern African Freedom, and activist organization working for divestment, began court proceedings to overturn the Attorney General's ruling. To date the case has not been resolved. In 1982, Kentucky Governor John Y. Brown sent a trade mission to South Africa to initiate economic ties. After numerous meetings with black legislators and leaders of the NAACP in the state as well as national anti-apartheid leaders, the governor reversed himself and decided not to seek economic linkages with South Africa. In still another state, non-legislative action occurred as far back as 1974 when the Attorney General of Alabama took action against the importation of South African coal because he maintained that the coal was produced by slave labor or indentured labor under penal sanctions (Shepherd 1977, 7). Thus, although the bulk of state government actions have been through legislative channels, other significant anti-apartheid actions also have been taken by executive branches.

Campaigns targeted at city governments have produced outcomes as interesting as those of state governmental activities. In 1975, the Washington, D.C., and Gary, Indiana, city councils were the first to adopt anti-apartheid resolutions recommending that city services and supplies not be purchased from a specific group of companies involved in southern Africa. Neither action was binding. However, a binding selective purchasing policy was passed soon thereafter in Madison, Wisconsin, in 1976. The cities of Berkeley (1979) and Davis (1978) had referendums in which the public voted to support divestment of operating funds as a means to contribute to anti-apartheid efforts. The Berkeley action was binding and affected approximately $4.5 million (ACOA, March 1983). The Davis action was not binding, but in 1980, the Davis City Council passed a resolution implementing the policy preference expressed in the referendum. In other actions, two mayoral candidates in Chicago announced in 1983 that they would not keep city funds in banks that sell Krugerrands, the South African gold coin. Subsequently, Chicago First National and Continental Illinois banks announced that they would discontinue Krugerrand sales.

Out of the 27 local governments entertaining anti-apartheid policies, 22 have passed one or more pieces of legislation. However, the city council of Cotati, California, has rescinded its action (Eager et al. 1983). In recent years, binding divestment legislation has succeeded in several major cities including Philadelphia, New York City, Boston, and Washington, D.C. Philadelphia became the first large U.S. city to pass a binding resolution prohibiting public employee pension funds being invested in corporations operating in South Africa and Namibia. The ordinance was passed unanimously, and by September 1983, securities worth $57 million had been sold. Another $50 million was expected to be divested in the next 18 months (ACOA, September 1983).

Although the New York City Council has not passed binding legislation on the issue of South African investments, the trustees of the New York City Employees Retirement System voted unanimously in August 1984 for gradual and conditional divestment. About $665 million of the $8.3 billion fund is invested in companies doing business in South Africa, but it is not yet known how much of this $665 million will be affected by the trustees' action. The divestment policy is to be implemented across five years as follows: after 15 months, stocks of companies doing business with the South African police or military, loaning money to the government, or refusing to sign the Sullivan

Principles will be sold; after two years, stocks of companies signing the principles but not allowing monitoring of compliance will be sold; after three years, those companies that do not achieve the highest rating in compliance to the principles will have their stock sold; and after five years, all companies will be divested except those whose activities "'are deemed by the trustees to be of substantial assistance to efforts to eliminate apartheid'" (*New York Times*, 4 August 1984).

Despite some attempts to veto the legislation, in February 1984 Washington, D.C., gained congressional approval to sell all its securities in corporations or financial institutions doing business in South Africa. About $65 million in securities will be affected when the law is implemented. Later in 1984, The Boston City Council voted to remove all city money deposited in banks lending to South Africa and all investments in corporations operating there.

The patterns of behavior that emerge across the cases where state or city governments consider anti-apartheid action are very interesting and useful for analytic purposes. When surveying the cases, one pattern that becomes evident is that of the presence or absence of a campaign pushing for such legislation. Some state and cities have experienced sustained organizing and lobbying by activists, whereas legislation in other states is a result of personal interests of a particular legislator or his/her staff. Examples of the former are the states of Connecticut, Massachusetts, Michigan, Minnesota, Oregon, and Wisconsin, and the cities of Hartford, Boston, Philadelphia, Washington, D.C., East Lansing, Madison, Berkeley, and Davis. In all of these cases it is possible to identify a particular group of people who are responsible for getting and keeping anti-apartheid legislation on the government agenda. In many of these cases, the campaigns were initiated by activists first at the city level (for example, Hartford, East Lansing, and Madison) and after successful campaigns in those arenas, then taken to the state level.

In places where there has been no campaign or group of activists pushing the legislation (for instance, Nebraska, Nevada, and Ohio; Cotati and Sacramento), there appear to be two principal sources for governmental initiative. First, some of the legislators or their staff have been involved in other anti-apartheid work outside the legislature or city council, often in some place other than their present geographic location. Or, they are close friends of people who are anti-apartheid activists. Because of their previous activities or those of their friends, they are linked into a communications network that continuously feeds them information about the nationwide anti-apartheid movement. They may have read in a national anti-apartheid newsletter about legislative activities in other states, or they may have heard such news through friends. Out of their own interest in anti-apartheid work, they initiated legislation in relative isolation from the active support and persistent backing of other activists. Legislation in Nebraska and in the cities of Cotati and Sacramento came about through such a process.

The second major source for governmental activity when there is no pressure group or interest group to sustain the effort is the targeting of potential local sympathizers and activists by national anti-apartheid organizations. For example, in 1980, TransAfrica systematically contacted over 70 black legislators across the country to discuss the issue of apartheid with them, inform them on anti-apartheid activities nationwide, and provide them with the text of a model divestment bill that they were encouraged to introduce. Later in 1981, two leaders of the national movement addressed a workshop on divestment at the annual conference of the National Black Caucus of State Legislators. In 1981 and again in 1983, nine national organizations concerned with anti-apartheid work sponsored a conference to which a number of state legislators and city council members were invited. Some public officials received financial subsidies in order to come. Many had sponsored anti-apartheid legislation, but others were there to learn how to do it. Legislative activities in Nevada, Ohio, Texas, and other places followed from these national organizations' initiatives.

Efforts at targeting state and local governments are likely to continue with significant momentum after these important successes in recent years. The impact of these campaigns will be discussed further in the following chapters. However, in order to continue our examination of the U.S. anti-apartheid movement as a whole and these campaigns in particular, it is useful to turn to analytic tools developed by scholars who study social movements.

Gerlach and Hine (1970) provide a framework within which to examine the structure of social movements, various groups contained within them, and the dynamics between the groups across time. These authors used the framework to investigate the black power and the pentacostal movements, and Cassell (1977) employed it in her observation of the women's movement. The framework outlines three characteristics that typify a social movement: Decentralization and polycephalous (many-headed) structure, segmentation, and reticulation. Decentralization and polycephalous structure mean essentially three things: there is no central command post or policy-making body for all of the movement; there are multiple leaders, no one of whom controls, regulates, or makes binding decisions for the entire movement (leaders are not even likely to know everyone involved in the movement); and there is no objective criteria for membership in the movement as a whole, although groups within it may have membership requirements (Gerlach and Hine 1970, 34–41).

Segmentation means that "the movement is composed of a range of diverse groups, or cells which grow and die, divide and fuse, proliferate and contract" (Gerlach 1983, 135). Segmentation occurs for a variety of reasons, some of which include competition among leaders or sects of participants, ideological differences, previous social and personal cleavages or geographic distance, and "an ideology of personal access to power . . . the assumption that individuals in the movement have direct access to knowledge, truth, and power" (Gerlach and Hine 1970, 41–55). Reticulation means that "diverse groups in the movement do not constitute simply an amorphous collection; rather, they are organized into a network, or reticulate structure through cross-cutting links, "traveling evangelists' or spokesmen, overlapping participation, joint activities, and the sharing of common objectives and opposition" (Gerlach 1983, 135).

There are a number of advantages for movements with these characteristics. Two are social innovation and minimization of failure. More innovation may occur because among the many groups within the movement "variation is maximized, options are explored, and new solutions may be found for various problems." Failures may be minimized because "decentralization maximized experimentation which may give a better chance of hitting on new solutions to problems" (Cassell 1977, 117). Thus, diverse movement organizations may form symbiotic relationships in which experimentation or new discoveries by one group may lead to another group's success in a campaign (Freeman 1975, 145). Other advantages are perhaps a maximization of strategic options, for example, hitting the target from several different vantage points at one time, and the movement's abilities to unite disparate elements for short term or single goal coalitions without forcing them to bind together in any permanent way. Furthermore, all movements have groups within them that range across a continuum of conservative to radical, depending on preferences about means and ends or their degree of institutionalization. When radical groups within the movement make demands, "middle-range or conservative groups, either purposely or inadvertently, use the radical action to spearhead their own drives and make their own demands and actions seem *comparatively* reasonable" (Gerlach 1983, 135, emphasis in the original).

Some of the disadvantages in such a structure, however, can be the duplication of efforts among groups that do not find themselves in a workable symbiotic relationship—most of whom usually cannot afford to waste resources in experiments or explorations of options that fail; group conflicts and factionalism; the ability of adversaries to "divide and conquer"; and the potential absence of a critical mass for any specific strategy to succeed.

The anti-apartheid movement fits very well in the Gerlach and Hine (1970) framework. It is characterized by decentralization in that there are several identifiable leaders of the movement none of whom can speak for or command the entire movement; by segmentation since localized groups with various life spans, degrees of institutionalization, goals, and strategies work on campaigns across the country; and by reticulation in that these groups form networks to share information and to work together on specific tasks. With regard to the campaigns discussed in the previous section, these concepts can be further illustrated with several examples.

Reticulation occurs in a variety of ways, one of which is that the state and local activities receive resources from each other and from national organizations. In most of these states, the local activists have called on experts from national groups to testify during legislative hearings, to lobby legislators, and to do educational work in their communities in support of the legislation. The national organizations also publish important information regarding strategies, updates on recent events in the United States and South Africa, and research on the apartheid issue and economic ties to South Africa. This occurs through newsletters, pamphlets, and books. In addition, they provide a communication node for persons wanting to check on current news. In most cases, however, even though nationally known persons may help initiate campaigns, there is no one at the national level who in any way directly organizes the ongoing work of these local activists or takes command over their decisions. There are also important differences and controversies among the groups in terms of ideology, composition and basis of their membership, strategies, legislative goals, and so on. That is, the work of these groups is also decentralized and polycephalous in nature.

For example, in Connecticut, the activist group (The Connecticut Anti-Apartheid Committee) has had a great deal of support and recruitment from labor unions, some of whose pension funds are directly affected by the anti-apartheid legislation. Church organization, black organizations, student groups, and other citizen groups have all provided important backing through endorsements, contributions, lobbying, and so on, but the core of the group and much of the organizational momentum comes from unions. In contrast, the Southern Africa Liberation Committee, the group responsible for a great deal of the legislative activity in Michigan, comes primarily from a university setting, as does the Madison Area Committee on Southern Africa. The groups are made up of faculty, staff, and students who since the early 1970s have not only been involved in legislative activities but also have pressed for and achieved university divestment.

In terms of ideological diversity, some groups conducting campaigns articulate their efforts as being part of a larger issue (human rights, the struggle against capitalism, and so forth) whereas others prefer to keep a more narrow focus specifically on the question of South Africa. The differences in ideology can have important implications for questions of strategy. Those who see anti-apartheid work as a part of the more encompassing struggle against capitalism often want to forge linkages and coalitions with groups working on more domestic issues such as workers' rights and conditions or discrimination against racial minorities. Those who prefer their work to be centered specifically on South Africa (or southern Africa) often do not view themselves or their work for racial justice in South Africa as an anti-capitalist struggle. Or, they see efforts to broaden the issue as a dissipation of their energy and a threat to their ability to appeal to their constituencies. They do not believe that the people whom they seek to mobilize will understand or be receptive to a critique of capitalism. Furthermore, the movement as a whole has experienced enough red-baiting that even some who view themselves as working in the context of anti-capitalist efforts want to keep the focus of anti-apartheid work narrow so as to avoid counter-productive public images.

Another contentious division in the movement that is somewhat related to the ideological issue is the degree to which the movement is mass-based; that is, the degree to which the campaigns educate and mobilize large segments of the American public. No one in the movement would deny that they would prefer to have backing by public opinion that clearly and decisively rejects apartheid. But in the midst of divestment campaigns, leaders have to make difficult choices about what concrete activities to pursue to achieve their goals, and they have to react to events that

are sometimes beyond their control. This leads to differences in strategies regarding how much time divestment
activists spend doing educational work or other activities
that will involve and convert large numbers of people. For
example, in some states and cities activists have discovered
that intense lobbying (which by definition is not highly
visible to the public) can consume all of their time and lead
to desired legislative outcomes. Thus a legislative victory
is achieved and policy elites will be fairly knowledgeable
about the issue, but the awareness of American people
about South Africa is likely to be changed very little.

Another controversy that illustrates the decentralized
and polycephalous nature of the movement is the racial mix
of the movement. It is impossible to discern without a
great deal of further research what exactly is the racial mix
of local activists who make up the hundreds of small anti-
apartheid organizations across the country. With one
exception, however, most of the major national organizations
are run and staffed by white people. Whatever the reasons
for this predominance of whites at the national level (and
they appear to be numerous and complex), it can have
important implications for their organizational ability or
inability either to mobilize black support for the movement
or to enhance authentic black participation in campaigns at
all levels. There is no operating consensus within the
movement about how to deal with this issue, and groups
across the country as well as the national organizations
differ in the degree to which they seriously attempt to
address it.

Despite these controversies and disputes there is a
great deal of cooperation among leaders within the movement. The movement does have coherence, and reticulation
is real. For example, most of the national organizations
came together to sponsor the two national conferences on
anti-apartheid organizing for state and local campaigns'
progress and needs. Several national conferences have also
been held in recent years for students and community
organizers. ACOA has called on its own staff as well as
leaders from the other organizations to be, in Gerlach and
Hine terminology (1970), the "traveling evangelists" to
speak or lobby in legislatures, city councils, or educational
events organized by local activists. And, national newsletters help to keep participants across the country current
on campaigns' successes and failures. But even the function of reticulation itself is an issue within the movement
because some local activists do not believe that they or
other "grassroots" organizers get enough support, aid, or
appreciation from national organizations.

Segmentation is also clearly demonstrated in the divestment efforts backed by organized anti-apartheid groups; that is, groups and individuals may coalesce for particular purposes or even longer term work; or, they may fracture into smaller units, each pursuing divestment work in its own way. One of the most interesting stories in this research demonstrates segmentation; it is about the dispersal of people from the group responsible for the city council selective purchasing resolution in Madison, Wisconsin, one of the earliest legislative actions in the country.

The name of the group was the Madison Area Committee on Southern Africa. An organization by that name continues to exist in Madison and continues to press for state legislation. Our concern, however, is with four people (two couples) who left the group and moved to jobs in different parts of the country. One couple moved to North Carolina (after spending some time in Africa) where they began working on the weekly news bulletin about Africa, *Africa News*. This bulletin carries stories about anti-apartheid activities across the nation and has highlighted news on state and city campaigns. In this way the couple made an important contribution to the divestment communications network.

The second couple moved to Michigan where they were pivotal in helping the Southern Africa Liberation Committee (SALC) there organize the drive for the East Lansing City Council resolution in 1977. They have also made vital contributions to the state anti-apartheid legislative campaigns, including the passage of the state anti-apartheid legislative campaigns, including the passage of the banking bill in 1980 and the university bill in 1982. A third couple who had been involved in SALC campaigns moved to California and have been a part of divestment campaigns there. Segmentation has occurred because, when people relocated, they left leadership positions in one place to spread their influence and become leaders in similar efforts in other places.

CONCLUSION

The Gerlach and Hine framework is useful in analyzing the anti-apartheid movement because it helps to dispel two important misconceptions about these efforts. The first is that the movement is conspiratorial in nature, controlled and manipulated by a clique of leaders who advocate policies and actions that on the whole would not be supported by the American public. The movement description in this chapter demonstrates, and analysis using this framework further confirms, that the movement is not monolithic or tightly controlled. In many respects it is community-based with people using institutions locally available to address this international issue they believe to be of great significance. This highly decentralized and segmented structure, however, has given rise to the second misconception: that the movement is so dispersed that it is completely disorganized, inefficient, and thus ineffective.

The framework helps us to see that diversity and proliferation of groups, goals, and activities as well as competition among ideologies and leadership does not automatically mean that the movement is weak, factionalized, or wasting energy on unnecessary duplication of effort. These problems may exist, but networking among groups and other aspects of reticulation keep the movement together in a workable whole with a structure that may have significant advantages. Some of these potential advantages have already been listed; other real ones will become clear in the discussion of the movement's impact.

The cases of anti-apartheid work in Connecticut and Michigan have been chosen to examine the question of impact in depth. This chapter has provided an important context of the larger movement within which to view these two sets of campaigns. The next chapter gives more context by discussing two topics: the degree to which economic sanctions efforts against South Africa can contribute to ending apartheid, and the responses made to the anti-apartheid movement in governmental, business, and other arenas.

NOTE

1. At this point, UNITA is aligned with the South African government, and together the two have held major sections of Angolan territory in the southern part of the country. UNITA would like to topple the MPLA government, and South Africa wants to make SWAPO inoperative by destroying it bases in southern Angola.

2

The Sanctions Debate

As was demonstrated in the previous chapter, one of the strongest thrusts in the anti-apartheid movement is that for economic sanctions. This chapter will analyze the potential for such sanctions as well as responses on the part of a wide range of institutions to this thrust in the movement.

THE POTENTIAL FOR ECONOMIC SANCTIONS

Despite the length and intensity of the debate over divestment and economic sanctions against South Africa, it has received surprisingly little scholarly attention. The lack of a broad base of rigorous analysis hinders efforts to evaluate the potential impact of sanctions and the theory of action of significance to this study. In general, a theory of action is an overall conceptualization of the relationship between the means (tactics, strategies) of a program, campaign, or movement and the desired end-states (goals, objectives) of that program, campaign, or movement (Patton 1978, 179–98). Often underlying the call for sanctions by anti-apartheid groups is a theory of action that asserts a relationship between the economic isolation of South Africa (the strategy) and the ending of apartheid (the goal). In order to achieve the purpose of this study—an evaluation of the performance of anti-apartheid divestment campaigns targeting state and local governments—this overall theory of action must be tested for its logic, plausibility, and underlying assumptions.

The success of sanctions in helping to end apartheid depends on many factors, some easier to anticipate and discuss than others. These factors include the goals desired by advocates, South Africa's vulnerability to outside pressures, the kinds of sanctions imposed, the number of countries, especially trade and investment partners, participating in the sanctions. Each of these factors will be discussed in some detail.

Goals

As has been shown, there is a wide variety of groups and people, both governmental and nongovernmental, who advocate either implicitly or explicitly some degree of economic isolation of South Africa in pursuit of an assortment of goals. Some see sanctions as a moral imperative against an evil system. Such persons maintain that no commercial benefits should accrue from interactions with a racist regime having an economy founded on modern-day slavery. Most people who take this position do not do so as purists, that is, they realize that in an imperfect and unjust world one cannot escape some degree of interaction with despicable political and economic systems both at home and abroad. But they want to take a stand, and they believe that to begin to rid the world of injustice, they must focus their energy somewhere. Therefore, why not focus it on one of the most odious of systems, the only constitutionally racist state in the world?

Some people desire sanctions as a way to express their support for black people in southern Africa, and especially for resistance movements engaged in guerrilla warfare there, such as the African National Congress (ANC), the Pan-Africanist Congress (PAC), and the South West People's Organizations (SWAPO) all of whom have called for the economic isolation of South Africa. Support for sanctions comes not because activists always have a thoroughly reasoned and logical theory of action with regard to how sanctions will end apartheid, but because authoritative persons and groups they respect and trust have requested their solidarity on the issue.

Many are engaged in these efforts because they believe such activities to be an efficacious way of raising consciousness and educating Americans or Westerners about racism, apartheid, and the role of corporations and governments in perpetuating these phenomena. Since the United States, Europe, and Japan are South Africa's most important economic partners, activists see sanctions as an

easily accessible issue from which to politicize a
their constituents on the broader questions of e(
racial justice.   Thus from this ideological var
advocating South Africa's economic isolation may
end in and of itself so much as a means or a
raise broader issues about the role of capitalism in the
world.

The goal of punishing or raising the costs of perpetuating apartheid for the South African government, whites,
or the system as a whole is foremost in the minds of some
sanctions advocates who want to impose deprivation or
embarrassment on the wrong-doers.   Sometimes particular
segments of the regime such as the military and police are
singled out as limited sanctions targets because of their
significant role in enforcing apartheid.   Regarding general
sanctions, however, critics correctly point out that those
who likely will suffer first and most from South Africa's
economic isolation are the Africans, the very ones sanctions
advocates hope to aid.   Therefore, these critics argue, the
punishment is misplaced.   Advocates respond to this criticism by pointing to the assertions of significant numbers of
black leaders themselves as illustrated in Table 2-1.   Such
leaders often assert that the South African black community
would prefer to endure the short-term increased hardships
of sanctions that might help end apartheid, than the long-
term debilitating and deadly effects of the racist system
they have experienced for centuries.

Some have goals of improved relations with black African states when they advocate a partial or total embargo.
Since support for the liberation of southern Africa has been
a cornerstone of OAU policy since its founding, and since
some governments like that of Nigeria and the frontline
states go to great lengths to demonstrate that support,
favoring some kind of sanctions, especially on the part of
governments, becomes a symbol and a signal of the desire
for better relations with Africa as a whole.

The goal usually assumed to be foremost in the minds of
those who advocate comprehensive sanctions is that of
ending apartheid.   This would be accomplished by imposing
economic hardship on the country as a whole, and especially
on the whites, to undermine their persistence in maintaining
the apartheid structures.   Sanctions are seen to be economic warfare, and coupled with the guerrilla war and internal
civil disturbances already in process, proponents hope to
rid the world of this form of racism.   That this goal is not
always the most pressing one for many advocates is important to note particularly when evaluating the success of
sanctions-related activist campaigns.   These activists may

TABLE 2-1. South Africa's Foreign Assets and Liabilities (Rand millions)

Year	Liabilities	Assets	Net Indebtedness	Net Indebtedness percent of GDP
1956	2,767	826	1,941	47.3
1960	3,121	922	2,199	43.7
1965	4,004	1,385	2,619	33.4
1970	6,017	2,400	3,617	29.9
1971	7,183	2,486	4,697	34.9
1972	8,255	3,072	5,183	34.4
1973	10,380	3,397	6,983	38.0
1974	12,757	3,814	8,943	41.0
1975	16,463	4,881	11,582	47.3
1976	19,830	5,022	14,808	53.8
1977	21,332	5,362	15,970	57.3
1978	22,886	7,777	15,109	52.7
1979	22,880	10,267	12,613	42.3*
1980	25,485	13,347	12,138	37.7*

*Preliminary
Sources: Republic of South Africa 1984, 356, 561; Spandau 1983, 110.

be able to achieve a great deal of what they set out to accomplish through calling for sanctions without attaining the comprehensive economic isolation of South Africa or the certain near-term end of apartheid. Activists as well as other advocates may also have varying combinations of these (or perhaps other) goals in mind when pursuing sanctions.

It is impossible to evaluate the logic, plausibility, and basic assumptions underlying all of this goal-oriented behavior. The focus here, therefore, will be on analyzing the theory of action of the last goal because it is the most significant in terms of what the white South African government has to win or lose. If sanctions advocates are correct that the economic isolation of apartheid will speed its demise, the white South Africans have a lot to lose; if the advocates are wrong and if this is their primary goal, they could be wasting a lot of time. It is beyond the capabilities of social science to predict accurately whether the advocated are actually right or wrong, but we can suggest whether their arguments seem rational and reasonable based on the data available to us; or, whether they seem beyond reasonable calculation and therefore a matter of faith.

The theory of action in the last goal asserts two basic causal relationships: (1) that sanctions will bring about economic hardship, and (2) that economic hardship, together with other forms of significant pressure such as guerrilla warfare and civil unrest, will significantly weaken the resolve of the South African government to maintain apartheid. The first assertion will be discussed later in this chapter. The second assertion is what concerns us now.

Although governments often behave as though they are confident of the desired outcome, Porter suggests, "there is neither logical reason nor historical evidence that political or psychological collapse inevitably follows economic hardship" (1979, 58). In his analysis of sanctions against South Africa, Porter chooses to ignore this aspect of the theory of action, but other analysts raise important questions about it. If we are to judge from previous experiences, in general there is reason to doubt that the desired political outcome can be achieved through the application of sanctions alone (Barber 1979; Doxey 1980; Wallensteen 1971). The failure of sanctions in bringing about a speedy end to white minority rule in Rhodesia (Doxey 1971; Porter 1978; Strack 1978) is often invoked as an analogy (although an imperfect one) to demonstrate the potential for a similar failure in South Africa. Some believe that sanctions would have effects opposite those desired by advocates—a white intransigence to domestic political change often referred to as a retreat "into the laager" (Ball 1977). There is some evidence that this occurred in Rhodesia (Doxey 1971).

This evidence is not conclusive, however. In his study of several sanctions cases, Barber (1979) suggests that economic isolation can make the target more susceptible to other kinds of pressures that might be significant in changing its behavior, and Strack (1978) asserts that eventually the sanctions against Rhodesia did contribute to the attainment of majority rule. Ferguson and Cotter dismiss the argument that heavy pressures would make whites intransigent by noting that the most rigid of the apartheid structures have been put in place during periods of relative political calm when the regime was free of external pressure, that is, lack of outside pressure has made the government intransigent and promoted the belief that the system will always survive (1978, 255–58). Myers et al. (1980, 69–81, 141–42) also argue that political and economic crises in South Africa have been accompanied by increases in cleavages and political dissent among whites and by proposals for significant alterations in apartheid structures. Therefore, the fear of a "retreat" or intransigence on the part of a large majority of whites may be ill-founded.

During political and economic crises, however, the government has been quick to quell dissent and crush the opposition it fears, even among whites. How much white dissent, civil unrest, emigration, and strong credible opposition would arise in times of severe economic hardship, versus how much increased loyalty and determination to protect apartheid against all odds there would be, is impossible to answer. An approximation to an answer is that sanctions (strong enough to produce significant economic hardship), coupled with other major pressures such as domestic black unrest or rebellion and intensified guerrilla incursions, could help rock the well fortified apartheid foundation. But, weak sanctions, or sanctions as a single source of pressure, are not likely to bring a speedy end to apartheid.

A crucial question is, therefore, can severe economic hardship be achieved through outside pressures on the South African economy? It is this question to which we now turn.

South African Vulnerability
to Outside Economic Pressures

Over the last 50–60 years the South African economy has undergone great structural change in a period of rapid industrialization. During this process the country has experienced greater participation in the world economy and has become even more dependent on trade and investment than before the development of manufacturing industries. There is a consensus among analysts that "foreign capital and foreign trade have been critical to the economic development of South Africa providing the foreign exchange required for industrialization and for the expansion of an increasingly capital-intensive economy" (Myers et al. 1980, 39; see also Barber et al. 1982; First, et al. 1973; Houghton 1976; Litvak et al. 1978; Porter 1979; Rogers 1976; Seidman and Seidman 1977).

In its trade the bulk of South Africa's exports are now and have been for many years raw or slightly processed minerals. The most important mineral exports are gold, coal, diamonds, platinum, uranium, iron ore, and cooper. Gold alone made up about 46 percent of total volume of exports (excluding re-exports) in 1974, and other minerals accounted for another 27 percent (Porter 1979, 587). In 1980, all minerals accounted for 76 percent of the country's total foreign exchange earnings of $26 billion. Gold is so important that for every decrease of $10 in the price of gold, foreign exchange earnings drop by about $220 million (Study Commission 1981, 130–36).

Unlike exports, the character of South Africa's imports has changed substantially since the beginning of the century, reflecting changes due to the industrialization of the economy. The percentage of imports in national income has remained relatively constant, about 20 percent of GDP (Houghton 1976; Porter 1979, 588), but imports of consumer goods have been declining proportionately while imports of capital goods have been rising. For example, in 1957 capital goods made up about 28 percent of imports, but in 1974 capital goods rose to about 42 percent. These goods (especially machinery and transport equipment) have been crucial to the industrialization of the South African economy. Because these particular imports are vital in providing much need technology, their importance is further heightened. One economist estimated that foreign technology accounted for 40 percent of South Africa's growth in gross domestic product from 1957–1972 (Myers et al. 1980, 39); another suggested that the figure was as high as 60 percent (Barber et al. 1982, 58).

Typically South Africa imports more than it exports. This problem is integrally related to its high need for capital equipment imports. From 1955 through 1982 the country experienced a deficit in its current accounts in 17 of those 28 years. Deficits in the total balance of payments also occurred in 17 of these years (Houghton 1976, 180–87, 292; Republic of South Africa 1984, 546). Legum explains that "the root cause of South Africa's economic problem lies, on the broadest level, in the inability of its production process to develop sufficiently to be able to supply its industries with modern machinery and equipment" (quoted in Litvak et al. 1978, 41). Porter (1979, 589) confirms that domestic industry provides "only the plant in which [capital equipment] is housed."

Because of its chronic trade and payments imbalances, foreign capital has been of considerable importance to South Africa. In 20 of the 29 years from 1946 to 1975, the economy experienced net inflows of foreign private capital (Houghton 1976, 182, 292). Between 1974 and 1976 alone, the flow of foreign investment to South Africa was enough to offset the current account deficit for those years (Myers et al. 1980, 39). The surge in the price of gold in 1979 and 1980 contributed to a balance of payments surplus of about $3.6 billion in each of those years, however. By 1981 the surplus had again become a deficit due to an increase in imports and a marked decline in gold prices. In order to rectify the imbalance, the South African government began borrowing. The amount of South Africa's foreign loans is estimated to have increased dramatically between 1979 and 1980, from $295 million to $794 million. In 1981, the country borrowed $479 million, and by early 1982, South Africa's debt was estimated to be about 13 percent of its gross domestic product (compared to 6 percent in 1980). In November 1982, the International Monetary Fund (IMF) approved a loan totaling $1.07 million, or which $680 million was made available immediately (UN Commission on Trans- national Corporations 1983, 4).

In the last decade, foreign loans have been vital to the South African economy for several additional reasons; the financing of state-owned corporations (parastatals) formed since the early 1970s to boost electricity production, port capacity, energy resources, and mineral exploitation; vast increases in government spending for military purposes since the mid-1970s; and at least a four-fold increase in the price of oil after the Arab oil embargo (Myers et al. 1980, 41–42). Litvak et al. (1978) as well as Barber et al. (1982) suggest that loans are particularly important to South Africa not only because they help finance economic develop- ment and military preparedness, but also because they have come during periods in which South Africa faced serious economic and political instability. Litvak et al. report further:

> In 1960 a peaceful crowd demonstrating against the pass laws was fired upon at Sharpeville. This Sharpeville Massacre, combined with other serious unrest in South Africa during 1960–61, caused a massive flight of foreign capital. Two hundred and seventy one million dollars was taken out of the country in 1960 and $36 million in early 1961. Foreign reserves dropped from $350 million to $245 million. The net outflow of foreign capital contin- ued through 1964. As South Africa entered a state of emergency, American banks came to the rescue and shored up the economy. Shortly after Sharpe- ville, financiers in the US put together loans add- ing up to $150 million. Foremost among these was a $40 million revolving loan offered by a consortium of ten American banks including Chase Manhattan and Citibank. . . . Despite the political crisis of the Angolan War and internal South Africa unrest since Soweto, US banks have again made their financial resources available . . . the amount of their out- standing loans to South Africa doubled between early 1975 and late 1976—a $1 billion increase.

> Commenting on the ability of the South African government to borrow from foreign banks, the *Financial Mail* stated a month after Soweto: "a unique feature of the market has been the support of US banks. Apparently more finance has come from this quarter than ever before."
>
> Between January and November 1976, $777 million was loaned to the South African government, state corporations and private businesses. The majority of these loans were reported after the black township uprisings in June (1978, 58–59).

South Africa's total foreign capital assets and liabilities for selected years since 1956 are shown in Table 2–1.

Most of South Africa's trade and foreign capital come from the West. Table 2–2 shows the value of South Africa's imports and exports with its major trading partners. About 80 percent of the country's foreign investment comes from Great Britain, the United States, West Germany, Switzerland, and France. In early 1979, total foreign investment was $26.3 billion; direct foreign investment was $11 billion, with $6 billion held by British interests (10 percent of Britain's worldwide direct investment), $2 billion by other European countries (Study Commission 1981, 133–34). By 1982, total direct foreign investment was a little under $16 billion. Although Japanese interests trade with South Africa, due to their government's restrictions, they do not have direct investments there. Japanese corporations get around this restriction by licensing South African wholly owned subsidiaries to manufacture their products. In 1981, for example, 35 percent of cars sold in the country were Japanese models assembled under licensing agreements (UN Commission on Transnational Corporations 1983, 11).

Direct investment by the United States in South Africa has grown a great deal over the last 30 years, as shown in Table 2–3. Although over 350 American companies have subsidiaries there, over 50 percent of U.S. direct investment is held by Ford, General Motors, Mobil, and Caltex Oil. More than 6,000 companies do business with South Africa, and U.S. financial involvement is far more extensive than direct investment. It also includes indirect investment, that is, U.S. holdings of South African companies' securities, which in 1982 amounted to about $7.6 billion, three times the amount of direct investment for that year (Africa Fund 1984; and Study Commission 1981, 134–35).

The amounts of foreign investment are impressive, but more impressive are the vital contributions this investment makes to the whole economy. As noted earlier, capital

TABLE 2-2. South Africa's Imports from and Exports to its Major Trading Partners (millions of dollars)

Imports From	1969	1970	1971	1972	1973	1974	1975	1976	1977	1978	1979	1980	1981	1982	1983
France	86	125	147	129	181	293	335	295	275	547	559	703	1,018	709	530
Germany	410	521	572	534	880	1,362	1,409	1,218	1,073	1,466	1,555	2,399	2,680	2,503	1,956
Japan	264	310	409	346	548	883	840	691	720	947	952	1,669	2,245	1,711	1,743
UK	699	785	939	764	909	1,210	1,494	1,185	971	1,200	1,491	2,242	2,467	2,029	1,669
US	519	593	658	605	760	1,193	1,341	1,460	1,125	1,137	1,478	2,527	3,021	2,484	2,178
World Total	2,992	3,566	4,039	3,658	4,736	7,225	7,592	6,769	5,910	7,215	8,362	18,327	21,015	19,576	14,587
Exports To															
France	60	56	54	74	100	99	125	171	246	318	418	524	529	415	442
Germany	144	153	154	172	275	468	573	544	595	767	1,085	1,029	885	785	785
Japan	212	253	255	336	353	521	661	592	737	876	1,129	1,551	1,591	1,533	1,366
UK	715	625	585	688	1,013	1,413	1,229	1,147	1,512	1,401	1,147	1,779	1,360	1,300	1,099
US	152	181	166	191	235	352	587	527	911	1,559	1,679	2,126	1,745	1,220	1,580
World Total	2,194	2,175	2,186	2,645	3,498	4,915	5,318	7,976	9,987	12,852	18,397	25,684	20,853	17,647	18,843

Source: IMF Direction of Trade Annuals 1971-84.

TABLE 2-3. U.S. Foreign Direct Investment in South Africa

Year	Total Direct Investment (millions of dollars)	Profitability of Investment (percent)
1950	140	
1955	259	
1956	288	
1959	323	9
1960	286	12
1961	311	13
1962	357	9
1963	411	10
1964	467	10
1965	529	15
1966	600	12
1967	666	12
1968	696	11
1969	755	17
1970	868	15
1971	965	11
1972	1,027	10
1973	1,167	18
1974	1,463	18
1975	1,582	9
1976	1,665	12
1977	1,792	11
1978	1,968	11
1979	1,906	19
1980	2,350	23
1981	2,619	19
1982	2,513	8

Notes: Profitability is defined as the rate of return; the rate of return is defined as the ratio of income to the total amount of foreign direct investment. Income is the sum of (1) interest, dividends, and earnings of unincorporated affiliates, and (2) reinvested earnings of incorporated affiliates.

Sources: Spandau 1983, 120; U.S. Department of Commerce, Survey of Current Business, 1958-83; U.N. Commission on Transnation Corporations 1983, 8.

equipment imports are crucial to the country since it is not able to supply the bulk of its own capital equipment needs. But beyond this, corporations have been involved in government programs designed to achieve the country's self-sufficiency in some strategic sectors of the economy (for example, energy). In addition, important sectors are dominated by foreign companies. In 1980, Myers et al. (39) reported:

> Five multinationals—Shell, British Petroleum, Mobil, Caltex and Total—collectively control close to 83 percent of the petroleum market in South Africa and generate 91 percent of the service stations. Volkswagen, Ford, GM, Datsun, and Toyota hold the major share of the automobile market; the sole South African company, Sigma Motors, has acquired 14 percent of the market by manufacturing Chrysler, Peugeot, Citroen, Mazda and Leyland cars. Mainframe computer sales are split between IBM and British-owned ICI, each with one-third of the market, and Burroughs, Control Data, Sperry Univac and Siemens play lesser roles. Only in mining and agriculture are the companies and operations primarily South African, and even in those sectors, some major international corporations such as Exxon, Union Carbide, US Steel, Phelps Dodge, Del Monte, Tate and Lyle, Rio Tinto Zinc and Newmont Mining play an important role.

United States bank loans to South Africa are also extensive (Klein 1978). Most of the loans have come from: Chase Manhattan, Citibank, Manufacturers Hanover Trust, Morgan Guaranty, and Bank of America. Many U.S. loans have been made through international consortia like the European-American Banking Corporation, and at times even regional banks have participated in loans to South Africa. United States bank loans to the South African government stood at $924 million at the end of 1977. As of June 1981, the amount had fallen to $278 million, but it rose again to $623 million by mid-1982. Loans to both the public and private sectors totaled $3.88 billion in 1982 (Africa Fund 1984; and Hauck et al. 1983, 128).

In summary, there is no doubt that trade and foreign capital, especially from the West, are of vital importance to South African economy. Does this mean that sanctions could bring about significant economic difficulty for the apartheid regime as many anti-apartheid activists believe they would? The answer to this question depends in large part on the type of sanctions imposed.

The Kinds of Sanctions Imposed
and the Number of Countries Observing Them

There are two basic kinds of economic sanctions with varia-
tions on each kind. The two are trade sanctions to prevent
imports and exports of goods, and capital sanctions to
prevent the import of financial investments. Within trade
embargoes there have been proposed bans on imports in
general and on particular imports (for instance, oil or
military supplies) as well as proposed bans on exports. In
an attempt to evaluate some of these proposals, Porter
created an economic simulation of the effects of sanctions on
the South African economy. His analysis of long-term
outcome concluded that if an embargo were to cut off South
Africa from importations of capital equipment, in the long
run "South Africa's growth should effectively cease.
Indeed, as time went and depreciation became relevant, the
output potential of South Africa would be reduced unless it
could rapidly develop from a very undeveloped base its own
capital goods industries" (1979, 590). Marvin (1964) comes
to the same conclusion. In addition, Porter asserts that in
the short run, the effect of sanctions on imports of capital
equipment could also have serious impact.

> How much impact would depend on the effectiveness
> of the embargo. If South Africa's imports were
> reduced by less than one-fourth, little economic
> damage would be inflicted—each one percentage
> point cut in imports would cause about a one half
> percentage point cut in GDP. Once imports were
> reduced by more than one-fourth, the damage would
> become more significant. The elasticity of GDP
> reductions with respect to import reductions rises
> to about one and one-fourth, as import reductions
> reach one-half. Should imports be cut by more
> than one-half, massive unemployment and relocation
> of white labor (as well as nonwhite labor) would
> have begun to occur (1979, 590).

Spandau (1983), a South African business analyst at the
University of Witwatersrand, basically agrees with this
conclusion based on his own investigation of the consequences of import sanctions.

In Porter's discussion of capital investment sanctions,
he claims that the cessation of foreign direct investment
could also hurt the apartheid economy's growth potential in
the long run. This result is primarily due to a consequent
reduction in the country's access to new technology and the

benefits of corporations' research and development. In the short run, however, this kind of sanction alone is not likely to have any severe impact, even on the balance of payments or on imports. This is in large part because the government would retaliate against investors. Myers et al. (1980, 138) enumerate the regime's strict foreign exchange controls put in place after the capital flight accompanying the disturbances surrounding Sharpeville (1960) to hinder corporations' withdrawal. Although foreigners have been freer since early 1983 to transfer capital in and out of the country, Porter (1979, 590–91) asserts that, in the event of sanctions,

> There is no possibility that South Africa would permit the actual physical withdrawal of the capital equipment which is the foreign net asset position in South Africa. Should foreigners attempt to unload the shares, loans, mortgages, etc. that represent claims on South African output, they would threaten disorder in the financial and foreign exchange markets of South Africa, but they would not reduce the economy's capital stock one iota. Of course, the financial disruption might make it difficult for South Africa to operate this capital at capacity. The most that "disengagement" can mean, therefore, is the cessation of new (and replacement) investment . . . basically a growth related [i.e., long-term] threat.

Porter and others dismiss the possibility of export sanctions against South Africa because the country has a very important commodity in fairly high demand with an easily disguised origin: gold. Also other important mineral exports could not be easily stopped for much the same reasons. Besides, Porter maintains, the only merit in stopping exports is to deny South Africa the foreign exchange to buy imports, and there are other ways of preventing imports that are not so troublesome.

With regard to commodity-specific import sanctions, Myers et al. discuss the case of oil but come to no definitive conclusion on the impact of a total oil embargo. They do suggest that at minimum, "economic growth would be retarded, new investment from abroad would slow to a trickle or cease altogether, and unemployment and the costs of living would rise" (1980, 140). Clearly, however, the South African government worries about such an embargo for the oil-poor country. After the 1973 OPEC oil embargo was put in place and then after the supplies from Iran stopped in 1979, the government instituted a series of measures designed to protect the country from the possibility of a well-enforced total oil embargo. The nation is reported to have stockpiles good for two to ten years in abandoned coal mines in the northern Transvaal. Plus, it is seeking with the help of American technology from the Fluor corporation, to expand its production of oil from coal through its parastatal SASOL (Myers et al. 1980, 140, 180). In recent years, however, there has been a relaxation in the programs designed to conserve supplies and reduce demand. This may suggest that the government no longer believes the supply situation to be critical (Barber et al. 1982, 57).

With regard to an embargo on another specific commodity, computers, Myers et al (1980, 141) suggest that the impact could again be serious. In an anecdotal analysis, the authors quote one banker as saying, "Without spare parts, our computers would be down within two years. Without computers, we need 2,000 trained bookkeepers. And where would we get 2,000 bookkeepers?"

In his evaluation of the impact of more general sanctions, Porter issues several caveats, some of which should be mentioned here. South Africa has never really prepared for sanctions in a concerted fashion. If the government should do so, the conclusions offered here would be altered by these new circumstances. He also suggests that the longer the world's governments take to institute sanctions, the more possibility the country has to prepare itself. In addition, Porter is concerned that "sanctions must work quickly, for they are increasingly averted by long-run adjustment" (1979, 585). He therefore asserts that the type of embargo with the greatest potential for damage is a stoppage of imports. And for this type of sanction to be most effective, it must be total—a cessation of all imports. "Partial sanctions achieve partial results" (1979, 584). It is this last point that raises still further concerns about the efficacy of sanctions.

In a report of their investigation into the possibilities and probabilities of sanctions, the Study Commission on U.S. Policy Toward Southern Africa (1981) concluded that among South Africa's major trade and investment partners, there is little or no likelihood that the European governments in power in 1981 would impose any further embargoes against South Africa. Furthermore, Israel and other governments have helped South Africa circumvent existing sanctions and would probably continue such aid in the event of stronger measures. Therefore, it is generally assumed that if any one of South Africa's major trade and

investment partners imposed any kind of trade or investment sanctions, others would and could simply pick up the
slack, getting a bigger share of a profitable pie. This
conclusion is perhaps drawn too quickly and too easily,
however, because there does not appear to be any serious
examination in the literature of the substitutability of
specific products and capital investments provided by any
one of the major partners. For example, there has been no
definitive study on how quickly and at what costs the South
African economy could recover from a partial or total imposition of sanctions by the United States.

What is fairly clear, however, is that, if judged by
their behavior in the UN, the governments of the United
States and Britain provide the biggest obstacles to further
embargoes against apartheid. Without the participation of
these two governments, whose nations constitute the largest
of South Africa's trade and investment partners, no sanctions efforts are likely to have severe economic consequences for South Africa. Based on the studies cited here, it is
reasonable to speculate that if these two governments
attempted to isolate South Africa economically without the
support of other partners such as Germany, France and
Japan, their actions alone could result in significant hardship for the apartheid regime. As stated earlier, however,
the United States government has never been willing seriously to consider any economic sanctions beyond the embargo on the sale of military items voted by the Security
Council in 1977. Britain has even closer ties of "kith and
kin" to South Africa and its policy makers show no signs of
willingness to go further in economically isolating South
Africa. Indeed, with the constructive engagement policy of
the Reagan administration, to which some European governments acquiesce, the ties that bind South Africa to the West
are only getting tighter.

Our overall conclusions about the potential impact of
sanctions must be cautious and qualified. If the goal of
economic sanctions were to be to bring severe economic
hardship to South Africa, to be most effective the following
conditions should be met:

1. At least one-half of the country's imports must be
stopped from entering the country; other economic isolation
measures such as the cessation of capital flows into the
country or commodity-specific embargoes—for instance,
oil—could potentially do serious long-term economic harm to
South Africa, but they are not as effective in the short-
term.

2. Enough governments and/or businesses must be willing to enforce the sanctions to achieve one-half reduction in imports.

3. Other trade and investment partners not enforcing the sanctions must not increase their supplies of imports.

If the goal of sanctions is ultimately to end apartheid by causing severe economic hardship, then one further condition must be met: the partial (as stated in 1 above) or total economic isolation of South Africa must be accompanied by other factors that threaten the foundation of apartheid. Such factors might include the following: From the world community—diplomatic pressures on the South African government; more vigorous enforcement of the arms embargo; cessation of all military and nuclear cooperation; humanitarian and/or military aid to the resistance movements; increased support to the front line states, and so on.[1] From the people in South Africa—increases in civil unrest or disobedience among whites and/or blacks, such as work stoppages and demonstrations; guerrilla incursions and acts of sabotage; refusals to serve in the military, and so forth.

It is impossible to predict what mix of these factors would end apartheid, but the effective economic isolation of the country, as designated in the conditions above, could be one factor to hasten the process.

There are several implications of these conclusions for divestment proponents whose goals are to speed the end of apartheid through the imposition of economic difficulty on the country. Their assertions that the apartheid regime would suffer considerable hardship if economic sanctions were enacted and affectively enforced are credible. Much of their activity has been focused on preventing direct investment, however, when prevention of trade (specifically exports to South Africa) may be the more harmful, although the more difficult, measure to impose. In that Western governments are not likely to institute trade or investment embargoes (as the activists are quite aware), any direct actions against businesses to pressure them to disengage from South Africa can only hope to achieve partial results—most likely results far short of the severe economic hardship desired. If pressures on businesses are persistently heightened, especially in Britain and the United States, so as to restrict their relations with South Africa to a greater extent than has been the case heretofore, the costs of acquiring goods necessary for maintaining growth in the South African economy probably will become higher and, at least, be of some inconvenience to the regime. But beliefs that such inconvenience or that piecemeal restrictions on business activities with South Africa could help bring about fundamental political change are, at this point, a matter of faith rather than reasonable expectation based on political and economic analysis. This leads to a con- clusion that most activists have long understood: the un- willingness of Western governments to take seriously the policy option of economically isolating South Africa is the major obstacle to imposing economic hardship on apartheid.

This conclusion is not likely to be a deterrent to activ- ists pursuit of sanctions-related goals. As stated earlier, a wide variety of goals other than bringing economic hardship to apartheid are the ones many activists pursue. To reit- erate, such goals may be one or more of the following: to take a moral stand, to express solidarity with southern Africa resistance movements, to educate constituencies about racism and the international political economy, to punish in some way those who perpetuate apartheid, or to improve relations with black African states. Therefore, the fore- going analysis of the impact of sanctions may be partially or totally irrelevant to anti-apartheid groups involved in sanctions-related work if they are principally seeking one or more of these other goals.

There are others, those outside the anti-apartheid movement, who seek to alter or abolish apartheid. They, too, operate fundamentally out of faith regarding change in South Africa, but their faith is that of basic belief in capitalism as a progressive force for improved race relations in the country. An examination of the degree to which these beliefs are rounded in sound analysis is our next task.

THE PROGRESSIVE FORCE ARGUMENT

The basic thesis of the progressive force argument has been around since the 1940s and has been put forward by both South Africans and people outside the country. Some have called it the Oppenheimer thesis after the English- speaking business magnate, Harry Oppenheimer, head of the Anglo-American Corporation. Barber et al. (1982, 81–82) state the argument succinctly:

> Economic growth itself, irrespective of its sources or its path, is the ultimate liberating force. In- equalities and injustices will inevitable be generated in the drive towards economic maturity. Unfortu- nately, the whites' historically determined monopoly of political power has given them the capacity to

make the blacks bear the brunt of this inequality, but a different socio-political structure would not have generated a lesser degree of overall inequality by virtue of being less racialistic. Capitalist countries pass through well-defined stages of development enroute to modernization. The particular growth-path will depend upon many factors. The sources of growth at any stage may be external demand, or the discovery of new resources, or advances in technology, or economies of scale. The rate of growth will depend upon the willingness to save and invest, and upon the availability of resources, including both skilled and unskilled labour. The distribution of the benefits will be determined by the ownership of resources and by the market structures which evolve. The growth process will progressively and inexorable thrust aside any political and institutional obstacles, since the cost of these, measured in terms of the benefits foregone, will become increasingly apparent and progressively less tolerable. In the case of South Africa, these obstacles include the whole apartheid structure, which will be gradually eroded in the economic sphere and ultimately, because of the consequent increase in the economic power of blacks in the political sphere as well. Because foreign trade and foreign investment are such important sources of economic growth in South Africa, they are an unqualified good. Any effects they may have on the distribution of power in the short run should . . . be ignored, because in the long run the ruling groups will recognize the need for reform and for negotiated compromise on the question of political rights, rather than put at risk their own living standards by curtailing the growth process.

The contention that capitalist economies, based on growth models of economic development, inevitably produce a high or even adequate degree of social well-being for the majority of the population has been under attack for some time in the social sciences among scholars who span the ideological spectrum (for instance, see Berger 1976). Therefore, there is no reason to accept the progressive force thesis on face value without a thorough investigation of how the political economy of South Africa itself has developed and is likely to develop in the near future. Such an extensive analysis is not possible here, but there are some brief responses to the argument that can be made.

Apartheid structures are rooted deeply in the country's history. The subjugation and control of Africans and the harnessing of their labor at cheap costs has been integral to South Africa's political economy long before the structure got its formal name in 1948. Apartheid has not been a phase or stage in the nation's development but one of its most important foundations. In recent years separate development has been significantly reinforced. The government has strengthened migratory labor policies, imposed more severe pass law restrictions on the majority of Africans, sought to bring some of the homelands to "independence," stepped up repression against dissidents, and forcedly removed Africans from "black spots" and other areas. At the same time, however, a small proportion of Africans have been given access to more skilled jobs and greater freedom of movement in the urban areas where some have long-established residence permits. Despite these small gains for a few, the plight of the majority is not improving and may be getting worse. Furthermore, these measures taken as a whole indicate that apartheid is not being dismantled in the face of continued industrial growth but is being made a more efficient instrument of that growth.[2] These recent government policies apparently aim to replace a highly stratified system in which class and race cleavages almost perfectly coincide—with whites on the top and blacks on the bottom—with another highly stratified system based solely on class, where whites remain on the top and, except for a few of the very privileged, blacks remain on the bottom.

Although the progressive force argument, like any thesis in social science, cannot be disproven absolutely, and although this analysis does not display its shortcomings in great depth, the preponderance of evidence suggests that "white domination will adapt to economic imperatives while retaining key features of apartheid. Progressive force advocates tend to exaggerate the demands of economic change and underestimate the durability of repressive institutions" (Litvak 1978, 36).

Those who argue against sanctions often also assert that, out of its own desires for a stable investment climate and a healthy skilled workforce, the business community in South Africa has been and will be an effective political lobby on behalf of improved conditions for blacks. An examination of both domestic and international business as a lobby in South Africa, however, does not support such a claim. Within South Africa, business lobbies rarely become active on issues outside a narrowly defined realm of rather specific business concerns. Their most intense and broadly defined political involvement came during the period of economic recession and political instability after the 1960 Sharpeville demonstrations and again following the 1976–77 disturbances in Soweto and elsewhere. This suggests that only during the years of disruptive political unrest and a sluggish economy did businessmen begin to question the government's apartheid policy. During the boom years of the 1960s and early 1970s business groups were fairly inactive in terms of their attempts to impact broad political, social, and economic issues. This inactivity results not only from the fact that businesses enjoy very favorable investment conditions but also because of swift and punitive political and economic retaliation by the government against those companies and business groups that have on occasion openly opposed government apartheid policies (Myers et al. 1980, 69–86, 141–42).

Therefore, opposition to sanctions based on an assumption that the international and South African business communities can be used for progressive and significant change in South Africa or the elimination of apartheid appears to have very little grounding in evidence. Despite the possibility of good intentions on the part of some businessmen, the business sector has shown itself historically to be very reluctant to oppose apartheid policies except under quite adverse conditions for brief periods of time with very modest proposals. That these sanctions critics want to pursue tried and failed policy options for change, as opposed to the untested and controversial sanctions option, is testament more to their allegiance to business than to the validity of their argument. In fact, across the years, apartheid has been good for business and business has been good for apartheid.

RESPONSES TO ACTIVIST PRESSURES

The evaluative purpose of this research is limited and will not adequately address the impact of the entire anti-apartheid movement in the United States or even the sanctions thrust within the movement. Some indications of overall impact will be discerned from the evaluation of the specific campaigns in Connecticut and Michigan discussed in Chapters 4 and 5. Nevertheless, it is important at this point to outline some apparent patterns of reaction to the movement by businesses, governments, and nongovernmental groups. These reactions shed greater light on the impact of the movement as a whole.

Business Responses

Adoption of a code of conduct for their subsidiary operations has been the most frequent corporate response to
pressures. The code of conduct, prominent in the United
States, the Sullivan Principles, has also been used by some
institutional investors as a criterion for divestment of their
holdings in businesses that do not adopt the principles.
The code is named after its founder, the Reverend Leon
Sullivan, a black Baptist minister from Philadelphia who is
well known for the U.S. community-based workers' training
programs that have prepared hundreds of thousands of
ethnic minorities for skilled work. Sullivan was named to
the Board of Directors of General Motors in 1971 as a result
of pressures on GM to include blacks on its board, and he
began at that point to challenge the corporation to withdraw
its business from South Africa. Across several years,
however, he was unable to convince anyone else on the
Board of his position, and out of frustration, he began to
develop the code of conduct for businesses operating in
South Africa. In March 1977, after close consultation with
corporate executives in a number of South Africa-related
firms, Sullivan announced his six criteria for fair employment practices in South Africa as shown in Table 2-4.
They already had the endorsement of 12 businesses with
South African operations, and they immediately began to
attain wide popularity in the U.S. business community. By
the end of 1978, there were 105 signatories, and at the
close of 1979, there were 135. In recent years there has
been a decline in the number of participating companies,
and at this point there are over 125 American businesses
that have pledged themselves to implementing the principles.
    In 1978, Sullivan amplified the code to require signatory
companies to support "the elimination of discrimination
against the rights of blacks to form or belong to government registered trade unions, and to acknowledge generally
the right of black workers to form their own union or to be
represented by trade unions where unions already exist."
In 1979, he added the demand that companies "assist in the
development of black and non-white business enterprises,
including distributors, suppliers of goods and services and
manufacturers." Corporations were also told to lobby the
South African government for changes such as the "aboli-
tion of job reservation, job fragmentation and apprentice-
ship restrictions for blacks and other non-whites" and to
"support changes in influx control laws to provide for the
right of black migrant workers to normal family life" (Myers

et al. 1980, 301–3; Schmidt 1980, 14–17). Further amplification came in 1982 and Sullivan stated on several occasions that companies should not only sign the principles but also adopt a policy of non-expansion in South Africa and not sell strategic goods to the police and military (Hauck et al. 1983, 99).

Sullivan established the International Council for Equality of Opportunity Principles to report on the progress of signatory companies and the Arthur D. Little Company, a Cambridge consulting firm, contracted to survey companies' compliance progress and report its findings every six months. After Sullivan was unable to obtain foundation support, signatories agreed to pay for the evaluation of company performance. They are assessed between $4,500 and $7,000 annually, the exact figure being based on worldwide sales (Hauck et al. 1983, 98, 101). Arthur D. Little sends corporations a lengthy questionnaire which their management fills out and returns to the consulting firm. The respondents are then categorized and reported as: [3]

Corporations in each category, 1981.

1.	Making good progress	34
2.	Making progress	32
3.	Needs to become more active	47
4.	Endorsers with few or no employees	22
5.	New signatories	10
6.	Non-respondents	21
7.	Signatories headquartered outside the U.S.	1
8.	Non-signatories	150

At first there were major difficulties in getting corporations to respond to the questionnaires, but the number of non-respondents decreased across time until 1982 when some companies began to perceive their negative ratings as a liability. Some still leave the most sensitive questions unanswered, but Sullivan and others have attempted to strengthen the reporting process. In addition to having signatories respond to the survey, Sullivan sent a team of observers to evaluate 25 companies' compliance in 1979. In 1982, a series of nine basic requirements was instituted. Those companies not meeting these criteria were placed in the third rating category (Hauck et al. 1983, 112–18).

Other codes of conduct have been developed by the European Community, Canada, and the Urban Foundation, a white South African business organization attempting to

TABLE 2-4. The Sullivan Principles

PRINCIPLE I: Non-segregation of the races in all eating, comfort, and work facilities.

PRINCIPLE II: Equal and fair employment practices for all employees.

PRINCIPLE III: Equal pay for all employees doing equal or comparable work for the same period of time

PRINCIPLE IV: Initiation of and development of training programs that will prepare, in substantial numbers, blacks and other non-whites for supervisory, administrative, clerical and technical jobs.

PRINCIPLE V: Increasing the number of blacks and other non-whites in management and supervisory positions.

PRINCIPLE VI: Improving the quality of employees' lives outside the work environment in such areas as housing, transportation, schooling, recreation and health facilities.

Source: Taken from Hauck et al. 1983, 155.

improve working conditions for blacks. The South African government has not interfered to prevent corporations from becoming signatories on any of these codes, and it even approved the final draft of the Sullivan Principles (Schmidt 1980, 47).

The Sullivan Principles and other codes have been widely condemned by many anti-apartheid activists and many black leaders in the United States and South Africa as being reformist, irrelevant to fundamental change in apartheid, and/or diversionary to the progress of divestment efforts. In 1982, the Motor Assemblers' and Component Workers' Union of South Africa labeled the Sullivan code as a "'piece-meal reform that allows this cruel system of apartheid to survive'" (*The Cape Times,* 19 January 1979). The 1979 U.S. Conference of Black Religious Leaders on Apartheid resolved "that the Sullivan Principles, though well-intentioned, are no longer sufficient and that the very presence of United States corporations in South Africa serves to legitimize the apartheid system of white supremacy" (Schmidt 1980, 107). Subsequently 58 black and white U.S. national church, labor, academic and other professional leaders signed a lengthy statement opposing the Sullivan code. In the statement they asserted that the principles "provided precisely what the companies were looking for: a guaranteed public relations success which promised maximum credit for minimum change." Although some corporate leaders take the principles seriously and devote significant time to their implementation, others basically agree with this claim. A manager of the Goodyear Tire and Rubber company's South African subsidiary said that Sullivan knocked divestment efforts "on their head . . . he has helped improve the image back in the U.S. of American companies in South Africa" (Business International 1980, 251). Another corporate official stated that "the Sullivan principles have been very convenient for American companies" (Hauck et al. 1983, 121).

In a lengthy analysis of the principles, Schmidt (1980) concludes that they are unlikely to have any significant impact on apartheid. Even advocates of the code, such as the Study Commission on U.S. Policy Toward Southern Africa (1981), assert that it is unlikely to impact or alter apartheid structures and will only make a positive impact on the lives of a very few blacks. Less than one percent of all blacks employed in South Africa work for American companies and one estimate suggests that only 58,000 black workers from a total black population of about 20 million are affected by the principles (Davis, et al. 1983, 551). The reasons for the severe limitations on the principles' potential are several. First, companies, by the admission of some of their own managers, are reluctant to comply, and since their compliance is monitored through self-reporting, it is impossible to know whether or not their reports are an accurate assessment of their progress. Second, some of the changes brought about through attempts at compliance have been hardly even disguised as cosmetic. Herman Nickel, the current U.S. ambassador to South Africa wrote in 1978 (72):

> In line with the Sullivan code, GM duly removed the offending signs from the lavatory doors in its Port Elizabeth plant, only to replace them with color-keyed doors; blue for whites and Chinese (the latter considered honorary whites for lavatory purposes), orange for blacks and coloreds.

The primary reason that the codes can have little impact, however, is because companies are forced to work within a legal and white trade union system in which blacks are denied citizenship and fundamental economic, political, and social rights in South Africa. The codes cannot and do not attempt to address themselves to the basic structures of apartheid such as the homelands, migratory labor, pass laws, and the complex legal restrictions on regime opponents, if they did, they would not be tolerated for long by the government. At best, the principles can contribute to the development of a small black middle class with greater stakes in the system, a development promoted by some segments of the apartheid regime itself and in the interest of corporations who need greater numbers of skilled black workers.

Other corporate actions regarding pressures to divest range from ending their business relations with South Africa to strong defense of their investments and refusals to yield to pressure. Polaroid is apparently the only corporation to have severed its ties with South Africa as a result of activists' pressures, although in early 1983, at least five corporations from the West sold their South African holdings. Analysts speculated that international opposition to investment played a role in these decisions (*Economist*, 25 June 1983). A number of other businesses have pledged not to expand their operations or, in the case of banks, make new loans. Examples of corporations that have at varying times in recent years announced that they would not expand their operations in South Africa are: Borg Warner, Burroughs, Control Data, Ford, General Motors, Gulf and Western, Johnson and Johnson, and Kimberly-Clark. Kodak announced a policy of no sales to the South African government. Citing anti-apartheid pressures as one of the factors in the decision, General Electric cancelled plans to invest in a $140 million coal-mining operation in the Kwazulu homeland.

Banks that apparently have made no new loans to the South African government or any of its instrumentalities are: First Chicago Corporation, Manufacturers Hanover, Morgan Guaranty, Wells Fargo, Harris Trust, Crocker National, First National Bank of Atlanta, Bankers Trust, Chemical Bank of New York, First National Bank of Boston, and Pittsburgh National Bank. Shearson/American Express, Merrill Lynch, and Sears, Roebuck and Co. have stated policies of not making loans to or underwriting the distribution of South African government bonds (*Africa News*, 31 May 1982; Myers et al. 1980, 307–11). Among the banks, only Chemical Bank and First National of Boston have adopted clear policies about no loans to the public sector, and Chemical Bank excludes the private sector as well. All the banks in Michigan (over 250) that serve as depositories for state funds have filed affidavits stating that they do not have existing loans to South African public sector or to

U.S. companies' subsidiaries there. However, none of the banks has ruled out trade-related loans (Hauck, et al. 1983, 125–37).

Unless they announce their reasons for the decision, it is difficult to discern whether company managers choose not to reinvest on the basis of activist pressures or because of the investment climate in South Africa. Recently some risk analysts have suggested that the long-term prospects for foreign investment in South Africa are not as favorable as before, and some investors have been hesitant to make commitments for more than five or ten years. These investors fear that skilled workers will be drained by the military draft and that companies will have to conform to strict laws regarding plant security. Nevertheless, at the same time, high growth in the market demand in the South African economy has stimulated corporate investment, which is rising, not falling. At least on a short- and medium-term basis, business executives appear to see no greater risk in doing business in South Africa than in many other parts of the world (Davis 1983; UN Commission on Transnational Corporations 1983, 9).

Corporate executives claim that due to activist pressures "they are forced to devote more time and energy to their South African operations than the scale of those operations would normally warrant." (Myers et al. 1980, 307) Another indicator of corporate attention to the issue is the number of business reports analyzing anti-apartheid efforts, such as those done by Business International (1980) and the Conference Board (Janger and Berenbeim 1981), or corporate brochures and advertisements explaining their South African operations. Citibank, General Motors and Dresser Industries are examples of corporations that have had concerted public relations campaigns to promote better images of their subsidiaries. In early 1984, the American Chamber of Commerce in South Africa sent a 20-page report to members of Congress explaining the chamber's attempts to bring positive change to South Africa. Another type of defense was made by Dow Chemical when it threatened not to make any more donations to Michigan State University if its stock was divested.

An important development related to divestment pressures is that some companies attempt to attract business on the basis of their policies of no or restricted ties to South Africa. Chemical Bank has received many institutions' deposits that were withdrawn from Citibank, and a number of investment firms promote their socially responsible (or "clean") investment services.

In all, business responses have been mixed. There

have been some restrictions of business relations with South Africa but no large-scale withdrawal of operations there. Many companies seem to have been inconvenienced by activists' pressures and most with operations in South Africa appear to pay close attention to the issue. As the Conference Board reports it: "There is one stubborn and intractable issue that will not go away—South Africa" (Janger and Berenbeim 1981, 22). But, so far, pressures have not mounted enough to threaten a crippling blow to corporations that remain tied to South Africa.

United States Government Responses

Within the U.S. government, response to divestment pressures has varied from one administration to another and from one part of the government to another. Officials within the Carter administration were willing to entertain the need for greater economic pressures on South Africa, and the most extensive trade restrictions ever instituted by the U.S. government were put in place in 1976–78. However, these officials were never willing to take the argument for full sanctions seriously. In the Reagan administration, the basic philosophy is one of greater conciliation and cooperation. In contrast to policies under Carter, the Commerce Department under Reagan has loosened restrictions on sales of non-military goods, computer and communications equipment, as well as aircraft and helicopters to the South African police and military. The value of licenses issued for such sales from 1981–83 ($28 million) was more than the value of similar sales in the 30 years from 1950–80 ($19 million) (*Africa News*, 30 January 1984). The current administration has also increased cooperation and exchanges on nuclear technology and voted in favor of a $1.1 billion loan for South Africa from the International Monetary Fund. The favorable vote came despite formal objection registered by 35 members of Congress and widespread protests by African, Middle Eastern, and other Third World governments.

The State Department and others in the executive branch claim that anti-apartheid activities have had little impact on governmental policy making and evidence from the Reagan administration would support this claim. Nevertheless, officials in several departments continue to monitor the movement, especially actions targeted at state and city governments, and the constructive engagement policy under Reagan may well have added momentum to these efforts, since activists have had no sympathetic allies in the administration. An outside consultant who subsequently became a special assistant to Chester Crocker, the Assistant Secretary of State for African Affairs, wrote a report on such activities for the State Department in 1981. Thus, even if the foreign policy and commerce bureaucracies do not adhere to the policies advocated by the anti-apartheid movement, they do pay some attention to it, and on several occasions officials have spoken out against the state governments' sanctions-related laws.

Although anti-apartheid activists historically have had more access to Congress than the executive branch, the level of congressional interest in South Africa has vacillated across time, and activists' impact has been mixed. One of the most important acts that Congress took regarding southern Africa was in 1971 when Senator Harry Byrd (Ind.-Virginia) offered a bill calling for suspension of U.S. sanctions against strategic materials supplied by Rhodesia. Sanctions were instituted by the United Nations against the illegal white minority government in 1968 at the initiative of Britain and with the support of the United States. At issue in the so-called Byrd amendment was the source of U.S. chrome imports. The only major source besides Rhodesia is the Soviet Union, and Byrd argued that the United States should not be dependent on its major antagonist for a strategic metal. The legislation was supported by chrome importers like Union Carbide, and anti-apartheid activists and their congressional allies were caught off guard. The amendment passed. In response, a major campaign was mounted by anti-apartheid groups, spearheaded by the Washington Office on Africa, and with additional pressure from the international community, the Byrd amendment was repealed in 1973 (Ogene 1983).

Congress went against the wishes of the anti-apartheid movement on another issue regarding the economic isolation of white minority regimes in 1971 when it assigned South African a sugar quota for the third time. The quota meant that the South African sugar industry had a guaranteed percentage of the U.S. market. Not only was the quota extended in 1971, but it was also increased. Although anti-apartheid activists fought the quota renewal, they were unsuccessful in convincing Congress (Ogene 1983).

High congressional interest levels and activity on South Africa often correspond to conflictful events in that country. The personal commitments of particular members of Congress also brought attention to apartheid. In their roles as chairs of the two Africa sub-committees, former

Representative Charles Diggs (D.-Michigan), between 1971 and 1973, and former Senator Dick Clark (D.-Iowa) in 1976 held a number of hearings on U.S. business relations with South Africa. Activists participated in these hearings, and they helped to lay a significantly better educational foundation for the introduction of a number of South Africa-related bills and resolutions between 1977 and 1984 in the aftermath of the Soweto uprisings and in response to increasing sanctions activity by state and local governments.

Much of the legislation was sponsored by members of the Congressional Black Caucus, especially Representative William Gray (D.-Pennsylvania). Other legislators active on the issue have been: Representative Stephen Solarz (D.-New York); former Senator George McGovern (D.-South Dakota); Representative Thomas Evans (R.-Delaware); Senator Paul Tsongas (D.-Massachusetts), and Representative Howard Wolpe (D.-Michigan), current chair of the House Subcommittee on Africa.

The bills and resolutions varied in substance including; endorsements of the Sullivan Principles; prohibition of certain bank loans; denial of foreign tax credits to American companies operation in South Africa; prohibition against further U.S. direct investment; tying IMF contributions to restrictions on its loans to South Africa; banning the importation of South African krugerrands (gold coins); and calls for U.S. sanctions against South Africa. One piece of binding legislation regarding business with South Africa that passed was a 1978 amendment to the Export-Import Bank Authorization Bill, the so-called Evans amendment. The amendment

> prohibited the Eximbank from granting financial guarantees or incurring any credits that would contribute to the maintenance of apartheid by the South African government . . . barred the Eximbank from guaranteeing any credits to the South African government or its agencies (including public corporations) unless the President of the United States determined that significant progress had been made toward the elimination of apartheid . . . [and] specified that no Eximbank facilities could be used to support any export to a private South African buyer unless the Secretary of State certified that the buyer had endorsed and was carrying out the goals of nonsegregation and equal employment outlined in the Sullivan principles (Hauck et al. 1983, 37).

The effect of this amendment under Carter was to cut off Eximbank credit guarantees and insurance programs for South African borrowers (Christenson 1981, 62),[4] but Reagan administrators have reached an informal agreement with the South African government whereby Eximbank financing can be resumed under the provisions of the amendment (Hauck, et al. 1983, 37). The only other law with such restrictions passed in late 1983. At that time Congress attached to IMF authorization legislation a provision that requires U.S. opposition to IMF loans to South Africa, unless a series of strict conditions are met (*Africa News,* 28 November 1983).

Another piece of legislation that passed the House was a resolution that denounced South Africa for Steve Biko's death and other repressive measures used against regime opponents. In addition, in 1982, Solarz offered a successful amendment to the foreign aid bill that provided "not less than $4 million" in scholarship funds for South African students who face educational discrimination in South Africa to pursue education in the United States. The program began in the fall of 1982. In fiscal years 1984 and 1985, educational assistance to black South Africans and training programs conducted by private groups in the homelands and elsewhere in the country received about $15.5 million. Much of the aid was a part of the constructive engagement effort on the part of the Reagan administration (Hauck et al. 1983, 42, 47; Washington Office on Africa, Winter 1984).

More hearings on the conflict in southern Africa were held in 1982, but this time the intent was to prove that the ANC and SWAPO are under the control of Soviet communists. Under the leadership of Senator Jeremiah Denton (R.- Alabama), the recently created Senate Subcommittee on Security and Terrorism investigated the linkages between the guerrilla groups and the Eastern bloc. Anti-apartheid activists fault the hearings for not acknowledging that the source of insecurity and terror in southern Africa is apartheid (Leonard 1983, 45).

Although activists appreciate congressional efforts to enhance anti-apartheid work, on the whole they have gotten only minimal support from Congress and thus have devoted only sporadic attention to targeting the House and Senate. However, South African interests worried enough about the activities of former Senator Clark and Representative Wolpe to join with others in efforts to unseat them. Clark lost his reelection bid in 1980, but Wolpe won his in 1982. With Clark, Diggs, and McGovern gone from Congress, anti-apartheid groups have lost important allies. (Leonard 1983, 185; Washington Office on Africa, Autumn 1982).

South African Responses

South Africans, both those sympathetic and those in opposition to apartheid, care a great deal about the anti-apartheid movement in the United States, the divestment issue, and the possibility of economic sanctions. The South African government maintains four official consulates and has permission for nine honorary ones in cities across the U.S. to promote friendly relations between the two countries (Republic of South Africa 1984). In other arenas, the 1978 exposure of the "Muldergate" scandal in South Africa (through findings by the official South African Erasmus Commission) revealed that Eschel Rhoodie, Secretary of the Department of Information, together with Prime Minister John Vorster, Minister of Information Connie Mulder, and General Hendrick Van den Bergh, head of the then Bureau of State Security, approved a plan to spend at least $73 million on projects to buy influence among politicians and media and to finance pro-apartheid groups around the world. The Commission claimed that the group's U.S. contact, John McGoff, a Michigan publisher, received at least $10 million to buy the *Washington Star*, but he got the *Sacramento Union* instead. McGoff denied the commission's charges, but he is well known to have been involved otherwise in promoting South African interests. He was under investigation by both the U.S. Securities and Exchange Commission and the Department of Justice for his South Africa-related activities, and in 1983 he consented to a court order banning him from future violations of certain SEC disclosure requirements (Hudson 1983; Washington Office of Africa, Summer 1982).

The South African government also spends a great deal of money each year on lobbying efforts in the United States. Three prominent firms that have represented South Africa are: Basin and Sears, the law firm of John Sears who was a presidential campaign manager for Ronald Reagan, for $500,000 a year plus expenses; Smaters, Symington, and Herlong for $300,000 a year; and Kimberly Cameron Hallamore for $63,000. Plus, four of the so-called independent homelands retain a least five lobbyists. At least three persons whose firms were paid lobbyists for the South African government have attained positions in the Reagan administration: Thomas Shannon, appointed presidential assistant for public liason; Donald de Kieffer, appointed to the office of U.S. Trade Representative; and Marion Smoak, appointed to work on African Affairs at the State Department (Leonard 1983, 169). Two nongovernmental organizations from South Africa that enhance relations between the two countries are the South Africa Foundation with John Chettle as director, and the U.S. Namibia (Southwest Africa) Trade and Cultural Council. Both are headquartered in Washington, D.C.

Although persons interviewed in the South African Embassy and U.N. Mission maintained that divestment campaigns have not directly harmed South Africa in any way, they admit that they keep a close watch over these activities and issue periodic reports on them. The government has even been worried enough to infiltrate anti-apartheid groups with agents and informers.

With regard to state and city campaigns, South Africans have been sent to lobby against divestment legislation in several states, South African interests paid Americans to lobby in their behalf, letters and supporting documents have been sent to state officials, South African Foundation officials have testified in hearings on some bills, and trips to South Africa sponsored by the government have been organized to show lawmakers the country firsthand. South African lobbying efforts against the Massachusetts divestment bill received a great deal of press attention (*Boston Globe*, 28 and 29 January 1983). In 1980, the Foundation published an extensive report on U.S. divestment activities, and in 1983, a second lengthy document on the divestment debate written by foundation director John Chettle was circulated widely. Chettle contended that divestment of state and city pension funds was illegal under U.S. law and financially unsound (see Chettle 1983 and 1984).

South Africans in resistance to apartheid both inside the country and outside monitor the U.S. movement closely. This is not as difficult as it might seem for those within South Africa because the media there give special coverage to anti-apartheid events in the United States. There even have been several stories on state divestment legislation in newspapers there. South Africans from inside and outside the country were interviewed for this research, and although all of them believe that the major dynamics for change in apartheid will come from within the country and region, they claim that they and others in opposition get an enormous boost in moral to know that U.S. citizens have joined them in the struggle against apartheid. Those in the country express a feeling of the breakdown of their isolation when they learn of international anti-apartheid activities.

Even though they do not have the resources of the South African government, representatives of the ANC and SWAPO actively promote divestment campaigns in the United

States through speaking tours and testimonies in hearings in various legislatures. Activists have often called on them and sponsored events for them to give their perspective on apartheid. Thus alongside the South African government's attempts to win friends in the United States are the resistance movements' attempts to do the same.

The United Nations Response

The UN Center Against Apartheid and Committee on Apartheid also monitor the U.S. movement closely and aid it in several ways. The Center publishes reports on anti-apartheid activities around the world and in the United States and provides a great deal of information to activists. In addition, members of the Committee have hosted receptions for activists when they held conferences in New York City, and UN facilities have been used for such meetings, including the provision of space for press conferences at meetings. With this support the UN gives the U.S. movement much-needed legitimacy.

Although all UN-related persons interviewed expressed appreciation for anti-apartheid efforts in the United States, one respondent was less enthusiastic about NGO contributions to attempts to end apartheid. In the end, he believed, government actions matter most.

CONCLUSIONS

This chapter has completed the context for analyzing and evaluating anti-apartheid campaigns targeted at state and local governments. These campaigns are a significant new thrust in an international and national movement that over a number of years attempted through a variety of means to increase the economic pressures on South Africa. As has been demonstrated, sanctions efforts have sparked a heated debate over the potential impact of the economic isolation of South Africa and have evoked interesting and significant responses from both opponents and proponents in governmental and nongovernmental groups.

The next chapter will present two frameworks within which to analyze divestment activities in Connecticut and Michigan. The following chapters then will examine campaigns in these states in depth in order to describe what happened, to analyze why events happened as they did, and to assess the campaigns' impact.

NOTES

1. For other suggestions on U.S. policy options, see Barber et al. 1982; Danaher 1980–81; Ferguson and Cotter 1978; Study Commission 1981; and Crocker 1980–81.

2. For further discussions of recent changes made in the apartheid structure: Leonard 1983; Myers et al. 1980; Saul and Gelb 1981; and Study Commission 1981.

3. According to the 1981 report. some corporations fit in more than one category.

4. Despite this legislation, U.S. exports to South Africa increased 30 percent in 1979 over 1978 levels. But the legislation may be more important to American banks who use Exim guaranteed loans as part of their reserve requirements and are therefore able to increase the level of their loans (Christenson 1981).

3

Frameworks for Analysis

Determining what factors produce successful campaigns or understanding why campaigns fail is a difficult undertaking. Evaluating their effectiveness is no easier. This study attempts to address these tasks through the comparison of two case studies. Two broad analytic frameworks are used to examine the cases. The first framework is designed to facilitate the discussion of why campaigns succeed or fail. The second aids in assessing their impact.

THE FIRST FRAMEWORK: INDICATORS OF WHY CAMPAIGNS SUCCEED OR FAIL

Because this study is about two specific sets of campaigns[1] carried out by small groups but conducted in the context of a much larger social movement, we will draw on scholarly literature that examines social movements and interest groups to provide insight into the variables that may be important to successful campaigns.

Sociologists tell us that the dynamics and impact of social movements are surprisingly understudied (Marx and Wood 1975), and interest group literature suffers from the same problem.[2] Many of the discussions evaluating impact are speculative in nature, although studies describing and documenting the activities of movements and interest groups are more empirical and plentiful. Despite this shortcoming, some of the variables suggested in the literature as related

89

to campaigns' success or failure can be grouped as follows:
(1) the types of goals pursued; (2) strength; (3) strategies and tactics chosen; (4) reaction and opposition; (5) the locus of the decision-making process targeted for influence; (6) the time it takes for the target to come to a decision. Few precise and consistent relationships of these groups of variables to effectiveness are spelled out in the literature, but a discussion of them provides useful guidance in narrowing the search for clues as to what makes campaigns more or less successful.

Goals

Movements or differing groups within the same movement seek varying degrees of change in their target institutions. Some groups desire total change, in which case they are usually labeled revolutionary or radical. Others desire only partial change and they are normally called reformist. Some groups may have a mixture of types of goals with only partial change sought in the immediate or short-term future and total change desired in the long run. No simple relationship exists between types of goals and chance of effectiveness. Groups seeking reform have failed in the past and revolutionary efforts have succeeded. Although many agree that greater degrees of change are harder to attain, Freeman (1975, 6) advises that both reformism and radicalism can have their pitfalls; that an uneasy tension exists between amount of change desired and the probability of achieving that change.

> Movements that conform themselves to the norms of behavior in order to participate successfully in political institutions often find themselves forsaking their major goals for social change. Longrange ideals are warped for the sake of shortrange gains. But movements that hold steadfast to their radical goals and disdain political participation of any king in an "evil" system often find themselves isolated in a splendid ideological purity which gains nothing for anyone. They are paralyzed by their own fear of cooptation; and such paralysis is in turn the ultimate cooptation as inactive revolutionaries are a good deal more innocuous than active "reformists." Thus successful movement must not only maintain a balance between its personal and political change, but also a creative tension between its "politics" and its "vision". It must keep well in mind where

it wants to go while accepting the necessity of often following a twisted and tortured road in order to get there.

Strength

Perry and Pugh (1978, 272) maintain that the strength of a movement or groups within it may have a bearing on success since "the strong movement has more alternatives than the weak one." There are a number of variables that together would indicate the strength of a campaign. Two such variables, which are rather obvious and to which Hughes (1978, 184, 211) points, are good financing and good organization. In examining the women's movement Cassell (1977) emphasized that a group with good organization may not achieve its goals, but a group without good organization is almost destined not to achieve its goals. Good organization consists minimally of some degree of formal structure, formal leadership, and a chain of command (Marx and Wood, 401). Thorough research on the issue under consideration, the persons making the decision, and their procedures, is reported by Cohen (1973, 203) and Milbrath (1967, 235–36) to be another variable important to effectiveness. To achieve sound research or to gain access to information, a group may need contacts within the decision making arena. Hughes (1978, 175) notes that inside contacts have been crucial to the success of some interest groups' efforts and at least helpful to others. Other indicators of strength listed by Marx and Wood (1975, 401) are number of adherents, degree of their commitment, power and prestige of adherents, support (or lack of opposition) of various noninvolved publics, interest groups and/or other movements, and ability to influence key decision makers or media. They also note that such variables do not necessarily all move simultaneously in the same direction (for example, mass membership could be in opposition to tightness or organizational structure).

Several authors assert that legitimacy and credibility of representation and activity on an issue lend strength and credence to an interest group's campaign. Cohen (1959, 12, 179) attributes lack of legitimacy as the cause of ineffectiveness of many civic and religious organizations while he notes it is the reason for success of many business groups. For instance, business organizations are seen as having a great deal of specialization in their area (Cohen 1973, 95–107), they have a great deal of expertise (Cohen 1959, 22; Hughes 1978, 211), and they are very practical and realistic in their policy recommendations (Hughes 1978, 211–16). In contrast, civic and religious organizations are seen by many whom they attempt to influence as being too idealistic and impractical (Cohen 1959; 1973), and they often claim to represent a very ambiguous or unbelievable constituency (for example, the people in the pews) (Chittick 1970, 214).

Strategies and Tactics

In analyses of how a movement might engineer its tactics for achievement of its goals, several authors agree: ". . . there is no *a priori* way of judging whether or not a tactic will be successful and there is no such thing as *the* successful tactic" (Wilson 1973, 235; see also Alinsky 1972, 138; and Perry and Pugh 1978, 272). Marx and Wood (1975, 403) assert that the absence of knowledge of which tactics will work under what circumstances results "partly from a lack of systematic study, partly from the historical uniqueness of each situation, and partly from the fact that what happens to a social movement may only be slightly related to its strategies.

However, in a text on social movements, John Wilson (1973, 236) describes three principles to guide the choice of effective tactics: breadth, simplicity, and flexibility. A tactic has breadth when it applies pressure to the target from a number of different fronts simultaneously, for instance, utilizing boycotts, stockholder resolutions, and workers strikes against a corporation all at the same time. Simplicity can be achieved by the leadership not imposing burdens on movement participants too heavy for them to bear and by the infusion of symbolic and pragmatic elements into the campaign. Flexibility means "avoiding total and irrevocable commitment to any given set of tactics, and it means foresight and planning for the reactions that a given set of tactics is likely to provoke. The first rule of flexibility is to avoid employing all the power at the movement's disposal in any given tactical campaign. . . . Without a reserve, the movement is devoid of retaliatory power and is likely to lose face and momentum. . . ." (Wilson 1973, 236).

Reaction and Opposition

A fourth set of variables important to effectiveness is the reaction to the campaign by targeted institutions, "bystander publics," and opposition. There appear to be, however, no clear generalizations about the nature of these relation-ships. Freeman (1979, 187) and Marx and Wood (1975, 401) all assert that for social movements these relationships are quite complex. Attempts by targeted institutions or opposi-tion to control a movement under some conditions can kill its effectiveness (or even the movement itself), whereas under other conditions such attempts can contribute to movement growth and attainment of goal. On the other hand, if the target has no reaction at all, or a reaction of ignoring the movement, this can dissipate a movement's efforts or cause movement groups to resort to extreme tactics. In addition, the movement's activities are located in a wider context, a society in which the public's reaction to either side might be decisive in determining the outcome. Favorable public opinion can help the movement obtain recognition from the target, and a negative view or lack of knowledge by the public may create the opposite outcome. Thus, movement campaigns often attempt to mobilize public support and/or sympathy through various tactics. "As a general rule, movements try to turn bystander publics into conscience constituencies who will supply the movement with additional resources, and try to prevent them from becom-ing antagonists who will discourage targets from responding to the movement" (Freeman 1979, 187).

The media may play an important role in helping the movement gain recognition from the public and/or the target institutions, and Molotch (1979, 91) maintains that "news coverage is critical to sustaining social movements." On the other hand, interest-group studies suggest that influence is most possible when the issue is *not* highly visible to the public, when the media do not show great interest, and when only a small segment of the populace is affected. (Kegley and Wittkopf 1982, 262).

Reactions by target institutions can vary from complete agreement with campaign demands, to minimal reform, to cooptation of the movement leaders, to repression, to sabo-tage and violent suppression (Perry and Pugh 1978, 278–79). If a target partially meets the demands of the movement such a response could satisfy the moderate follow-ers enough to keep them from supporting greater demands by participants committed to achieving more than reforms or partial changes. The outcome of coercive reactions (for example, repression, sabotage, violent suppression) is difficult to predict, and again, the public and media would seem to be important factors moderating the effects of these coercive target responses. If there is some degree of support or sympathy for movement goals among the public and media, the use of coercion can backfire and lead to greater support for the activists.

In discussing interest groups and opposition, Cohen (1973, 144-45) asserts that "counterveiling" opinions or a great deal of conflicting interest-group activity can leave the target free to take almost any position on an issue. If there exists no prevailing opinion across the concerned groups, there is no consensus to which the target must react. The interest groups counter-balance each other so as to moderate or weaken each other's effectiveness. Sometimes the outcome of such situations is that a decision will be delayed for further study. In such a situation, the interest group with the greatest degree of persistence would seem to have a greater chance of affecting the final result.

Locus of Decision

The targets of most interest-group activities are governmental bodies, but within that one large category of targets are several different kinds of decision structures. Cohen (1959, 1973, 78–126), Hughes (1978, 199), and Milbrath (1967, 250) all maintain that interest groups have greater access, and thus more potential for influence, when a decision is being made in the legislature or with legislative consultation rather than when the executive branch has sole jurisdiction. A legislature is more accessible primarily for three reasons: it is a body of elected representatives who to some degree can be held accountable by their public constituencies; there are more rewards and punishments available for use by interest groups when dealing with the legislative branch; and the legislature often takes longer to make decisions than does the executive branch because of its committee system, public hearings, and so forth; interest groups, therefore, have more time to make their input.

Time

The length of time a campaign target takes to make a decision can be very important to effectiveness, Hughes (1978, 213) and Milbrath (1967, 249) agree that longer time (more than a month according to Hughes) allows for more input by interest groups and therefore more chances to have an impact. Short-term efforts are likely to be effective only if they are massive. This suggests, too, that the nature of the situation can be important. In crisis situations, for example, decision time is likely to be very short with little opportunity for interest-group input. The relationship between time and effectiveness actually may be more curvilinear, however, since extremely slow decision making may lead to diversions or dissipation of energy for the interest group, or it may allow time for significant opposition to arise.

Summary

This discussion of social movement and interest group literature leaves us with a list of variables that scholars suggest might be important in determining whether campaigns succeed, partially succeed, or fail. As has been noted, however, few clues are given about the precise relationships between effectiveness and these variables, or about the relative importance of the variables in relation to one another. Indeed, in some cases the literature suggests contradictory relationships. Therefore, their use in this study will be for heuristic purposes rather than for the purpose of detailing specific hypotheses. In order to give some structure to the list, the variables can be divided into what Herbert Simon (1969) calls the inner environment—the sphere of potential direct control by the movement organizations involved in the campaign; and the outer environment—everything else relevant to the campaign.[3] Table 3–1 lists the variables drawn from the previous discussion in these two categories.

THE SECOND FRAMEWORK:
DEFINING EFFECTIVENESS
AND DESIGN OF THE EVALUATION

Defining effectiveness and choosing a design for the evaluation are integrally related, and to deal with both this study employs an adaptation of what House (1980) labels the goals-based approach to evaluation. One of the difficulties in using literature about evaluation is that much of it is focused primarily on evaluating social service programs, rather than NGO political campaigns. Nevertheless, House and others point out general considerations that must be taken into account in evaluations, and they are useful for this study.

House (1980) discussed a total of eight broad approaches to evaluation.[4] The goals-based approach was chosen here for two reasons: it is suitable for examining the data available (for example, the data are not quantitative and

TABLE 3-1. Variables for Analyzing Campaign Success

Inner Environment

1. Goals
2. Tactics
3. Strength
    a. Number and kinds of organizations involved in the campaign
    b. Degree of involvement and commitment of each organization
    c. Number and degree of involvement and commitment of individual participants
    d. Amount of coordination among the organizations in the campaign
    e. Financial resources
    f. Staff resources
    g. Research efforts and amount of information gathering
    h. Support from groups and individuals outside the campaign
    i. Contacts with key decision makers
    j. Legitimacy and credibility
    k. Leverage over the targeted institution or decision makers

Outer Environment

1. Reaction and opposition to the campaign
    a. From the targeted institution or decision makers
    b. From other organizations or counterveiling campaigns
    c. From the media
2. Target: the type of decision-making arena involved
3. Time available to the campaign

---

thus other approaches such as systems analysis that use quantitative techniques are inappropriate), and it provides a standard or criterion for determining effectiveness: the goals of the participants. Other standards might be created, as in a goal-free evaluation, but since any standard is arbitrary, I preferred to have the activists themselves impose the set of criteria rather than my imposing it for them. Therefore, effectiveness is defined as whether or not the campaign has met its own goals; or, to allow for more subtlety in analysis, the *degree* to which the campaign meets its own goals.[5]

Participants in the divestment campaigns often have multiple and even conflicting goals, as is evident from the discussion of the larger movement. The goals may be long-term or short-term in nature, and not all goals may be apparent. Through interviews with participants and through reviewing organizational documents I have arrived at an interpretation of the proponents' goals. In order for a goal to be included on the list of goals in the following chapters, unless it is in an official document like organizational minutes, at least two people must assert it. That is, if only one interviewee has a particular goal, it is not included in the list. All goals are listed despite the potential conflicts between them, but the conflicts are then discussed. The goals are divided into categories of short-term (defined as less than a year), medium-term (one to two years), and long-term (three or more years).

This study goes beyond the technique of goals-based evaluation in two ways. The first is that all discernible outcomes are examined, whether or not they are related to campaign goals. The second is an analysis of the campaign theory of action. As discussed in Chapter 2, the theory of action involves the means (strategies, tactics) undertaken by the campaign to reach its desired end-states (goals) (Patton 1978, 179–98). To evaluate the theory of action is to assess whether or not there is reason to believe, given the information available, that the campaign can work to accomplish what its adherents want. The overall theory of action regarding the probable impact of various types of economic sanctions against South Africa has already been discussed. The two case studies will relate this overall theory of action to the specific campaign goals and strategies employed in Connecticut and Michigan.

CONCLUSION

With these two frameworks to organize the analysis, we now move to consider anti-apartheid activism in two locales—how the campaigns accomplished what they did and what their impact has been.

NOTES

1. *Campaign* is defined as a coherent set of activities by persons and organizations directed at achieving a specified outcome. This definition is similar to that given by Cohen (1959) for an issue.

2. The distinction between the concepts of *interest group* and *social movement* is not always clear, and for these purposes it is not particularly pertinent either. Interest group is defined by Zeigler and Peak (1964, 3) as an organized social aggregate that seeks political goods that is incapable of providing for itself. *Social-movement*

organizations (SMOs) have been defined as "the carrier organizations that consciously attempt to coordinate and mobilize supporters" of social movements (McCarthy and Zald 1973, 2). One distinction between the two is that not all social-movement organizations attempt to have an impact on political process, whereas all interest groups do; for example, some social movements are only interested in personal change in their participants, not change in societal institutions (for example, Pentacostals). Another distinction is that interest groups are often *directly* affected by the outcome of political process which they try to influence (for example, business groups lobbying for less governmental regulation, or church groups lobbying for continuation of their tax-exempt status, and so forth). In contrast, social-movement organizations are often *not* directly affected by the outcomes they seek (for example, students protesting the Vietnam War even after the draft had ended). In addition, SMOs are more transitory than interest groups in many cases, interest groups tending to be highly institutionalized.

3. Simon's work in the *Sciences of the Artificial* (1969) has been adapted for use as a policy engineering framework by Bobrow (1972) and Sylvan (1979). I am employing only certain aspects of this engineering framework in this study.

4. Other approaches discussed are: systems analysis, decision making, goal-free, art criticism, professional review, quasi-legal, and case study.

5. Examples of evaluation criteria or standards other than goals are: evaluating consumer products for *safety,* evaluating social services on the basis of the *needs* of their recipients, evaluating professionals on the basis of criteria established by their *profession.* For example, no outside standard for evaluating anti-apartheid divestment campaigns was apparent.

4

The Connecticut Case Study

On 1 June 1981 the Connecticut General Assembly gave final
approval to the most far-reaching divestment legislation
ever passed up to that time by any governmental body in
the United States. The bill provided that no state funds
were to be invested in corporations or banks doing business
in South Africa. The Senate voted 25 to 10 for the bill,
and the House of Representatives endorsed the legislation
by a margin of 101 to 35. Despite such overwhelming
legislative support for the act, Governor William A. O'Neill
yielded to intense pressure from large businesses in Connecticut and vetoed it.

To demonstrate some degree of sensitivity to particular
segments of his party and his eagerness to be counted as
an opponent to racism and apartheid, O'Neill appointed a
task force to formulate investment legislation that he hoped
would satisfy business, maintain sound investments, and
placate anti-apartheid activists. The task force recommendations were adopted in their entirety by large majorities of
both houses in the General Assembly in April 1982 and
subsequently were signed into law by the governor. Although it falls short of what the previous bill was intended
to achieve, the activists' goal of full divestment, this law
stands as an important precedent for state action on divestment.

This chapter will analyze the history of anti-apartheid
legislation in Connecticut, the implementation of these bills,
the variables that contributed to their passage, and their
impact.

LEGISLATIVE HISTORY AND IMPLEMENTATION

In four years the General Assembly has entertained five different bills on the state's investment in corporations doing business in South Africa. Three of these acts have passed the legislature and two have become law; two died in committee.

The first bill was introduced in 1979 by Representative Boyd Hinds, a white civil rights activist and legislator from Hartford. The Finance, Revenue, and Bonding Committee[1] held hearings on the legislation but never reported it out of committee. It is not surprising that divestment legislation was introduced in the Connecticut General Assembly at that time. For several years, especially in the aftermath of the 1976 Soweto riots, other institutions in the state had been targets of anti-apartheid divestment campaigns, and some of them had yielded to these pressures to varying degrees. At least four colleges and universities in the state had taken positions on the investment of their funds in South Africa-related companies,[2] and in 1979 Yale University decided to sell $1.5 million worth of J. P. Morgan and Co. bank stock because of the bank's loans to the South African government (Myers et al. 1980, 339–71). Corporations located in Connecticut had been under attack for their South African presence, and the Hartford City Council had begun facing the issue in 1978 as a result of efforts by a group known as City Workers Against Apartheid.

In addition to this state legislative work on South Africa, Hinds had been involved in a variety of other anti-apartheid activities. Operating from a civil rights organization in Hartford, he submitted stockholder resolutions on South Africa to Connecticut businesses, devoted energy to the Hartford City Council divestment campaign, and brought the question of the financial links between South Africa and state funds to the attention of Lieutenant Governor Killian. Killian, who was trying to win black and liberal support in a Democratic party primary campaign against Ella Grasso, advocated divestment in his campaign platform. The concept of disengagement from South Africa, therefore, was nothing new in the state, and for some like Representative Hinds, it was a part of on-going civil rights commitment.

Proximity to New York City is also a factor that makes Connecticut susceptible to activism on apartheid. A number of organizations devoted to change in South Africa are located in New York, and many anti-apartheid campaigns have been conducted there. Connecticut proponents of divestment have had easy access to the resources of these organizations (such as speakers, research, and so forth) as have activists in other northeastern states. In general, the Northeast has experienced a higher concentration of anti-apartheid activity than any other region of the country. Thus Hinds's legislative initiative in 1979 was an extension of similar proposals confronting other institutions in the same environment.

Unrelated to the introduction of Hinds's bill was the formation in August 1978 of the Connecticut Anti-Apartheid Committee (CAAC). Several recent college graduates who had been participants in anti-apartheid work on their campuses were eager to continue their previous efforts toward isolating South Africa. Spurred by a remark of Lieutenant Governor Killian reported in the press that state pension funds were invested in companies operating in South Africa, the group began making plans to lay the groundwork for legislative action. They wanted to build a broad, multi-racial coalition of support for such efforts among labor unions, churches, and community organizations. Unaware that Hinds's bill existed, they deliberately focused their work on educational and consciousness-raising activities about South Africa and the role of U.S. corporations there. These efforts were intended to show how people in the United States might express their solidarity with South African blacks and help achieve change in apartheid. Their goal over the next several years was to achieve complete withdrawal of all Connecticut state funds from corporations doing business in South Africa.

In the first year and a half the CAAC, with a nucleus of between six and ten people on their steering committee, was devoted to a wide range of educational and support-building activities: distributing fliers and pamphlets, getting endorsements from community leaders, showing films, sponsoring conferences and speaking engagements with black South Africans and Americans with expertise on southern Africa, writing newspaper articles, holding social and cultural events focused on South Africa, doing research on Connecticut investments and the issue of sanctions against South Africa, and obtaining support and endorsements from organizations around the state. These activities were not randomly targeted throughout Connecticut but were specifically focused on organizations and networks where people in the CAAC already had contacts and credibility. Most of the CAAC steering committee have strong ties with labor unions, and some serve in leadership positions in their unions. Others are well known for their involvement in voluntary organizations.

Because this group was well connected with labor

groups, community organizations, and churches, and because each person devoted a great deal of time to the work
(two to three nights a week), the committee achieved impressive accomplishments by early 1980. Among the early
endorsers of the CAAC calling for divestment legislation
were the Connecticut State Labor Council, the Hartford
Labor Council, Operation P.U.S.H. of Hartford, the Hartford NAACP, and a number of state representatives.
Unions representing state employees whose pension fund
investments were at stake also endorsed the campaign: the
Connecticut State Federation of Teachers, the Connecticut
Education Association, and District 1199 of the New England
Health Care Employees. In addition, the CAAC had established three branch chapters in Hartford, New Haven, and
Waterbury and was publishing a monthly newsletter with a
mailing list of 500 people. Well-publicized events such as
speeches by black South Africans prominent in resistance
movements drew 80 to 100 people from across the state. In
addition, the CAAC provided speakers or films for other
groups interested in hearing more about South Africa. The
committee received some media coverage, especially when
they brought in well-known speakers, and the group was
responsible for a regular column on South Africa in the
weekly Hartford *Inquirer,* the largest black newspaper in
the state.

More about the nature of these educational and organ-
ization-building activities and the people conducting them
will be covered later in this chapter. The foregoing description, however, should serve to demonstrate that a
significant amount of publicly visible activity was ongoing,
and the group was building a substantial amount of organizational support.

In early 1980, Representative William Dyson, a black
school teacher from New Haven and a Democrat, introduced
the second bill to insure that no monies were invested in
corporations doing business in South Africa. The monies
involved are primarily pension funds, although some other
minor investment funds did exist. Again, the CAAC was
unaware of Dyson's intentions to submit this bill. Although
the committee had attempted to hold a group discussion on
divestment legislation with a number of legislators in
October 1979 (cancelled due to a special legislative session
called by Governor Grasso on the day the meeting was to
be held), it had no ties to Dyson at the time. He initiated
the act without prompting from the committee but with the
support of the legislative Black Caucus.

The CAAC soon learned of the bills' existence, however, and although the group was unprepared at that point

to launch a major lobbying effort in the General Assembly, members testified in support of the legislation when the Appropriations Committee held hearings. The bill met opposition in committee and in order to get it passed, Senator Sanford Cloud, a lawyer from Hartford, a Democrat, and the only black senator, amended it to include the Sullivan Principles, for example, to require divestment from all corporations doing business in South Africa that have not adopted the Sullivan Principles. Dyson, who admits that he knew very little about the Sullivan Principles, their effectiveness, or the controversy surrounding them, agreed to the amendment as a means for getting favorable committee recommendation. The CAAC was very disappointed with the revised bill. The group would have preferred to let it die in committee again and organize stronger backing for another attempt at full divestment the next year rather than see the precedent of adopting the Sullivan Principles as a criterion for investment. But momentum for the legislation was already established.

Another important actor in Connecticut's divestiture debate, Henry Parker, the state treasurer and a prominent black politician, indicated his support for the bill as amended. He believed that the Sullivan Principles were a positive, if minimal, first step that the state could take. The legislation passed the Senate with no apparent difficulty but met obstacles in the House. Dyson attempted to amend the act to remove the Sullivan Principles provision after discussions with the CAAC that convinced him that the principles were ineffective and a bad precedent. His amendment failed. Other more conservative representatives wanted to apply the same standard of morality in investment decisions to other issues: the conflict in Northern Ireland and the seizure of American hostages in Iran. It is not clear whether these attempts at extending the concept of divestment were offered in good faith or were intended to so overload the bill that it would be defeated. The outcome, however, was that the bill was finally passed with the following amendment:

The state Treasurer shall insure that state funds are not invested in any corporation engaged in any form of business in Iran which could be considered to be contrary to the foreign policy or national interests of the United States, particularly in respect to the release of all American hostages held in Iran. (Section 3–13g, Title 3, Chapter 32, Connecticut General Statutes)

To implement this legislation, the Treasury Department conducted research to discover which companies investing in South Africa had signed the Sullivan Principles. Officials discovered that the state owned stock in fourteen companies that they believed would be affected by the law. Letters were written to these companies indicating that their stocks or bonds would be sold unless they became Sullivan signers. The treasury wanted to use the legislation as leverage to urge companies to endorse the Sullivan Principles rather than having the state simply abandon their stock immediately. Through correspondence, the department found out that three of the fourteen companies had become recent signatories, some had too few employees (fewer than ten) to qualify for the Sullivan Principles, and others held less than 50 percent ownership in the South African subsidiary and thus could not control its policies. Exceptions were made for corporations in these last two categories, and in the end, seven corporations' securities were sold. Table 4–1 illustrates the companies whose stocks were sold. By waiting until the prices went higher than the original purchase prices, the state earned about $2 million from the sale.

TABLE 4-1. Corporations Divested in Implementation of 1980 Sullivan Principles Legislation

Baxter Labs	Owens Corning
Dresser Industries	Pepsico
IMS International	Teneco
Lubrizol	

One company whose stock was divested sent a hostile response to the treasurer's office. Dresser Industries, noted for its refusal to sign the Sullivan Principles and for its public relations campaigns justifying its South African investments, wrote an antagonistic letter. Ironically, Dresser was simultaneously applying to the Connecticut Development Authority for a loan to build a facility in the state, but no anger from either party spilled over into the deliberations about the loan.

Meanwhile in other arenas, the CAAC methodically continued its educational work and gathered more endorsements. The committee also researched corporate involvement in South Africa, the extent of the state pension fund investment in these corporations, and the financial impact on the portfolio of selling the stocks and bonds of these companies. The information from this research was reported to legislators and was considered by the CAAC as fundamental to laying the groundwork for another attempt at comprehensive divestment in 1981. In June 1980, the committee sponsored a dinner and guest speaker in commemoration of the June 1976 Soweto uprisings by black youth in South Africa. Dumisani Kumalo, an exiled South African black journalist, was the featured speaker. The CAAC used the occasion for fund raising and building support for their 1981 legislative drive. Over one hundred people from across the state attended.

In September 1980, at the invitation of Henry Parker, the Reverend Leon Sullivan came to Connecticut, to the state where his principles had become enshrined in law. The occasion was a Conference on Social Responsibility sponsored by the Treasury Department and held at Connecticut General Life Insurance Company, one of the insurance companies known for its shareholder activism. The conference focused on two subjects: corporate social responsibility in minority recruitment in the United States; and South African investments. The Reverend Sullivan gave the keynote address for the sessions on South Africa.

Sullivan took the opportunity to preach a warning on U.S. investments in South Africa to the corporate managers, government officials, and academics gathered to hear him. He emphasized that not enough corporations had signed the principles (at that point 140 out of 350 U.S. companies with affiliates in South Africa had signed). He complained that the signatories were moving too slowly in their implementation, and he advocated no new or expanded investments and no bank loans to the South African government. Threatening to abandon the principles in favor of total divestment, he shouted, "Let it be heard in corporate boardrooms in America that their affiliates in South Africa must either shape up or ship out" (Lowery 1980, 1).

Apparently Sullivan's reception was polite, somewhat cool, and even awkward at moments. Some people present had expected more sympathy from him for a corporate perspective on the issue, and his overbearing, loud style offended some. What the speech accomplished, however, was unmistakable clarity that even Sullivan himself felt the principles were problematic. This gave some confirmation to the critique of the principles the CAAC had been making all along. What the conference as a whole accomplished was to reinforce the legitimacy of using social criteria in addition to prudent financial criteria for investing state funds. Treasurer Parker had gone on record to affirm the 1980 legislation as "a first for state governments in the country, [and] an important addition to Connecticut's public policy on investment" (Connecticut Office of the Treasurer 1982, 19).

Passage and Veto of Full Divestment Legislation

The next significant event in the history of Connecticut's anti-apartheid legislation was the introduction in January 1981 of two divestment bills. The acts were worded differently but were substantively the same. Both required the withdrawal of all state investments from corporations or banks doing business in South Africa. The addition of banks made the bills different from the previous legislation in 1979 and 1980. The two bills' authors were Representative Dyson, who had become the chair of the legislative Black Caucus, and Representative Abraham Giles, a black representative from Hartford. Dyson's bill was referred to the Appropriations Committee and Giles's to the Finance, Revenue, and Bonding Committee. Because there was a better chance of getting Giles's bill out of the Finance Committee, proponents concentrated on facilitating its passage and allowed the Dyson bill to die in the Appropriations Committee. The text of Giles's legislation is shown in Appendix B.

This time the CAAC was well prepared and ready to devote considerable energies to the passage of this legislation. The group's persistent educational efforts had paid off in the form of at least fifty individual and organizational endorsements (see Table 4–2). The research efforts bore fruit when CAAC Chairperson Christy Hoffman was able to give sophisticated and reliable testimony on the effectiveness of the Sullivan Principles, the financial impact of divestiture on state investments, South African black support for corporate withdrawal, and the nature of U.S. companies' involvement in South Africa. Three other people related to the CAAC also testified at the hearings: a representative of District 1199 of the New England Health Care Employees Union, a representative of the Connecticut State Federation of Teachers, and the immediate past president of Hartford's AFSCME Local 1716.

No one testified in opposition to the bill and throughout the legislative process no organized opposition was apparent. Several lobbyists for business concerns say they knew about the legislation but were burdened by other priorities. Believing that its chances for passage were not very high, they decided to watch the bill but not work to oppose it. Other business lobbyists claimed that the act simply slipped by them unnoticed. In any case, at that point no one was coordinating business interests. In addition, both proponents and opponents recognized the emotionally charged atmosphere surrounding the bill. The debate was cast so that anyone opposing the act risked being perceived and labeled a racist. No business groups wanted to risk such a label even though some felt their best interests would be served if the bill were defeated.

The CAAC activists lobbied intensively for the bill in the last weeks prior to its passage. Two members of the CAAC steering committee, Christy Hoffman and Peggy Buchanan, spent every evening after work for about three weeks talking to legislators about the bill. Representative Dyson personally introduced them to key leaders in both houses and gained access for them to people who were otherwise difficult to reach, especially in the last weeks of a legislative session. The two were able to provide information that many legislators desired and were perceived as expert and persuasive. Every legislator interviewed remembered their presence and saw it as significant in the passage of the bill. Representative Dyson and other Black Caucus members also lobbied for the bill among their colleagues.

In an action unrelated to the divestment debate, Treasurer Parker had announced that $450 million worth of stock from pension funds' portfolios would be made available to finance mortgages in Connecticut, instituting the YankeeMac program. With this action Parker reinforced a point that he had made publicly on several occasions: pension funds could be creatively and prudently invested in a way that would allow their participants to receive benefits before retirement. The first objective of the program, however, was to diversify and stabilize the portfolio. The CAAC activists pointed to this program as proof that profitable alternative investments could be found and that as a matter of principle, the funds ought to be invested as far as possible within the state and not in South Africa.

Two objections that threatened the bill's adoption arose within the legislature after the bill had come out of the Finance Committee. One was that, due to prevailing high interest rates, the state might incur a loss of funds if forced to sell its fixed securities in the near future. Therefore, an amendment was added to the bill by Representative Giles to insure that divestment would not force the state to incur a financial loss. The second objection was that the act was too comprehensive. It was to apply to investments in companies doing business in *or with* the

TABLE 4-2.   CAAC Endorsements

Labor Organizations

J. Brown, President, New England Health Care Workers, District 1199
Hank Murray, Educational Director, UAW
John Wilhelm, Secretary-Treasurer, Local 217, Hotel and Restaurant
    Employees Union
Connecticut State Labor Council (AFL-CIO)
Greater Hartford Labor Council (AFL-CIO)
Meriden Labor Council (AFL-CIO)
Waterbury Labor Council (AFL-CIO)
New Haven Labor Council (AFL-CIO)
Bristol Labor Council (AFL-CIO)
Hartford Area Coalition of Labor Union Women (CLUW)
New Haven Federation of Teachers, Local 933
Connecticut State Federation of Teachers
Young Workers Liberation League
AFSCME Local 1716
International Association of Machinists, District 91
International Association of Machinists, Local Lodge 707
International Association of Machinists, Local Lodge 1746-A
United Auto Workers, Connecticut State CAP

Church Organizations

Inter-Denominational Ministers Alliance, Hartford
North United Methodist Church, Hartford
American Friends Service Committee, Connecticut

Black Organizations

Afro-American Cultural Center, New Haven
Hartford NAACP
National Council of Negro Women, Hartford

Anti-Apartheid Organizations

City Workers Against Apartheid, Hartford
Visiting Nurses Association, Anti-Apartheid Committee, Hartford

Others

United States Representative Toby Moffett
Mayor George Athanson, Hartford
State Representative Boyd Hinds
Committee of 24, Hartford
Spanish Action Council, Waterbury
Vieques Support Committee, Hartford

TABLE 4-2. Continued

Others Continued

New Haven People's Center
Peace Center, New Haven
Pearl Street Community House, Waterbury
John Del Vecchio
Edwin Vargas
Hartford Peace Coalition
Hartford Chile Solidarity Committee
Coalition for a Just Society
Homefront, Hartford
United Farmworkers Support Committee, New Haven
New Haven Puerto Rican Solidarity Committee
Puerto Rican Socialist Party, Hartford
Rudy Arnold, City Councilman, Hartford
State Representatitve Thirman Milner
The Guardians of the Hartford Police Department
Connecticut Education Association

Republic of South Africa. It would apply not only to companies with subsidiaries in South Africa but also those that trade with South Africa. Some legislators felt that it might even be interpreted to apply to companies whose products were sold by a third party to South Africa. This was considered a serious problem of definition and an impossible provision to regulate. Giles proposed another amendment that simply removed the words "or with." For some the definition as amended was still not clear enough, and it was to arise as a major difficulty later. But the bill was adopted 101 to 35 by the House and 25 to 10 in the Senate.

Once the act was passed, the organized opposition began. Business leaders from major banks, insurance companies, industries, and law firms in Connecticut lobbied both the treasurer and governor in meetings that were reportedly undetected by the CAAC or legislative proponents. A list of businesses represented is shown in Table 4-3. Persons interviewed who were present at these meetings were generally reluctant to admit that they were there and were hesitant to give the names of others present. There was some hesitancy to be associated with the push for the veto. The delegation asserted a number of arguments against the legislation and in favor of a veto:

1. Foreign policy is the preserve of the federal government; the state should not be involved in making foreign policy.

2. Their businesses are good corporate citizens of the state and those that have investments in South Africa are signatories of the Sullivan Principles; this legislation would punish and stigmatize them along with the less conscientious businesses which are not involved in attempting to bring about what these men see as positive change for blacks in South Africa.

3. The legislation was inconsistent with important U.S. sectors of opinion with regard to South Africa, for example, the official governmental foreign policy, a recent Rockefeller Commission report (Study Commission 1981), and the Reverend Sullivan's organization.

4. Other responsible and palatable options for taking a stand against apartheid were available, and this group was willing to help search for them.

5. The bill was too comprehensive, removing many large U.S. businesses from the portfolio and virtually all large banks.

6. The definition of "doing business in South Africa" was ambiguous, and therefore, the legislation was sloppy.

7. The measure would likely have a negative impact on investment income and appropriate diversification of the investment portfolio.

8. The act would create a bad business climate in Connecticut and discourage future investment.

9. The legislation was considered and passed in haste without due consideration for its impact on businesses in the state or the state's pension fund investments.

The validity of these arguments is mixed. The assertion about the ambiguity of defining "doing business in" seemed to be the most serious. The treasurer would have had the authority to provide a clear definition once the bill became law, but the business group was not willing to leave him with that responsibility. There was also some legitimacy in claiming that the impact of divestment could have a potential negative impact on the investment portfolio. The specific impact on Connecticut's pension funds was unknown. Although the CAAC had provided expert analysis from a pension investment study on divestment in California (Baldin et al. 1980) and from an investments analyst to prove a benign if not positive effect, no official and definitive impact study had been done specifically on Connecticut's portfolio. Some officials seemed to think that divestiture would make little difference to the funds, but

TABLE 4-3. Connecticut Businesses with Investments in South Africa

Company	Activity	Product sold to/in South Africa	Sullivan Signatory
Air Express International Corp., Stamford	Sales	Air freight	No
Chesebrough-Pond's Inc., Greenwich	Manufacturing/Sales	Cosmetics	No
Echlin Manufacturing Co., Branford	Manufacturing/Sales	Automotive parts	No
General Electric Co., Fairfield	Manufacturing/Sales	Locomotives, applicances	Yes
Grolier Inc., Danbury	Marketing	Educational and reference materials	Yes
Heublein International, Farmington	Sales	Kentucky Fried Chicken	Yes
International Playtex Inc., Stamford	Sales	Women's undergarmets	No
Loctite Corp., Newington	Sales	Adhesives, chemicals	Yes
Olin Corp., Stamford	Manufacturing/Sales	Swimming pool chemicals	Yes
Perkin-Elmer Corp., Norwalk	Sales	Sophisticated measuring devices	No
Richardson-Vicks Inc., Wilton	Manufacturing/Sales	Drug products	Yes
Remington Products Inc., Bridgeport	Distributor	Shavers and accessories	No
The Stanley Works, New Britain	Sales	Handtools	No
Stauffer Chemical Co., Westport	Sales	Agricultural chemicals	No
Texasgulf Inc., Stamford	Exploration	Gold, platinum, chrome	No
Union Carbide Corp., Danbury	Mining	Chrome, vanadium	Yes
Uniroyal Inc., Middlebury	Sales	Tires	Yes
United Technologies Corp., Hartford	Manufacturing/Sales	Elevators	Yes
Xerox Corp., Stamford	Sales/Service	Photocopying equipment	Yes

Source: American Consulate General, Johannesburg, 1979 List of American Firms, Subsidiaries, and Affiliates in South Africa; 1981 Fifth Report on the Signatory Companies to the Sullivan Principles

the lack of an authoritative analysis left reasonable doubts in some peoples' minds.

The business group's argument regarding the haste with which the legislation was considered is not valid, but only an indication that some business lobbyists were either caught off guard or did not want to enter into the legislative fray. The state's interference with foreign policy assertion is weak because, although it has foreign policy implications, the state was essentially regulating its own investment policy. The other arguments are simply opinions, which the business community predictably holds in a very contentious debate. From the proponents' perspective, on the other hand, the point of the legislation was to lump all corporations that have subsidiaries in South Africa together, regardless of their position on the Sullivan Principles. Proponents had argued in the legislature that the principles are useless for creating fundamental change in apartheid and serve only as a facade for businesses.

The governor found the business group's arguments persuasive, and their pressure worked. Although he made no public statement before the bill's passage, Treasure Parker wrote a long letter to the governor describing his meeting with opponents and indicating a list of options to pursue on the issue other than signing the divestment act into law (Table 4–4). He was a known proponent of corporate social responsibility, and his letter was couched in language indicating support for the concept of divestment; but Parker's signal was unmistakable. As one of the leading black politicians in the state, he gave O'Neill plenty of room to veto.

Coincidental with the discussions between business leaders, O'Neill and Parker, was another event which would affect the outcome of this entire political process. The event was the initial planning of an itinerary and agenda for a group of South African religious leaders being brought to the state by the Episcopal Diocese of Connecticut. Being concerned about the issue of apartheid and having witnessed the divestment debate in the state, diocesean officials decided to invite twelve South African Christians of all races to Connecticut to interact with church members and others. The purpose was not only to expose both black and white Americans to South Africans and apartheid but also to expose South Africans to Americans in a variety of settings and occupations. On the planning committee for the South Africans' visit were two persons who had been involved in discussions about the recent legislation with the treasurer. One was Dr. Edythe Gaines, Commissioner for the Public Utilities Control

TABLE 4-4. List of Governmental Options from State Treasurer Parker's
Letter to the Governor

• Formulate a task force similar to one in California in order to
consider appropriate, alternative, anti-apartheid action.

• Review the possibility of new Connecticut legislation which would
build upon our state's important Sullivan Principles bill, by requiring not
only that corporations doing business in South Africa be signers of the
Priniciples as a condition of investment, but also that they get a good
rating in the audit conducted for Doctor Sullivan by the Arthur D. Little
Company.

• Review other possible legislative solutions, perhaps in harmony
with the recommendations of the Study Commission on United States Policy
Toward Southern Africa, which released its report this spring. That report
opposes disinvestment but favors restricting expansion and new investment
in South Africa.

• Initiate a corporate campaign, led by Connecticut-based Sullivan
signatories, to convince recalcitrant corporations in Connecticut and the
country to sign the Sullivan Principles.

• Review the possibility of adopting state policies aimed at making a
positive contribution to the success of Zimbabwe, because the success--or
failure--of this nation will have great bearing on the future of South
Africa.

Authority, a close personal friend of Henry Parker and a
prominent black leader in the state; the other was Isaac D.
Russell, a lawyer. Russell had a long-standing interest in
South Africa, and while on a six months leave he had
worked in Johannesburg for the Urban Foundation. The
Foundation is a white South African business organization
formed after the Soweto riots in 1976, which attempts to
upgrade the standard of living for certain segments of
blacks.

With input from Gaines and Russell, the planning committee decided to hold a conference on appropriate responses from Connecticut government and business to apartheid,
and with the help of Parker they asked the governor to
cosponsor it. In addition to the South African church
leaders, the conference would host governmental leaders,
business leaders whose companies had investments in South
Africa, and the CAAC activists. The committee saw itself

as providing an arena in which ethical questions could be discussed separately from the pressures that accompany the legislative process. The conference also provided an opportunity for O'Neill to demonstrate an interest in the issue in the aftermath of the veto. Thus some who were advising the governor to veto the bill were also helping to provide him with alternative actions to pursue. Believing that the issue was a legitimate one in need of further study, they arranged the next step in a continuing examination of the relationship between state investments and apartheid.

The governor vetoed the bill on 1 July 1981. His veto message maintained that the measure "is too sweeping in nature and does not provide the State of Connecticut with a positive step-by-step mechanism to achieve this goal." He stated that the legislation would "punish a number of state firms who have been engaged in meaningful actions to support the human rights of South Africans" through the Sullivan Principles which, he continued, "are minimum standards by which corporations should operate in South Africa regarding minority [sic] employment practices" (O'Neill 1981). Other problems he cited were the definition of "doing business," the definition of "reasonable time" in which the treasurer could implement the bill, and the potential of negative impact on investment returns.

The veto message carried a reference to Parker's letter and further pledged

> to provide the leadership which will insure the necessary incentive to end apartheid and carry out the good intentions of House Bill No. 5740 in a more effective manner. The following will be done: 1. I will ask the corporations of the State doing business in South Africa to further explore appropriate actions to end apartheid; 2. A review will be made of current Connecticut legislation for the purpose of strengthening the "Sullivan Principles" concept; 3. A complete impact analysis of divestiture will be undertaken to determine the results which such action would have on the State pension investments (O'Neill 1981).

CAAC members report that they were completely caught off guard by the veto. Lobbying the governor was something the committee never considered necessary to a successful campaign. Confident of the outcome, the members celebrated the legislative victory at their second annual Soweto commemoration dinner in June. Shortly after the veto, however, the group quickly mobilized a campaign to

override it. Members wrote letters to legislators responding
to each of O'Neill's objections; they wrote and provided
information for newspaper articles; they were interviewed
on radio; and the committee held a press conference. A
case study of the campaign published in a pamphlet by the
American Committee on Africa describes the post-veto
activity as follows:

> At the press conference members of religious, civil
> rights, community and labor organizations spoke in
> favor of the bill. This was the broadest display of
> public support yet to come together and was con-
> sidered very successful. Operation P.U.S.H. of
> Hartford and the Hartford Black Ministerial Alliance
> became particularly active at this time. Telephone
> calls and other lobbying were at their peak in terms
> of broad participation. The Committee argued that
> the Governor had shown himself to be easily in-
> fluenced by business, [and] that the state was
> being governed through backroom deals. . . .
> (ACOA, January 1982, 4)

But the attempted override failed. After an emotionally
charged debate, the House voted 81 to 61 to override.
This was 20 votes short of the necessary two-thirds majority. The CAAC and legislative proponents readied themselves for another round the next year.

The Episcopal Diocese held its conference on Connecticut governmental and business response to apartheid in
October 1981. Present were eleven South African religious
leaders. The twelfth, Bishop Desmond Tutu, an Anglican
bishop and prominent African leader, was not allowed to
come by the South African government. His passport had
been revoked when he advocated corporate withdrawal from
South Africa in a previous trip outside the country. As
stated earlier, representatives of the treasurer's office, the
legislature, businesses, CAAC members, and local churches
were also present. It is not clear what the planners might
have expected the South Africans to say in such a gathering, but what they said was not what business executives
wanted to hear. They gave a stinging critique of the
Sullivan Principles as irrelevant to meaningful change in
South Africa, and although they refused to risk their own
safety back home by commenting publicly on the divestment
question, "they indicated a lack of enthusiasm for foreign
investment in their nation. . . . They said foreign investment helps only a tiny percentage of the South African
black work force" (Cohen 1981). The participants in the

one-day conference left having heard that this group of South Africans did not believe foreign investment was helpful in their struggle against apartheid. Ironically, the governor had cosponsored a conference that placed in question his own position regarding state investment and South Africa.

The Governor's Task Force
on South African Investment Policy

To help carry out the tasks to which he had pledged himself in his veto message, O'Neill appointed a Task Force on South African Investment Policy in December. The charge to the Task Force was

> to review the State's current legislation with the objective of strengthening the Sullivan Principles' concept; work closely with businesses and corporations which do business in South Africa; and analyze the impact of divestiture on state pension funds (Connecticut Office of the Treasurer 1982, 4).

Fourteen persons were named to the Task Force and Parker was asked to chair it. The distribution of members was as follows: two corporation executives; two bank executives; two lawyers, one from an insurance company and one from a large law firm; two executives from investment firms; two representatives from labor unions; two legislators, one of whom was the chair of the legislative Black Caucus; and Edythe Gaines, an influential black politician mentioned earlier. Notably missing from the list were representatives of the CAAC, although the two labor union leaders were both members of CAAC, and one was its chair, Christy Hoffman. Five of the members were black. The members' names and institutional affiliations are shown in Table 4-5. Note that many of the names are familiar ones in this story. O'Neill had received help in putting the Task Force together from Parker and Cloud among others. Although the group represented a diversity of opinions on the issue, total business representation outweighed representation from other arenas. But, as will be explained later, there turned out to be no unanimity of opinion among business interests.

From 25 February 1982 to 21 April 1982, the Task Force accomplished a formidable and colossal assignment. Some Task Force members' estimates of their time devoted to

TABLE 4-5. The Governor's Task Force on South African Investment Policy

---

The Honorable Henry E. Parker
Task Force Chairman

Sanford Cloud, Jr., Esquire
Counsel
Aetna Life & Casualty
Hartford, Connecticut

Allan R. Nelson, Vice President
Connecticut General Investment
Management Company
Bloomfield, Connecticut

Christy L. Hoffman
AFL-CIO
Waterbury, Connecticut

The Honorable William R. Dyson
State Representative
New Haven, Connecticut

Dean J. Patenaude, Vice President
Connecticut Mutual Insurance Co.
Hartford, Connecticut

Doctor Edythe J. Gaines, Commissioner
Public Utilities Control Authority
New Britain, Connecticut

John Fussell
United Auto Workers
Waterbury, Connecticut

Isaac D. Russell, Esquire
Day, Berry and Howard
Hartford, Connecticut

Peter deWilde Shapiro, Vice President
The Connecticut Bank and Trust Company
Hartford, Connecticut
President, The Urban League of Greater Hartford, Inc.

The Honorable Abraham L. Giles
State Representative
Hartford, Connecticut

Frank Stanley, Senior Vice President
Hartford National Bank and Trust Co.
Hartford, Connecticut

William W. Hamilton, Manager
International Communications
General Electric Company
Fairfield, Connecticut

Russell T. Semelsberger
Vice President
Otis Elevator Company
Farmington, Connecticut

Note: At points during the proceedings, Jack Hughes substituted for
Russell Semelsberger and Frank V. Donovan substituted for William Hamilton.

meetings, consultations with allies outside the Task Force,
phone calls, research, and so forth, range from a low of 50
to 60 hours to a high of 80 to 100 hours. The level of

participation by almost all members was high, and every member interviewed expressed surprise at the degree of commitment sustained across the two months. At first the question of time line and when the finished product was to be reported was unsettled. The treasurer hinted that the work could go beyond the spring, past the closing of that year's legislative session in June. Several members, however, expressed their frustration at such a suggestion and urged that the work be accomplished as quickly as possible. They wanted to try to submit a report, and if appropriate, attempt to get legislation passed in the current session.

The group began its work by holding an orientation session for a full day. The agenda covered the topics of an overview of South Africa and apartheid, the role of U.S. corporations doing business in South Africa, and the effectiveness of the Sullivan Principles. Persons addressing these topics were well known experts, and they brought a variety of perspectives to the discussion. Some were advocates of economic sanctions against South Africa and corporate withdrawal while others fully supported the Sullivan Principles approach. None were in favor of making investment decisions based on financial criteria alone.

Later in the deliberations the Task Force spent a half day hearing reports from consultants hired to study the impact of complete divestiture on the state's portfolio. These reports provided an analysis of the most extreme policy the group could recommend. Anything short of complete withdrawal of investments from corporations in South Africa was assumed to have a less momentous effect on investment risk and return. Three investment management consulting firms ran computer models comparing the current portfolio to two hypothetical portfolios: a so-called "sanitized" portfolio without corporations that have investments in South Africa, and a "standard" portfolio designed to provide a control group of investments (using the Standard and Poor 500). The purpose was to measure the difference in degree of risk involved in each set of investments and the rates of return. A low-risk portfolio is considered to be one in which holdings are diversified across a wide range of businesses or places for investment (for example, auto industry, banks, electronics, oil, and so forth) and across types of investment (for example, stocks and bonds). Diversification means that the entire portfolio is not vulnerable to a possible negative trend that any one segment of the market might be experiencing at any given time.

With some slight differences, the three reports concluded with substantially the same results. They suggested that the sanitized portfolio would be less diversified than the other two, and thus potentially was more risky. One consultant noted, however, that the increased risk was not significant. The reports also agreed that there were slightly higher returns in the sanitized portfolio, although again, one firm said the differences were not significant. The third common conclusion was that divestment would require withdrawal from the larger, more financially stable companies, focusing the portfolio on lower market capitalization (smaller) companies. In recent years these companies typically had yielded higher returns but were generally considered to be potentially more risky investments. The findings of one study were summarized as follows:

> In conclusion, the exclusion of the unacceptable companies from the mutual equity fund will not have any negative impact. In fact, the study has shown the "sanitized" portfolio to outperform both the original portfolio and the market (Connecticut Office of the Treasurer 1982, 34).

A second, less positive analysis concluded:

> Reducing the universe of stocks to non-trading corporations [corporations not invested in South Africa] substantially increases portfolio risk while potentially increasing returns. Possibly of greater importance is that it removes the larger, more financially stable companies as potential alternative for selection by the State's Investment Managers. This hindrance could have a substantial negative impact on the portfolio's future behavior (Connecticut Office of the Treasurer 1982, 32).

What the Task Force itself concluded from these reports was that using social criteria for investment decisions did not necessitate abandonment of prudent financial criteria or responsible fiduciary behavior.

Besides contracting with these consultants for their analyses of the impact of divestment, Parker solicited comments from seven investment advisors from the state's employees retirement plan whose firms are responsible for investing about one-half of the state's pension funds. The common conclusion of these seven reports was that complete divestment, in the words of one report, "would seriously restrict the universe of available equity investments for the Connecticut Employees Retirement Plans" (Connecticut Office of the Treasurer 1982, 45). Two advisors noted, however, that their investment approach already emphasized smaller, less institutionally recognized companies and thus complete divestment would be less burdensome to them. Several mentioned a preference for the Sullivan Principles approach, and one advisor asserted that smaller companies should not be considered more socially responsible.

> These smaller companies which do not currently have any connection with South Africa should not be given credit for their socially responsible actions because for the most part the only reason they do not deal in South Africa is their size and not any conscious decision on this social matter. As these companies grow and increase their markets, there is every reason to believe that they will do business in South Africa if it is profitable for them to do so. The proposed bill [i.e., full divestment] gives no credit to the companies that are acting in a socially responsible matter [sic] in their dealings with South Africa and favors companies who, because of their size or product line, have no current business in South Africa (Connecticut Office of the Treasurer 1982, 48).

Therefore, although the conclusions of the consultants' formal studies on the whole were mixed, the investment managers were adamant in insisting that it would hinder their normal investment approaches and decisions.

Negotiations over specific recommendations consumed most of the Task Force efforts. A wide range of alternatives were considered, as shown in Table 4–6. The CAAC was primarily responsible for proposing option E, and Russell suggested option D. The origin of the other alternatives is not known. From this list the group settled on an approach fairly quickly. The Sullivan Principles would be kept as a criterion for investment but other criteria would be added. This resolved the most fundamental question underlying the Task Force work—whether or not the state would withdraw its investments from all corporations with South African operations. The response was no. What remained was to decide the additional criteria. This final chore proved to be the most contentious aspect of the group's work.

Basic to defining the criteria was the old problem of clarifying "doing business." Giles had attempted to take care of this difficulty in the legislature by amending his full divestment bill. His amendment had intended the definition to apply to companies with subsidiaries in South

TABLE 4-6. Legislative Options Considered by the Task Force

A. Recommend that the State Legislature adopt a resolution condemning the practice of apartheid in South Africa and expressing its concern to the White House on current United States policy toward the government of that country.

B. Recommend that the State of Connecticut not purchase any goods or services from any United States corporation doing business in South Africa.

C. Draft legislation that would improve on the Sullivan Principles.

D. Draft legislation improving upon the Sullivan Principles and requiring social development expenditures.

E. Draft legislation keeping Sullivan Principles and requiring no sales to the military, plus the following:

   1. no sales of strategic materials to the government or its agencies;
   2. no discharging of employees for striking;
   3. no investment in homelands or growth points;
   4. recognition of unions.

F. Support the existing bills but defining what "doing business in South Africa" means.

Source: Connecticut Office of the Treasurer 1982, 8.

Africa. The Task Force followed the same basic sentiment when it settled on this meaning for the term: "conducting or performing manufacturing, assembly, or warehousing operations within the Republic of South Africa" (Connecticut Office of the Treasurer 1982, 16). The more difficult problem came when the group applied the definition to banks and financial institutions such as insurance companies (many of which are based in Connecticut, some being investment agents for the state). Would the state be required to cease investing in a bank that loaned money to a corporation "doing business" in South Africa? Would such a loan constitute the bank's "doing business" in South Africa? Because of the enormous administrative burden of enforcing a broad definition, the group decided to be more lenient with financial institutions by defining their doing business as "lending money to the Republic of South Africa or any agency or instrumentality thereof" (Connecticut Office of the Treasurer 1982, 16). Russell, who offered the definition, knew that it would make the entire Task Force package much more palatable to the bank representatives, but at least one industry representative questioned this outcome. He believed the banks had bought their way out of the controversy while leaving the industrial and commercial sectors to suffer. Tempers flared, and if there had previously been a united front among business interests, there was now a sizable crack in it.

A second major issue that caused a great deal of tension concerned a criterion of sales to the government, police, and military in South Africa. The CAAC through Hoffman had proposed that all companies with sales to the government or military be disqualified from the portfolio. The two corporate executives whose companies, United Technologies Corporation (UTC) and General Electric (GE), have subsidiaries in South Africa practicing such sales objected vehemently to this idea. Hoffman got no support for her proposal except for the second labor representative. Her fall-back position was to suggest no sales of "strategic" products or services to the government, police, or military with the term *strategic* defined as: armaments, aircraft, vehicles, or computers, and spare parts and services with respect thereto. In order to clarify the definition in a manner acceptable to the corporate representatives, William Hamilton amended the definition with the phrase: "as defined in the Export Administration act and also as defined by the joint actions of the U.S. Departments of State and Commerce."

The Exportation Administration Act was passed in 1978 under the Carter administration as a means of compliance with the 1977 United Nations Security Council Resolution 418 banning the export of military equipment to South Africa. The United States representative voted in favor of Resolution 418 and it is binding on all UN members. Under Carter, the Export Administration Act prohibited the exports of all goods and technology to the South African military and police, but, as mentioned in Chapter 2, under the Reagan administration, in March 1982 the prohibition was altered significantly to allow sales of various kinds of electronic equipment, computers, medical goods, and other items to the South African government. Being close monitors of U.S. foreign policy toward South Africa, both Hamilton and Hoffman knew of this very recent change in regulation. Because it now allowed a wider range of products to be sold to the South African government, Hamilton proposed it for use by the Task Force. For the same reason, Hoffman rejected it. Not knowing specifically what the Export Administration Act entailed, the remainder of the committee was reluctant to approve Hamilton's amendment.

Another amendment was suggested by Jack Hughes, a UTC representative. He suggested that the group use the International Traffic in Arms Regulations (ITAR: U.S. Code of Federal Regulations, Chapter 22, Part 121) to define their recommendation. This regulation authorizes the president to exercise control over exports to all countries of arms, ammunition, and implements of war listed in the provision. Whereas for U.S. government purposes the ITAR applies to exports, the Task Force would be suggesting its use under Connecticut law as a standard to apply against subsidiaries of U.S. corporations in South Africa. After seeing copies of ITAR, the group was willing to accept it as a definition of arms with the added clause "and data processing equipment and computers sold for military or police use or for use in connection with the pass system" (Connecticut Office of the Treasurer 1982, 16). Because subsidiaries of U.S.-based computer firms (for example, IBM, Control Data) supply a great deal of computer equipment to the police and military in South Africa (unhampered by the ITAR provision) and because these sales have been repeatedly criticized by anti-apartheid activists, Hoffman and the other labor representative wanted to ensure these companies would be excluded from the portfolio.

The debate over the definition of the term strategic was especially virulent and threatened to cause the demise of the whole effort. During those particular meetings the industry representatives almost resigned from the Task Force, and the reluctant CAAC members had to be coaxed by Parker and Cloud to accept the final compromise (Table 4–7) as the best attainable solution. The underlying issue at stake was, of course, whether or not the state would be able to invest in the largest employer in the state, UTC, and another major corporation headquartered in Connecticut, GE. The intention of the CAAC was to get as many South Africa-related companies as possible excluded from the portfolio, if necessary including any Connecticut-based corporations, but the UTC and GE representatives were not idly going to witness the state's implicit condemnation of their operations. In the end, Hoffman and Russell agreed to accept a definition that would include UTC and GE in the portfolio in order to save the possibility of reaching a final product—a rather broad set of divestment criteria applicable to a number of other corporations and banks.

A third major area of contention was what the Task Force would report as its conclusion from the divestiture impact study report. Parker wanted the Task Force to reassert and affirm the consultants' findings that total divestment would substantially reduce the universe of available investments. Hoffman objected, arguing that the consultants had also found a slight positive gain in returns and were in disagreement over the impact of reduced investment opportunities. The issue was one with important ramifications for Connecticut and, as we will see, for other anti-apartheid actions targeted at pension funds. That is, can the fiduciary responsibility be carried out responsibly with a divestment policy? In the end, the Task Force report stated the opinions of the consultants and advisors in a straightforward fashion without taking a position on their findings. Similarly, it describes the opposing viewpoints on the Sullivan Principles.

After these two intense and at times rancorous months of work, the Task Force submitted to the governor an 81-page report of its activities with its unanimous recommendations which are shown in Table 4–7.

Meanwhile in the legislature, in consultation with Parker, Representative Stolberg, co-chair of the Finance Committee, had a bill ready and waiting as a vehicle for legislative action on the Task Force proposals. In order to get the issue before the legislature but not to preempt potential Task Force recommendations, the bill was a repeat of the previous year's legislation. Although there had been hearings (with a number of the CAAC members testifying again and business interests bringing their first testimony on the issue), no one was convinced that the act would pass as it stood. With the Task Force recommendations, however, the legislation, House Bill 5975, was passed by overwhelming majorities in both houses and signed by the governor. The bill is shown in Appendix B.

Implementation of the 1982 Law

Immediately after the bill became law, the Treasurer's Office began work on its implementation. Discussions were held with a number of organizations that research and monitor corporate social responsibility issues or South Africa in order that the department could begin developing research files and data exchanges. Letters and questionnaires were sent to all corporations and banks in the portfolio advising them of the new law and asking for information on their policies related to business in South Africa and, if they had business there, their Sullivan Principles rating. Banks were asked for policy statements on their South Africa

TABLE 4-7. Task Force Recommendations

STANDARD I

That the State Treasurer disinvest from those corporations doing business in South Africa which have not obtained a performance rating in the top two categories of the Sullivan Principles rating system prepared by the Arthur D. Little Company.

STANDARD II

That the State Treasurer disinvest from those corporations doing business in South Africa which supply strategic products or services for use by the government or for use by the military or police in South Africa.

STANDARD III

That the State Treasurer disinvest from those corporations doing business in South Africa which fail to recognize the right of all South African employees to organize and strike in support of economic or social objectives, free from the fear of dismissal or blacklisting.

ADDITIONAL RECOMMENDATIONS

A. That the State Treasurer, in administering a law inclusive of these recommendations, may require a social audit of corporations doing business in South Africa.

B. That the State Treasurer consult with the Investment Advisory Council in developing, interpreting and administering any policy relating to these standards.

DEFINITIONS

"doing business in South Africa"

> Conducting or performing manufacturing, assembly, or warehousing operations within the Republic of South Africa or, if a bank or other financial institution, lending money to the Republic of South Africa or any agency of instrumentality thereof.

"strategic products and services"

> Articles desinated as arms, ammunition and implements of war as described in 22 C.F.R. - 121, (U.S. Code of Federal Regulations) and data processing equipment and computers sold for military or police use or for use in connection with the pass system.

Source: Connecticut Office of the Treasurer 1982, 3, 16.

lending practices. A summer intern was hired to begin work on the law, and a new position, Investment Officer-Social Compliance, was created for management of the treasurer's corporate social responsibility program, a program broader than implementation of the South Africa law. Barbara Reid was appointed to the position and began work in February 1983. Reid had worked for the department for eight years and was well acquainted with corporate social responsibility issues. The Investment Advisory Council, a body charged with advising the treasurer on all matters related to investments, met a number of times to monitor implementation and to begin the divestment process.

Of the 230 corporations in the $2.7 billion portfolio, 70 (with securities worth over $350 million) were doing business in South Africa. A process was developed for determining the schedule of divestment for any companies not meeting standards of the new law. An "avoid list" was created for those not in compliance. No new securities are purchased from companies on the avoid list, and if the company cannot be convinced to comply with the law, its securities will be sold. If a corporation comes into compliance, it is taken off the avoid list. Furthermore, if a company whose securities have been sold comes into compliance at a later date, it will become eligible for the portfolio again. Therefore, review of the South Africa related investments is a dynamic process that requires constant monitoring to determine companies' eligibility for investment, divestment, of reinvestment.

In order to give companies an opportunity to comply with the law, the treasurer is willing to act patiently, negotiating with a business about its activities before withdrawing an investment. Parker and his staff interpret the law as intending to encourage positive change in the social and environmental practices of the companies, and they want to sue it as leverage to improve business operations in South Africa to the fullest extent possible.

By mid-1984, the Treasurer's Office was confident that it had established a fair and consistent process to monitor and act on the first standard, rating in the top two categories of the Sullivan Principles. The results are shown in Table 4-8 which displays for the first two years of implementation the companies whose securities, under this standard, were sold, put on the avoid list, or reapproved for investment. Net gains from divesting the 23 corporations listed in the first section of the table were about $5.58 million.

One of the ironies of this story is that both UTC and GE, two companies with representatives on the Task Force

TABLE 4-8.   Implementation of Standard I: Corporations with Securities
Sold, Put on the Avoid List, or Reapproved for Investment

Corporations Whose Securities were Sold*	Reason for Sale	Date
Air Products and Chemicals	Non-signatory	1/83
Alexander and Alexander	Non-signatory	1/83
American Can Company	Rating	7/84
American Home Products	Non-signatory	1/83
Baker International	Rating	4/84
CBS, Inc.	Rating	4/84
Celanese Corporation	Rating	1/84
Coca Cola Company	Rating	9/83
Cooper Industries	Rating	12/83
Dun & Bradstreet	Non-signatory	1/83
Eli Lilly and Company	Rating	1/83
International Minerals and Chemicals	Rating	7/84
Loctite Corporation	Rating	7/84
Martin Marietta Corporation	Non-signatory	1/83
Measurex Corporation	Rating	7/84
Motorola	Rating	1/83
Nabisco Brands	Rating	4/83
Nalco Chemical Company	Rating	7/84
A.C. Nielson Company	Rating	7/84
United Technologies	Rating	12/83
Upjohn Company	Rating	4/83
VF Corporation	Non-signatory	1/83
Warner Communications	Rating	1/83

Avoid List	Reason	Date
Tenneco	Rating	12/83
Warner-Lambert Company	Rating	12/83

Reapproved for Investment after being on Avoid List or Sold	Reason	Date
American Home Products	Signed the Principles	1/84
Coca Cola Company	Received Acceptable Rating	1/84
Cooper Industries	Received Acceptable Rating	1/84
Eli Lilly Company	Received Acceptable Rating	1/84
General Electric	Received Acceptable Rating	4/84
Minnesota Mining and Manufacturing	Received Acceptable Rating	12/83
Nabisco Brands	Received Acceptable Rating	1/84
United Technologies	Received Acceptable Rating	1/84

*Most of these corporations had been on Avoid List prior to being sold.

127

that developed the standards, were put on the avoid list and UTC securities were sold. UTC has two subsidiaries in South Africa, one with an acceptable rating and one without. The second later came into compliance and the company was reapproved in January 1984. GE has six subsidiaries in South Africa and only one was out of compliance because it is not a Sullivan signatory. GE owns only about 25 percent of the subsidiary and could not force it to sign the principles. However, it does subscribe to the European Community Code and has received a favorable rating in that system. In negotiating with the parent company, the Treasurer's Office agreed to reapprove GE if the subsidiary made more progress in implementing certain labor practices in South Africa. GE was restored to the acceptable category in April 1984.

Treasury staff admit that they have not made a great deal of progress in implementing the other two standards in the law or the provision pertaining to banks that make loans to the government or its agencies. To begin enforcing the standard on labor unions, the office has sent its list of potential investments to the African-American Labor Center, associated with the AFL-CIO, for its reaction. The center has representatives in South Africa. Staff also consult experts in research organizations and the anti-apartheid movement to learn about labor relations in specific corporations.

Implementing the standard on bank loans and on sales of strategic products and data processing equipment has proven more difficult. The Treasurer's Office wrote to all corporations to learn of their practices in these areas, but the information is hard to get. Banks and computer companies are reluctant to give out detailed information on business transactions they believe to be proprietary in nature, although they will make public general policies regarding sales to the South African government, police, or military. For those corporations (mostly banks) that have a general policy of not doing business with the South African government, there is no problem. But from the treasurer's perspective, *not* having such a policy is insufficient reason for divestiture. Therefore, the staff face the fairly burdensome task of finding out information about detailed transactions that the companies do not want them to have (for example, what kinds of goods and services are sold to which government agencies or parastatals).

To facilitate the process, the treasurer asked for an advisory opinion from the Connecticut Freedom of Information Council to see if his office could keep the necessary information confidential, using it only for the purpose of implementing the law. The opinion declared that such confidentiality was possible. All of this correspondence between the Treasurer's Office, the companies, and the Freedom of Information Council took almost two years.

From the perspective of the CAAC, implementation was proceeding much too slowly. The committee wanted to do something to hasten it. Members had agreed to give the process a year before making decisions about further action, but their goal for the state still remained that of full divestment. In the fall of 1983, over 15 months after the bill had become law, the group decided to approach legislative leadership about the possibility of reintroducing a full divestment bill. Stolberg, by this time Speaker of the House, advised them instead to propose amendments to tighten the existing law. Through the Finance, Revenue, and Bonding Committee, the CAAC introduced four amendments:

1. that the definition of strategic products and services include data processing or computer *supplies* sold or *leased* for military or police use, *or to agencies of the South African government that perform research and development, or for use in the production of arms and related materials*;
2. that the reference to the pass system in this definition be expanded to include the book of life, which is the identification document carried by all non-Africans; (only Africans are required to carry passes);
3. that all vehicles sold or leased to the South African military or police and all petroleum products sold for military use be added to the standards for divestment; and
4. that all corporations and banks be required to provide the state with information regarding compliance.

The amendments were of two types: one to clarify the intent of and to close loopholes in the law (paragraphs 1, 2, and 4), and the other to expand the law beyond the original standards (paragraph 3).

With regard to the first type, the CAAC was disappointed that, from their perspective, Parker had been enforcing the letter but not the spirit of the law. They saw any corporation that failed to declare a policy of not doing business with the South African government, military, or police as ineligible for state investment. Furthermore, they interpreted the law as prohibiting investments in businesses aiding military-related research or administration of the book of life. If corporations were reluctant or refused to disclose the necessary information, the CAAC maintained that such inaction was sufficient reason to divest without further negotiation. There was no need, they argued, for corporations to have protection from public disclosure under freedom of information procedures. The corporations should bear the burden of proving themselves eligible rather than the state going to great lengths to make their case for them. Some corporations that were violating the standards according to the CAAC but who securities were still held by the state were: IBM, Control Data, Hewlett Packard, Xerox, Citibank, NCR, and Sperry. However, the last two were on the avoid list for non-disclosure of information. The CAAC based its assessment on documentation, also available to the treasurer, that details the relationship of U.S. corporations, especially computer companies, to the South African government (see NARMIC 1982).

With the second type of amendment, the committee wanted to expand the definition of strategic products. The South African subsidiaries of U.S. automobile companies sell vehicles to the police and military, but because such vehicles do not fit the definition in the ITAR code of "armed or armoured vehicles . . . and vehicles fitted with, designed or modified to accommodate mountings for arms . . ." the companies meet the second standard. CAAC members argued that a looser construction of the law would disqualify the car companies such as GM and Ford from state investment, but they knew Parker would not interpret the law in this manner. Therefore, they wanted to spell out the more rigid requirement. The amendment on petroleum products was entirely new but, CAAC members believed, well within the spirit of the law since the law was intended to distinguish between corporations that make the greatest contribution to apartheid and those that do not.

Hoffman spoke on behalf of the CAAC in hearings by the Finance Committee on the proposed amendments in March 1984. Parker and Reid also testified. The later two maintained that they had no fundamental disagreement with the amendments intended to clarify the law, but that there simply had not yet been enough time to implement it fully. They also assured the Finance Committee that corporations would be divested if they continued to refuse disclosure of information now protected from public scrutiny under freedom of information procedures. Parker promised a full report on the process in later months.

Parker and Reid objected, however, to the substantive amendments to broaden the definition of strategic, arguing that it potentially could bring significantly greater risk to the portfolio. Without further study on its implication, they opposed it. CAAC members believed that the only corporations eliminated from potential or actual investment by the expanded definition were Ford, GM, Mobil, and Texaco. The first three of these companies are in the Connecticut portfolio but Texaco is not. Nevertheless, the committee did not press its case.

No major campaign was mobilized by the CAAC to get the amendments passed and they died in committee. The group did not have much enthusiasm for pressing the amendments because they hoped at some future point to try again for their real objective, full divestment. The proposals, however, had served the useful purpose of holding the Treasurer's Office publicly accountable for its activities, and the committee hoped such pressure would hasten and broaden implementation.

In subsequent months, the Treasurer's Office made more progress on enforcing the second standard, the one on strategic products. By July 1984, the securities of NCR Corporation and Sperry Corporation had been sold for a net gain of $1.27 million, putting total gains from divestment at about $6.85 million. These two businesses had been on the avoid list for non-disclosure of information, but as of August 1984 no other computer companies were on the avoid list. Neither were there any banks on the avoid list, and the CAAC is still pressing for divestment of those corporations that its members believe should have been removed from the portfolio already.

In other arenas, after passage of the 1982 law the CAAC continued its on-going activities of speaking engagements, sponsoring educational events, and commemorating special occasions in the history of black resistance in South Africa. In addition, Hoffman was invited by the American Friends Service Committee to participate in its educational tour on South Africa in the Iowa Democratic Party Caucuses. She also was invited and attended the August 1983 UN Second World Conference to Combat Racism and Racial Discrimination in Geneva, Switzerland.

The Treasurer's Office has been providing a number of state and local governments (for example, Iowa, Washington, D.C., New Jersey, Oregon, Nebraska, Ohio, Florida, Pennsylvania) and various other organizations with information on Connecticut's anti-apartheid law. Parker also spent time in Iowa and Maine at the National State Treasurer's Conference speaking about the Connecticut experience. Parker is more than ever convinced that the state's moderate law is a very good means for taking a significant stand on apartheid and pressuring companies in South Africa to change for the better. He prefers the route of taking the time to negotiate with companies and to examine exhaustively all possibilities that they are not aiding apartheid, rather than the easier route of divesting when there is any doubt about their eligibility for the portfolio. His office also continues its longstanding activities on voting its proxies in corporate responsibility shareholder resolutions.

Summary

The history of the political process on the question of state investments and apartheid demonstrates that three different policy outcomes were achieved in three years: a partial divestment law using the Sullivan Principles, a vetoed full divestment bill, and a second partial divestment law designed to strengthen the first. The story of how Connecticut addresses the issue will continue to unfold, but at this point it is important to analyze why these outcomes occurred. What factors are responsible for the passage of the various pieces of legislation, the veto of the 1981 act, and the formulation of the Task Force recommendations? The next section of this chapter will examine this question.

WHY THESE OUTCOMES

To help structure the analysis of why divestment legislation succeeded in varying degrees in Connecticut, the list of variables introduced in Chapter 3 (Table 3–1) will be used. The variables serve as clues for investigation rather than as precise indicators. As in Chapter 3 they are divided into two categories: the inner environment, the sphere of potential direct control by the organizations involved in the campaign; and the outer environment, everything else relevant to the campaign. The campaign leading up to the passage of the 1981 full divestment bill, the governor's veto, and activists' post-veto efforts are investigated in some depth using the variables. A less structured approach will be taken in analyzing the task force negotiations, which are not considered to be a campaign on the part of the activists. The passage of the 1980 bill will be examined only briefly since there was no campaign organized to promote it either.

The 1980 legislation containing the Sullivan Principles lays the foundation and sets a precedent for future governmental action on apartheid, but its passage is the result primarily of the efforts of a few black legislators backed by the legislative Black Caucus. Because the bill was amended in committee to include the Sullivan Principles, it met virtually no opposition. Although many felt it was the right thing to do, the law also was something the rest of the legislators could "give" to the Black Caucus in a routine political exchange. The CAAC had testified on the bill and urged its passage, but the group had not mobilized its supporters or lobbied on behalf of the measure. The bill passed with little notice and by itself does not provide a very interesting study of political processes.

The 1981 Campaign: Goals, Theory of Action, Target, Time, and Context

In contrast, the 1981 full divestment bill was the object of a long campaign and fascinating process. To establish why the campaign got as far as it did, it is important to understand where it was intended to go—that is, its goals. The campaign goals are listed in Table 4–9. They have been discerned through interviews with proponents in the CAAC steering committee and the Black Caucus and from a list of goals published by the CAAC as its aims for 1980.[3]

All proponents in the campaign are not agreed on all the goals they seek. Everyone emphasizes that the issue of apartheid is the focal point of their work, and there is no disagreement about the goals having to do directly with apartheid or U.S. investments in South Africa (for example, numbers 1 through 11). There is disagreement, however, about goal 12 because in it apartheid and U.S. investment in South Africa become vehicles for raising larger questions about the structure and organization of the United States and South African economies as well as the world economy. Some proponents, especially those in the labor unions, see goal 12 to be as important as 1 through 11. The analysis underlying it provides a framework through which to view their entire effort. Other proponents, especially those in the legislature and community organizations, regard goal 10 as secondary to their central concerns (embodied in goals 1 through 11). This disagreement over goals is essentially an ideological conflict also present in anti-apartheid efforts elsewhere in the country. The CAAC deliberately subdued it in the interest of pursuing a broad coalition of supporters.

The goals in Table 4–9 have been structured into categories of short- medium-, and long-term to try to take into account variation in the time needed to attain them. A time dimension is crucial to judging effectiveness since some goals are intended for quick achievement, whereas others remain a lifetime vision. For purposes of this study,

TABLE 4-9. Connecticut Proponents' Campaign Goals

Short-term

   1. For proponents to express solidarity with the struggle of blacks and others in South Africa resisting apartheid;

   2. For proponents to take a principled stand against apartheid and U.S. corporate investment in South Africa;

   3. For proponents to draw attention to the issues of apartheid and U.S. corporate involvement in South Africa;

   4. For proponents to continue support for the Patriotic Front (of Zimbabwe) and SWAPO (of Namibia) through educational work (articles, newsletters, and so forth) and, if necessary, with other actions;

   5. For proponents to show support for anti-racist actions here in the United States whenever possible;

Medium-term

   6. For the state to take a principled stand against apartheid and U.S. corporate investment in South Africa;

   7. For proponents to achieve complete withdrawal of state investments from corporations with investments in South Africa and from banks making loans to the South African government or its parastatals;

   8. For the state to express solidarity with the struggle of blacks and others in South Africa resisting apartheid through divestment of its pension funds;

   9. For the combined actions of the national anti-apartheid movement to constrain any further U.S. government or corporations' cooperation with and support of the South African government;

Long-term

   10. For proponents and the state to contribute to the ending of apartheid;

   11. For proponents and the state to contribute to the world-wide anti-apartheid movement's efforts to completely isolate South Africa economically;

   12. For proponents to raise the consciousness of working- and middle-class people in Connecticut about the structure and behavior of multinational corporations with regard to:

     a. their support for apartheid;
     b. U.S. government facilitation and defense of their operations;
     c. the similarities of anti-corporate struggles in the U.S. and abroad, especially in South Africa.

---

short-term is considered to be less than a year, medium-term one to two years, and long-term three or more years. The goals are identified with proponents, the state, or the national anti-apartheid movement in the United States. Proponents hold and advocate all these aims, but they hope to accomplish some themselves and others they want to have the state or the total movement accomplish.

In the context of the discussion of goals in Chapter 1, proponents' goals for the state require substantial change in Connecticut's investment policies. As suggested in Chapter 3, the assertion of social movement literature generally is that groups seeking greater degrees of change have less likelihood of achieving their desired outcomes, whereas those seeking lesser change have a better chance at succeeding. Therefore, from the beginning the CAAC faced a big challenge.

The short- and medium-term goals feed into the long-term goals and, together with strategies and tactics chosen, these nearer objectives provide a route by which proponents hope eventually to achieve the most distant aims. As was discussed previously, the combination of these means and desired ends is the theory of action for the campaign. The goals list suggests several theories of action, only one of which, the most prominent, will be examined in detail. The group has chosen to target an institutional investor, the state, as a means of putting pressure on corporations involved in southern Africa. Together with similar actions by other anti-apartheid groups in the United States and worldwide, they hope to convince these corporations to disengage from South Africa and the United States government to consider sanctions. They believe that such disengagement or sanctions, combined with the dynamics of internal resistance and other pressures inside the country, will help end apartheid.

In order to achieve state divestment, the group chose to focus a campaign on the legislature, pressing it to pass full divestment legislation. A variety of tactics were used to mobilize support for the legislation and convince legislators to vote for it. CAAC members along with others who supported their cause held educational and cultural events; communicated within their network with a monthly newsletter; wrote newspaper articles and letters to the editor; held press conferences and demonstrations; spoke on divestment at other organizations' meetings; endorsed other organizations' anti-racist work; solicited endorsements and other support from organizations and their leaders across the state; researched the issue; lobbied, testified, suggested amendments for the bill; and negotiated for its passage inside the legislature. In the process of mobilizing support for the legislation, the group wanted to make its own moral stand public and tried to convince others to do the same.

Part of the process in a goals-based evaluation is to discern whether or not the activists have a logical theory of action. Could one reasonably expect that what the proponents want to accomplish can be accomplished through the route they have proposed? Does any sequence in the theory require a leap of faith rather than a rational understanding of the issues? Judging the logic of any proposed strategy for political change is difficult, and outcomes are not predictable with high degrees of accuracy. Using the best evidence available, however, the logic and rationality of a theory of action can be tested.

This evaluation will begin with the last segment of the CAAC theory of action, the destabilization of the South African regime through sanctions. Many in the general anti-apartheid movement assert that the imposition of economic sanctions on South Africa and corporations' withdrawal of their investments is one means for speeding an end to apartheid. Although sanctions and corporate withdrawal are not the only factors that the movement participants believe will bring down apartheid, some argue that such economic pressure can be an important complement to resistance efforts inside the country. This working assumption and the nature of U.S. corporate investments in South Africa have been discussed and analyzed in Chapter 2. The CAAC operates out of this same understanding of the issue, and the group's theory of action reflects its attempt to contribute to the wider pressures for sanctions. No segment of the movement is isolated and participants believe their efforts combine to create a powerful force. In applying the discussion of the divestment debate in Chapter 3, we can suggest that the CAAC theory of action is a mixture of rationality and faith. The theory has the best chance of holding if sanctions are imposed by all nations' governments. Anything short of comprehensive international enforcement preventing trade and investment in South Africa leads to less confidence in the theory, and activists understand this. They have always maintained that their movement must be international to be effective, and INGOs exist to try to coordinate efforts across national boundaries. The activists in Connecticut believe that their work will aid the entire movement's pressures toward sanctions and that these smaller contributions will accumulate to be large forces.

Targeting institutional investors to achieve enough pressure on companies to cause their withdrawal from South

Africa is a strategy chosen by anti-apartheid activists to maximize the leverage exerted on the corporations. Since institutional investors hold more stocks and bonds than individual investors, and since the former are more accessible to activists than the corporations themselves, the choice makes good sense. However, pressures and hassles from stockholders are peripheral to the factors that lead a company to make international investment decisions—that is, unless the pressures are great enough to cause the corporation financial harm in some form. There is potential for such a cumulation depending on the number and size of activists' campaigns, and some businesses clearly worry about such possibilities. Should that potential be realized, one could expect serious consideration of withdrawal from South Africa by corporate executives.

The first parts of the CAAC theory of action, the process of getting a state legislature to pass a bill, are easier to assess. The strategies and tactics are standard procedures commonly believed to aid in producing a desired legislative outcome and draw public attention to an issue. These are not the only strategies available, but they are logical and rational ones. The early sequences in the theory of action, therefore, are the most dependable ones. The later sequences are not only more difficult to judge, but they are also more reliant on a combination and accumulation of pressures from arenas completely outside the influence of the CAAC members. That such pressures will accumulate is a matter of activists' faith in the total movement.

Another of the variables to be considered as significant in facilitating or hindering a campaign is the arena targeted. In this case, the arena probably helped activists' efforts. Instead of going directly to the companies that invest in South Africa to pressure them to withdraw, or to the Treasury Department to convince officials there of the need for divestment, the activist chose a more accessible forum—the legislature. Being a large public arena with a responsibility to pay some attention to citizens' concerns, the legislature provided easier entree for the CAAC. The group knew several legislators who were already sympathetic and they hoped to convince more.

Time was also on their side. Since late 1978 the committee had been organizing for a mobilization of effort by a large number of people. Members had not been willing or ready to attempt such a mobilization in early 1980 when the Sullivan Principles bill was being considered. But by early 1981 they were prepared, and a few legislators were still interested in pursuing full divestment with them. In addition, by 1981, the issue was no longer new to the legislature, and few legislators were unaware of or caught off-guard by the activists' interest in pursuing it. Legislators also did not seem to be so saturated with the issue that they could not tolerate it being raised again. Therefore, timing seemed to facilitate the campaign.

As suggested earlier, it should be no surprise that the Connecticut legislature was targeted for such a campaign. It is a logical arena into which to carry a question that was being promoted in other institutions nearby, and receptivity had already been demonstrated. Other contextual elements need to be noted as well. During this debate, and for over half of the last twenty years, the Democratic party has controlled both houses of the General Assembly and the governorship (Jewell and Olson 1978, 34). Within the General Assembly in 1981 there were three black senators (out of 36) and seven black representatives (out of 151), and the state treasurer, an elected official, is also black. The number and proportion of black legislators is not high, but one could assume that among the ten there would be some sympathy for full divestment. The state work force is heavily unionized, and activists report that there are a number of groups in Connecticut working on a wide range of social issues that might be considered liberal or leftist. The networks among these organizations seem to be fairly good because there is overlapping leadership in some cases and deliberate attempts to maintain good communications across groups. Since Connecticut is geographically a small state, state-wide organization and mobilization for activists' causes is easier.

All of these factors would seemingly characterize Connecticut as being fertile ground for a legislative divestment campaign. Any conclusion about the state's positive propensity to accept such legislation, however, should be tempered with an acknowledgment of the importance of business interests to the state, especially in the southern part, near New York City. A number of large corporations, many of them multinationals, are headquartered in Connecticut. Table 4–3 illustrates which of these companies have investments in South Africa, and one can easily assume they are not receptive to the idea of withdrawing their investments. Therefore, whereas a lot of contextual factors in Connecticut appear to help the CAAC achieve its goals, others hinder it.

The 1981 Campaign: Strength

One of the major inner environment variables that should

affect the outcome of a campaign is its strength. Strength is actually a multifaceted and complex set of variables that deserves thorough examination. The CAAC was able to develop a great deal of strength in many areas as it entered and conducted its 1981 campaign. One of those was a very broad coalition of endorsers and supporters outside the legislative arena. Table 4–2 lists these endorsements.

As was stated previously, the CAAC began soliciting support in late 1978. Members would attend other organizations' meetings, discuss the issue of apartheid and U.S. corporate involvement in South Africa, and request endorsements. They also held their own events often featuring well-known speakers or entertainers from South Africa (for example, Dumasani Kumalo, an exiled journalist; Thozamile Botha, an exiled black labor and community organizer; Jennifer Davis, an exiled white economist and Executive Director of the American Committee on Africa). The events always focused on apartheid and the U.S. connection to it, but they also were designed to encourage people to socialize with one another, have fun, and enjoy each others' company. These events were usually cosponsored by union, community, or university organizations. The events paid for themselves and even helped to raise funds. The committee operated all its activities on a budget of about $1,500 per year.

Gaining access to a wide range of organizations and their meetings was not difficult for the CAAC. Most of the core group (about six to ten people) are active in and hold leadership positions in other organizations. For example, two persons mentioned earlier, Christy Hoffman and Peggy Buchanan, are well connected in other groups. Hoffman, twenty-nine, is a machinist in a Pratt-Whitney (United Technologies) jet engine factory and is the Steering Committee chairperson in the plant's local International Association of Machinists. Buchanan, thirty, is a Connecticut state employee doing training workshops for other state employees; she is also in leadership in the Connecticut State Federation of Teachers (a public employee union) and works closely with other activist groups, one focused on feminism and another on El Salvador. The CAAC nucleus is composed of other persons similarly well known for their involvement in community organizations in Connecticut. Thus to promote their educational efforts and to gain support for the campaign, the CAAC called on their acquaintances in these various networks.

Another factor that aided in achieving endorsements was the single issue focus of the campaign. The committee was very deliberate in not allowing its work to branch out into other issues or even other aspects of the issue of racism. Although the question of broadening their focus was discussed several times, the group decided to resist it. Other organizations were already working on some of those other issues that were enticing to the CAAC members, and they felt that the divestment campaign alone was plenty to handle. The committee also was determined not to fall prey to sectarian in-fighting among themselves, a problem that characterizes some leftist groups. The nucleus of the CAAC was not all of one ideological persuasion, and most felt that achieving a successful campaign necessitated appealing to a wide range of people of varying political perspectives. If you were committed to the withdrawal of U.S. corporations from South Africa, you were welcome in the group. This single-issue ideologically open policy cost the group a few of its participants who wanted to promote a broader issue and a more narrow ideology; but it helped to gain the committee a wide range of supporters devoted to its principal goal.

To maintain its network of supporters, the CAAC kept frequent communications with them. The committee distributed fliers with the names of endorsing organizations and supportive statements from many of their leaders. Educational materials were also disbursed, and a newsletter was sent out monthly to a list that by 1981 had five hundred names on it. The four-page newsletter carried articles on events in Southern Africa, anti-apartheid activities across the United States, and committee activities and announcements. The newsletter as well as special mailings were used to alert supporters of legislative committee hearings and upcoming votes in committees or in the House or Senate. Press conferences and statehouse rallies were also held at crucial junctures in the campaign.

The committee had a number of good vehicles for communications, an outstanding network of contacts, and some very articulate spokespersons. However, to sustain campaign momentum across three years required more than good means of communications; it also required a convincing message. What could the CAAC tell people to persuade them that they should care about the exploitation of black people in a country half-way around the world? This question of relevance was one of the most difficult tasks the group faced.

The arguments about U.S. corporations' support for apartheid through their presence in South Africa and through the products they provide to the government and the economy in general are familiar ones in the anti-apartheid movement. The CAAC asserted that the state workers' pension funds should not be benefiting from investments earned through a racist system; that citizens could both demonstrate solidarity with South African blacks and contribute to changing apartheid by demanding divestiture of those pension funds. This argument was not sufficient, however, and the committee took it further. They brought it home. As Hoffman (1981) put it:

> It's important, we found, to draw connections between what is going on in South Africa and what is going on in the U.S. . . . It's important to draw the connections between the fact that Uniroyal in Naugatuck, Connecticut has closed down its plants, and Uniroyal in Naugatuck, Connecticut has also invested in the Bantustans of South Africa; that Olin has had a very long and bitter strike with its workers in New Haven, Connecticut and it is selling guns to South Africa; and that banks are redlining our communities and are making loans to South Africa. . . . These connections have been very important for us to draw for the people we are reaching out to. . . .

Asserting that workers and people in general in Connecticut had something in common with South African blacks and that they all had reason to be angry at the same companies was a convincing message, especially to unions. The persuasiveness of the message, combined with strong means of conveying it, mobilized a lot of organizations to add their support to the campaign as seen in Table 4–2.

Campaign strength consisted not only of the broad coalition of endorsements the CAAC generated outside the legislature but also of supporters inside the General Assembly. The Black Caucus continued to be persistent backers of divestment legislation in general, but some had to be persuaded that the 1980 Sullivan Principles bill was not sufficient. The caucus members interviewed admitted that at the time of the Sullivan Principles amendment they knew very little about the principles and were willing to use them simply to salvage the legislation. Once they learned details about the principles from the CAAC, they were ready once again to promote full divestment. The CAAC requested Representative Dyson to reintroduce his bill, although he would have done so without the request, and Representative Giles introduced his legislation without the group's encouragement. Dyson now chaired the Black Caucus, and his credibility in the House as well as his leadership in encouraging the divestment concept among legislators proved to be crucial, as will be seen later.

Outside of the Black Caucus, the CAAC was able to win support among other legislators as well. Particularly significant support came when the group convinced the leadership of both the Finance and Appropriations Committees that the legislation should be passed. The campaign, therefore, gained a great deal of its strength from the number and kinds of supporters both inside and outside the General Assembly.

A second major source of campaign strength came from the CAAC steering committee. The assets its members bring are devotion to the work, skillful leadership, credibility and legitimacy among both supporters and adversaries, and carefully nurtured supportive relationships among themselves. The members' devotion to the work is demonstrated in several ways. One is that half of them have been in the steering committee since the founding of the CAAC in 1978. These people have given a great deal of time to anti-apartheid work both in terms of years and in terms of the daily requirements of keeping the organization going. Those interviewed reported that they regularly spent at least two nights a week and often many Saturdays on CAAC tasks. It is also not uncommon for members to take off time from their employment for committee activities. Thus the commitment level in the steering committee was very high.

The members' connections to other organizations have proven useful in gaining endorsements from the CAAC, but these organizations have made another contribution as well. They have been arenas in which the group could acquire valuable leadership skills. Most of the persons in the steering committee have been activists and leaders among activists for over five years. They have had a great deal of experience in a variety of organizations, and they are well known in these other activist groups for their skills, their determination, and their commitment to a broad range of social justice issues. They pay close attention to details of organizing, and they are consistent and reliable in their work. For example, they know how to raise money to underwrite CAAC activities and publications; they know how to carry out thorough research both on the issue itself and on how to promote the issue; they are articulate and accomplished public speakers; they are tenacious and persuasive negotiators; and they demonstrate good political judgment by reacting to and molding events in the political environment to fit their needs and by creating their own events to further their cause. These various leadership qualities have brought credibility to them as individuals and legitimacy to their work in the eyes of both friends and foes.

In addition, the steering committee functions as a group to foster good relations among themselves. Some are good friends and it is not unusual for them to spend time together outside of CAAC work. On observing one of their meetings it was evident that they are careful to consider every person' opinion. In consensus style, if someone has misgivings about a decision, the group takes that doubt seriously and re-examines the question. The meetings seem to be well planned (for example, a written agenda) and they are run efficiently in terms of sticking to the subject at hand until a decision is reached. Differences of opinion do arise, but the group seems to manage its conflicts fairly well.

Therefore, as suggested by social movement and interest group literature, the strength of a campaign makes a significant contribution to its effectiveness. In this case strength lay principally in the widespread support the CAAC was able to generate for divestment and in the committee's skillful and committed leadership.

The 1981 Campaign: Strategies and Tactics

Once the campaign had momentum its proponents had to map their legislative course carefully and adapt it as events unfolded. Two elements they found necessary to passing a bill were testimony on its behalf and lobbying. Hoffman testified for the CAAC in both the Appropriations and Finance Committees where Dyson's and Giles's bills were placed. She spoke against the Sullivan Principles and explained why the 1980 bill would not suffice for state investment policy. She also addressed the issues of the financial implications of divestment for the pension funds, the nature of U.S. corporations' investments in South Africa, and the support among black South Africans for economic sanctions. In the Finance Committee, she answered several questions on these various topics. Some representatives of CAAC endorsers testified, too, including persons from District 1199 of the New England Health Care Employees Union, the Connecticut State Federation of Teachers, Hartford AFSCME Local 1716, and the University of Connecticut School for Social Work.

The testimony served the purpose of defining the issues, providing vital information to decision makers, and giving evidence of support for the legislation. Excerpts of some of the testimony were put into a handout and distributed to all legislators. The testimony also functioned to begin casting the question as basically a moral one. Potential opponents began to realize that to raise objections was to risk being perceived as a racist.

Representative Dyson proved to be crucial to the CAAC lobbying effort both when the bills were in committee and once Giles's legislation was favorably reported out. Hoffman and Buchanan estimate that they spent every evening for about three weeks at the Capitol talking to legislators about the bill in the period just before it was up for a vote. During that time Dyson accompanied them to legislators' offices, introduced them, and requested that his colleagues spend some time with them. He gained access for them to the Democratic leadership in both houses, to committee leadership, and to other influentials. He also regularly provided information on which legislators were reluctant and which ones had further questions on the measure. The two CAAC representatives would then target these people. Once the bill reached the point of floor debate, these two even helped the bill's backers prepare their arguments.

Simultaneously with their lobbying efforts, Hoffman and Buchanan were providing other CAAC members with information about lawmakers who needed outside pressure to help persuade them. Representatives from the committee's endorsing organizations would then be asked to call or write these legislators requesting their support. This persistent lobbying effort paid off in that every legislator interviewed remembered Hoffman's and Buchanan's work, and two persons said they believed it was a principal reason the bill was successful.

Two tactical decisions that facilitated passage were the choice to go with Giles's bill rather than Dyson's, and Giles's last minute amendments to narrow the scope of the act and ensure protection from financial loss. Giles's legislation was heard in the Finance Committee where it stood a very good chance of being reported out favorably, due in some measure to the active support of the Committee Co-Chair, Representative Irving Stolberg. Dyson's bill was placed in the Appropriations Committee and its chances were slim. Thus the proponents chose to abandon Dyson's bill and push for Giles's. The amendments Representative Giles added to his bill facilitated its passage, but they were not sufficient to take care of doubts that would be raised later. Insufficient attention to nuance and precision in the wording of the legislation was a tactical error in the campaign.

The 1981 Campaign:
Reaction and Opposition

The nature of the reaction to a campaign from a number of
quarters can be crucial to the effectiveness of the activists'
efforts. Reaction in this case was on the whole positive or
neutral, and there was no organized opposition to the bill
during the General Assembly's consideration of it. Since
the only pressure was from proponents, legislators had free
rein to pass the legislation with little concern about who
might be antagonized by such an action.

In the General Assembly the bill was seen as a "little"
bill in that it did not command a great deal of attention
throughout the legislature, but neither did it go unnoticed.
Majority and minority leaders in both the House and Senate
were well aware of the measure, but they did not devote a
lot of time to it because it did not have a lot of complications to be worked out. It was a relatively "easy" piece of
legislation that did not get into trouble.

The question of whether or not state governments
should get involved in foreign policy matters arose during
the debates and discussions around the bill. When asked
about this in interviews, the lawmakers responded in two
ways. Many said that essentially the issue is not a foreign
policy issue but one of how the state regulates its investments. The state government may choose the criteria it
wants for such regulation, and if decision makers choose
not to invest in companies present in South Africa, it is
simply a matter of managing monies in a socially responsible
and morally satisfying manner.

When pressed, however, almost all respondents agreed
that there was a foreign policy dimension to the issue.
They all said that foreign affairs are normally peripheral to
the responsibilities of state governments except in rare
cases. Some international issues become significant as
matters of principle, and the legislature decides to make a
statement about them. As Senate Majority Leader Schneller
put it:

> . . . when a state legislature feels that it's impor-
> tant enough to make a statement on any issue, I
> feel it should do so—whether it's a bilateral nuclear
> arms freeze, whether it's equal rights for women,
> or whether it's that this country should impose
> sanctions against a nation that is carrying out a
> policy we feel is totally undemocratic and totally
> against our philosophy.

If state legislatures should take stands on important issues, what makes the issue important? For the Connecticut General Assembly, apartheid and investments became significant because a group of people persisted in pressing the question. Although the CAAC kept it alive and in the attention of decision makers, for many legislators the fact that the issue meant a great deal to the Black Caucus became an additional rationale for passing it. Legislators reported that they typically will support a bill if it does not adversely affect their constituents (whoever the constituents are defined to be); it it is helpful to some of their colleagues in the legislature (the Black Caucus in this case); and if it is generally in line with their political philosophy. In many respects like the 1980 Sullivan Principles law, the divestment bill was seen as something that the legislature could give to the caucus without much political or financial cost.

During the bill's consideration in the Assembly neither Governor O'Neill nor Treasurer Parker took a public position on it. Parker spoke privately about the bill with a few legislators, but there is no trace of any reaction by O'Neill during the legislative process. The legislators interviewed reported that they did not anticipate his veto. Although Parker had established precedents of using social criteria in addition to financial criteria for investments and he had actively promoted the concept of corporate social responsibility, his first responsibility as state treasurer and sole fiduciary for the pension funds is to see that these monies get the highest return from the safest investments. Typically (as will be seen in the Michigan case) money managers are very reluctant to have others continually tampering with how they make their investments. Had Parker testified on the legislation, he would by necessity have taken the position that a divestment policy would reduce the number of available investment opportunities for the state. In the absence of an expert analysis on what this might mean for the funds, such testimony probably would have harmed the campaign. He was under enormous pressure from his black colleagues to remain unopposed to the legislation.

In addition, one Treasury Department official claims that, like some segments of the business community, people in the department were caught off guard by the momentum of the bill. They did not believe it had a very good chance of passing and (except for Parker) had not paid much attention to it. They became aware that a response from Treasury might be appropriate only after the legislation had passed the House. Before they could muster an analysis, the act had passed the Senate. Therefore, due to the combination of a somewhat unaware bureaucracy and the political imprudence of a black treasurer opposing legislation sponsored by the Black Caucus, an important source of potential opposition to the bill was quieted.

CAAC members had met with the treasurer twice in April after the bill was out of committee. At one meeting they took a pension analyst with them to lend credibility to their assertion that state investments would not be harmed by the legislation. This meeting may have helped Parker understand the dynamics of the issue better, and he expressed appreciation for CAAC work. More persuasive pressure, however, came from the Black Caucus. The committee did not attempt to lobby O'Neill, and although it is not clear that their arguments would have fallen on sympathetic ears, failure to lobby was another mistake in the campaign.

Another arena of reaction that can facilitate or harm the progress of a campaign is the media. A regular column on South Africa was sponsored by the CAAC in the *Hartford Inquirer,* a weekly and the largest black newspaper in the state. The *Hartford Advocate* printed a lengthy story on the Hartford City Council discussions about pension fund investments in South Africa as early as 1978, and both daily papers, the *Advocate* and the *Hartford Courant,* carried a story on the continuation of these same City Council discussions in 1980. These daily papers, however, did not pay much attention to the state divestment campaign until the veto in July 1981. Therefore, the state's major media did not seem to significantly help or hinder the CAAC efforts.

The last notable source of reaction and potential opposition that needs examination is the business community. There are two explanations for why there was no organized business opposition to the 1981 bill while the Assembly was considering it. One is that there was no common concern among business interests about the bill. Some segments were aware of it, monitoring it, and even providing notice about it to interested parties. For example, the Connecticut Business and Industry Association (CBIA) watched the legislation with interest. CBIA is a business organization with 5,000 Connecticut companies as members. One of its primary purposes is to serve as a lobby for business concerns, and there are four full-time lobbyists on the staff. Almost every large corporation in the state is a member of CBIA, but most of its members are small companies. Although CBIA paid attention to the 1981 bill and even reported on it in a newsletter, the association took no active role in opposing it for three reasons:

(1) most CBIA members were not affected by the legislation; the big corporations that would be affected had their own lobbyists who had expertise on the issue and could pursue the matter if they chose to do so; none of these big businesses requested help from the association at the time, and the CBIA lobbyists decided to simply wait and see what happened; (2) these lobbyists had a number of other pressing issues that would affect most of their members (for example, unemployment compensation, taxation) to consume their time; (3) the divestment legislation was politically sensitive; if it were necessary to oppose it, the lobbyist did not want to risk the association being labeled racist by coming out against it; if the big corporations felt it necessary to oppose the bill, their lobbyists could help take the heat and risk the label.

In retrospect from the other side, some of the lobbyists from the large companies complained that CBIA should have taken more of a lead in opposition. Part of their role, said one person, is to absorb some of the controversy for the business community at large. The problem was, however, that there was no united business interest on the issue. There was a big business-small business split because small businesses had no concern at all about the legislation.

The second reason for no corporate opposition in the legislature was that the corporations' lobbyists misjudged the bill's chances for passage. The lobbyists interviewed were all aware of its existence but were unaware of the amount of support it was receiving. Since a similar bill had been amended to their satisfaction the year before, they felt confident that the Assembly would simply let this one die. Opposing it as a matter of principle could be interpreted as a racist reaction, and in their estimation there was no other reason to oppose it. They did not believe the bill had a chance, and no one alerted them that it did until the House had already passed it. Thus another sector from which one would have expected sophisticated and determined work against the act was virtually silent.

In summary, the 1981 CAAC legislative campaign succeeded because the CAAC had created a strong campaign, making known to the legislature a political climate sympathetic to full divestment; the Black Caucus had given the act impetus in the Assembly, and together with the CAAC had generated momentum for its passage; and, hearing no significant objections, legislators decided to yield to proponents' pressures. The media's small attention probably facilitated passage since it was not enough to alert and alarm the opposition, and proponents had enough time and a sufficiently conducive political climate to organize a great deal of support. This campaign demonstrated impressive CAAC organizing and lobbying skills to achieve a fairly radical goal. Table 4–10 provides a digest of the variables that contributed to the effectiveness of their efforts. The committee had only a month to celebrate, however, before their victory became a defeat.

Post-Passage Reaction and Opposition: The Veto

Immediately after the legislation got Assembly approval, large corporations and business associations mobilized their forces and requested meetings with both the treasurer and the governor. Some sent letters requesting the governor to veto the bill. The decision-making arena had shifted and now the companies, among friends, could say behind closed conference room doors what they had been unwilling to say in the legislative debate. A list of some of the corporations and organizations represented in the lobbying effort is shown in Table 4–11. The arguments made by this group against the bill have already been discussed but the participants' reasons for opposition need further analysis. As was noted earlier, those engaged in pressuring O'Neill to veto the bill were reluctant to have themselves identified. And, because the process was a closed one within a small group, the dynamics of what occurred are not easy to discern. The broad issues raised are clear, however, and can be discussed.

Table 4–3 lists the large businesses in Connecticut that have investments in South Africa. These industries are important to the economy of the state, and one of them, United Technologies, is the largest single employer in the state. To be placed on a proscribed list of investments is, in the view of corporate executives, an accusation of bad corporate citizenship. It is, as some put it, a slap in the face. Since most of these companies were Sullivan signatories, they felt they were doing their share for progress in South Africa. They wanted to be rewarded rather than punished for their efforts because compliance with the principles was costing them money, time, and headaches. They had already confronted the issue of their investments in South Africa in other arenas, and they did not accept or succumb to the critique that their operations bolster apartheid. The Connecticut businessmen interviewed said that the withdrawal of state monies from their stocks and bonds was not likely to affect the value of those securities nor would it convince them to pull out of South Africa. Divestment would also not make them take their plants, factories,

TABLE 4-10. Summary of Variables Significant in the Passage of the 1981 Legislation

---

Inner Environment

1. Goals: required a great deal of change
2. Tactics and Strategies:
   a. extensive and expert testimony
   b. persistent lobbying
   c. access to legislative leadership
   d. negotiations and compromise over language in the legislation
3. Strength:
   a. broad coalition of endorsements and supporters inside and outside the legislature
      (1) numerous educational events
      (2) members' access through networks to large number of organizations
      (3) individual members' reputations for legitimacy and credibility
      (4) single-issue focus of the campaign
      (5) frequent communications with supporters
      (6) credible and salable (relevant) argument in favor of divestment
      (7) extensive research on the issues and how to press for the Committee's position
      (8) Black Caucus support, and support of other influentials in the legislature
   b. highly committed and skilled CAAC leadership

Outer Environment

4. Reactions and Opposition:
   a. Legislature: receptive to being persuaded to pass the bill
   b. Treasury: no opposition and no activity on the bill
   c. Governor: no opposition and no activity on the bill
   d. Business: no active opposition and little activity at all
   e. Media: little attention
5. Target: large and accessible
6. Time: began the campaign two years prior to its heaviest thrust; had about three years total
7. Generally conducive political environment in the state despite the heavy business influence in Connecticut

---

and headquarters out of the state. What it would do, however, is give them a bad image, and in general the whole concept made them very angry. The state has no

TABLE 4-11.   Partial List of Businesses or Business Organizations that Lobbied for the Veto

Aetna Insurance Corporation	Day, Berry and Howard Law Firm
Connecticut Bank and Trust	General Electric Corporation
Connecticut Bankers' Association	Hartford National Bank
Connecticut Business and	Insurance Association of Connecticut
Industry Association	Union Carbide
Connecticut General Life	United Technologies Corporation
Insurance Company	

business, they believe, in pronouncing where they should or should not conduct their international affairs.

For banks, the image problem was even more significant and the legislation was more stringent. If the state could not hold investments in banks that lend money to corporations doing business in South Africa, the state probably could hold no bank securities at all. This would be a condemnation of the whole financial sector. Furthermore, banks and insurance companies are entrusted with the management of some of the state's portfolio (about half the funds are managed outside the Treasury Department). The legislation would curtail the range of investment possibilities open to them and would interfere with their standard investment philosophies.

Thus big business and the business associations finally came in a united effort to persuade the governor to protect their interests, and they found a sympathetic audience. Divestment proponents and opponents interviewed agree that O'Neill is well known for his sympathy for business concerns and his relative lack of sympathy for labor issues. This corporate pressure together with the go-ahead from Parker proved effective, and O'Neill complied by vetoing the bill.

Why the veto was not overriden is fairly easy to explain. Although initially caught off guard by the veto, the CAAC and Black Caucus rallied their forces and continued their pressure for full divestment. They received a great deal of help from their supporters and the media. Whereas the press has been relatively quiet during the first consideration of the bill, no fewer than nine articles and editorials on the veto appeared in the major newspapers within the twenty days between the veto and the Assembly trailer session. Most of the articles reported the events in a straightforward fashion whereas the editorials were generally sympathetic to divestment. But now the group faced counter pressures from business lobbyists, the leadership's pressure for party loyalty, and the widespread perception that a suitable outcome could still be achieved through the Task Force the governor promised to appoint. The Task Force provided a middle option for those who wanted it. No matter how morally significant the bill had been in its initial passage, that significance diminished considerably for majority leaders and Democratic Party legislators when party faithfulness and gubernatorial embarrassment were at stake. Overriding vetoes in Connecticut is difficult and rare, and although the bill originally passed with majorities large enough to defeat a veto, the legislature sustained this and all O'Neill's vetoes. Some level of support for the bill was evident, however, when a majority voted favorably for the override.

The Task Force Work and Recommendations

Although far short of requiring complete divestment, the Task Force recommendations represent the most comprehensive set of criteria for *partial* divestment yet achieved by any legislative body in the U.S. Every Task Force member interviewed marveled that the diverse group had achieved unanimous proposals so far reaching. A combination of factors seems to account for this outcome.

One was leadership provided by Parker and Edythe Gaines. Parker was described by several members as forceful in style and determined to achieve a workable product, even if it meant having a number of meetings at inconvenient hours. To have the Task Force fail would have been a disturbing political embarrassment for himself and the governor in an election year, and the press was already predicting an inconsequential outcome. Gaines proved to be a skilled mediator and negotiator. Members report that on several occasions at crucial junctures she was responsible for maintaining communications between opposing factions. She found middle ground between seemingly irreconcilable points of view. In addition, there were two members from the business community, Shapiro and Russell, who were accustomed to this kind of work—tasks that require skill in bridging the corporate-civic gap. Both had had previous experience in making a link between the two sometimes disparate worlds, and they enjoyed doing it.

The commitment level of participants was another factor contributing to the success of the Task Force. The amount of time donated has already been mentioned. Besides attending meetings, the members were submitting drafts of their own ideas, marshalling the resources of their organizations to provide research for options being considered, and holding sub-group caucuses to consolidate positions. Why so many of the fourteen were willing to go to such lengths for this group is only partially explicable. Some are highly involved with the issue of U.S. corporate investment in South Africa as a priority in their lives for personal reasons (for example, Hoffman) or for professional reasons (for example, Hamilton). Others were very committed to helping the leadership in the state resolve a very sticky issue (for example, Gaines, Cloud). Besides being interested in the issue, a few were fascinated with the process and enjoyed being in the fray (for example, Russell). And some, of course, saw their firms' reputations at stake (for instance, Hughes, Semelsberger, Shapiro).

Another significant reason for the Task Force staying together was the business representatives' unwillingness to be blamed for its failure. One industry representative admits to having wished in the middle of the process that the labor representatives (CAAC) would get frustrated enough to walk out. He wanted the Task Force to fail. He felt confident that no total divestment legislation would get past the legislature again because, in the next round, the business community would fight hard and publicly against it. If the Task Force failed and there was no possibility of passing new legislation, there would be no change in the status quo—the treasurer would continue to abide by the 1980 Sullivan Principles bill. Although this man wanted it to fail, and although at points he and other business representatives were contemplating resigning, he was not willing to be the catalyst for its failure. He wanted the proponents to provide the catalyst.

In the beginning Hoffman and Fussell (the other labor representative) were unsure that they would remain on the Task Force. They took a "wait and see" attitude. As the lack of legislative support for another full divestment bill became clear, they decided to stay and achieve as much as possible. Parker had sent a letter to the General Assembly leadership requesting a delay in consideration of any further divestment legislation until the Task Force reported. Even though the CAAC had been pushing for a repeat of the previous year's legislation, the group soon realized that the chances of such an outcome were growing smaller. Therefore, Hoffman and Fussell were not to play the role others wanted them to play in breaking up the Task Force, and as the process progressed, all parties seemed to acquire even greater reasons for sticking with it.

The CAAC could have gained one more vote for their side by demanding an official representative in addition to Hoffman and Fussell as labor representatives. Another vote probably would not have mattered for the most difficult decisions, however, because they were ultimately resolved by negotiation rather than majority rule.

Hoffman and Fussell are credited by several members as being responsible for the report going as far as it does. A number of members had been willing to settle for a Sullivan Principles approach. One such participant said, "We went further than we thought we would, and I think she (Hoffman) backed off somewhat." Hoffman especially was perceived as composed, very intelligent, competent on the issue, a hard-nosed opponent, and a negotiator with exceptional political judgment. One business representative said, "She's very crafty. . . . I only wish she were on our side." She and Fussell provided the cutting edge. The 1981 campaign had tested their organizing and lobbying skills but the Task Force tested their mettle in the rigors of face-to-face confrontations and negotiations with their opponents. They pushed their proposals to the brink and then backed off, so that the end product had much more substance and merit from their perspective than many people, even CAAC constituents, expected.

Hoffman and Fussell are both personally very committed to achieving complete withdrawal of state funds from corporations investing in South Africa, but they were also receiving pressure from the more leftist elements among their constituents. The CAAC steering committee had been criticized for spending too much time on legislative processes and not enough time doing further educational and organizational development in communities. Constituents were also questioning the committee's participation on the Task Force since many were convinced it could only yield anti-apartheid rhetoric and more sophisticated Sullivan Principles.

The committee justified its legislative work and Task Force participation in several ways. Their 1981 campaign had proven that, with the right combination of favorable forces and hard work, the legislature could be a fruitful arena for achieving their goals. Now that the decision-making process had been removed from the Assembly into a more closed arena, their work would become more difficult in many respects, but there was still potential for a constructive, although not completely satisfying, outcome. Other arenas through which to pressure companies were either more closed (for instance, direct pressure on corporations themselves) or less resourceful and powerful (for example, university or church investment portfolios). The legislature and state government were both relatively accessible and in command of millions of dollars in South African-related investments. And, succeeding in the passage of the 1981 bill demystified the legislative process for committee constituents and demonstrated the power of their organization. "Playing politics" and all the concomitant compromise and negotiation had become necessary, but it also had proven useful. The group was not sure it would remain committed to working in the legislative arena, but at the time of this writing it was still determined to achieve full divestment. Members had begun to evaluate their work over the last several years and assess what new directions, if any, they would now take. The impact of the Task Force process and resolution on the cohesion and internal dynamics of the CAAC is as yet unknown. The core group seems to be in solid support of Hoffman and Fussell's work in the Task Force, but the compromise reached may have a negative impact on CAAC's relationship with some of its constituents.

With the CAAC representatives pushing the Task Force to the limits of criteria acceptable to the businessmen, the Task Force recommendations were, in sum, a result of Parker's determined leadership, a few members' mediation at crucial points between the opposing factions, and everyone's commitment to staying with the process. In the end, the CAAC and the business group really had no choice but to stay with the process. Neither wanted to be blamed for its failure, and neither wanted the state to act without them present to protect their interests.

Looking in retrospect across the last several years, the CAAC campaign was, in all likelihood, not sufficient by itself to produce the various outcomes related to anti-apartheid issues. Clearly, however, it was a necessary and pivotal driving force. Without the CAAC efforts Connecticut would not have the divestment legislation it now has; nor would the 1981 bill have passed. Analyzing these variables and their causal relationship to the outcomes, however, only partially fulfills the intent of this research. The next section will discuss the impact and importance of these consequences.

IMPACT AND EFFECTIVENESS

All political processes have intended and unintended consequences; some of these consequences are immediately evident and others are not so easily detected. Although all of the traceable outcomes of the CAAC campaign will be discussed in this section and in part in the conclusions of the last chapter, effectiveness will be defined using the goals-based approach to evaluation discussed in Chapter 2. That is, the degree to which the campaign met its own goals is the degree to which it was effective. The goals and theory of action have already been discussed, and the theory of action has been evaluated. Together these posit what proponents *would like* to happen. The campaigns' effectiveness and impact must be judged on what actually *does* happen. Table 4–12 lists the known outcomes of the entire political process that dealt with the anti-apartheid legislation. These outcomes are categorized according to their principal recipients.

Table 4–13 contrasts the proponents' goals with outcomes to demonstrate achieved, partially achieved, and unachieved goals. Three of the goals—expressing solidarity with those resisting apartheid (1), taking a principle stand (2), and drawing attention to the issue (3)—are seen to be achieved by the proponents because of the outcomes of having widespread recognition of the Connecticut divestment process in the state, in the country (among those attentive to the issue), and among South Africans. Goal 11, that of proponents making a contribution to the worldwide anti-apartheid movement, is listed as both achieved, partially achieved, and unachieved. This is because a number of outcomes do make such a contribution, but because no corporations have withdrawn from South Africa directly as a result of the Connecticut process and because some have been convinced that staying in South Africa can do some good, divestment has not fulfilled all that proponents had hoped that it would. The Connecticut legislation, however, does appear to be one of the factors considered by GE in its ongoing assessment of its operations in South Africa, and therefore, the goal is also listed as partially achieved.

The goals related to having the state take a principled stand (6), withdrawing investments from corporations doing business in South Africa (7), and expressing solidarity with those in resistance to apartheid (8) are all seen as partially achieved or unachieved—partially achieved because in the end the state did not do all that activists wanted it to do, and unachieved because of the particular outcome of the governor's veto. Goal 9 can only be assessed in the context of the entire national anti-apartheid movement, and whether or not activists participated effectively in other anti-racist actions (5) or will ultimately contribute to the ending of apartheid is unknown. Also, it is impossible without further research to evaluate the educational and

TABLE 4-12. Partial List of Outcomes in Connecticut

For the State Government of Connecticut

Legislature

1. The General Assembly took a principled stand with all three bills.
2. The 1981 campaign convinced many legislators that the Sullivan Principles are inappropriate and inadequate for bringing change in South Africa; these legislators experienced a change of attitude.
3. Some legislators now receive public relations materials from the South African government.
4. Some legislators dispensed the Task Force report to interested persons inside and outside the state as an example of a good model to follow.
5. Some legislators take an active interest in hastening the implementation of the law.

Executive

6. Top elected officials (the governor and treasurer) and their staffs have spent considerable time on the issue.
7. The Treasury Department has assigned one full-time staff person to implementation to the 1982 bill, a process closely monitored by the activists.
8. The entire process has put the Treasury Department in communication with several corporate responsibility groups and groups researching South Africa, for example, IRRC, ICCR, and the Corporate Data Exchange.
9. Some stocks and bonds were sold in implementing the 1980 legislation; a number of others have sold or put on the avoid list in implementing the 1982 legislation.
10. The department monitors closely companies with investments in South Africa whose stocks are not sold to ensure the state can lawfully keep their securities.
11. Department officials provide outside managers (of part of the state's portfolio) with a proscribed list of investments so that these managers can comply with the law.
12. The treasurer discussed the Task Force Report and the 1982 legislation with other state treasurers at a 1982 Northeast States' Treasurers Conference; he spoke on the legislation in Iowa and his office has provided a number of states and local governments and other organizations with information on the Connecticut experience.
13. The treasurer was able to submit to the governor a unanimous Task Force Report from a group with widely opposing opinions.
14. The governor vetoed the 1981 bill.
15. The governor was perceived to anger black and labor elements of his party with the 1981 veto.
16. The governor and treasurer were perceived to be pleasing a wide

TABLE 4-12.   Continued

range of politically active groups with the Task Force Report, through it
they took a stand against apartheid without alienating business, labor, or
the proponents.

For Business

17. Over $75 million in stocks and bonds have been sold by the state;
no Connecticut bank securities are likely to be sold, and few companies'
securities have been sold for violation of standards other than the
Sullivan Principles Standard.

18. Business executives (especailly those on the Task Force), business
lobbyists, and their staffs spent a great deal of time on the issue.

19. Business executives from corporations with South African
investments are required to fill out forms and reply to correspondence from
the Treasury Department if they want the state to keep their securities.

20. The business community in general was publicly criticized for not
engaging in open debate on the issue in 1981.

21. Some business representatives on the Task Force have dispensed the
Task Force Report to interested persons inside and outside the state as an
example of a good model to follow.

22. Some business people report a change in their attitudes about the
issue; they no longer believe that a company can claim its presence in
South Africa is good in and of itself; these people have become convinced
that corporations must sign the Sullivan Principles or some comparable code
of conduct if they are to remain in South Africa.

23. Some business people and the treasurer report that their belief in
the Sullivan Principles as an appropriate and adequate policy for corporate
responsibility in South Africa has been reinforced.

24. No corporations have announced any withdrawal of their investments
in South Africa as a result of Connecticut's governmental actions.

25. A General Electric South African subsidiary, Southern Sphere
Mining, withdrew from a $138 million mining venture in the Kwazulu homeland
citing the state of Connecticut's new investment policies as one of the
reasons for its withdrawal.

26. The Connecticut Bank and Trust and the Hartford National Bank, as
members of the Private Export Funding Corporation, stopped leanding money
to South Africa (prior to the Connecticut divestment campaign).

For the U.S. Government

27. The U.S. State Department, the Department of Commerce, and the
Africa subcommittee staff in the House and Senate are aware of the state's
action; (see Chapters 2 and 4 for further discussion).

For South Africa

28. The South African Embassy and U.N. Mission are aware of the

TABLE 4-12. Continued

---

state's actions and have attempted to infleunce the process; (see Chapters 2 and 4).

29. The South African press reported on the state's actions.

30. Representatives of the resistance movements are aware of the state's actions and have attempted to influence the process; they have communicated their approval to the CAAC.

For the Anti-Apartheid Movment

Nationally

31. Local and national groups across the country have taken a great deal of interest in the Connecticut campaign; the ACOA chose it as a case study for publication and distribution through its networks.

CAAC

32. The CAAC focus on the legislative arena brought it criticism from leftist elements in its constituency.

33. The group was forced to adapt to circumstances that took the issue out of an open forum (the legislature) into a small, closed decision making arena (the Task Force).

34. The group was perceived to be pressing for a principled cause.

35. Through the entire process the Committee gained credibility and legitimacy for the organization and for individual leaders from supporters, from opponents, and from interested observers.

36. The group gained a large number of endorsements and support for its campaign.

37. The group disseminated information and spoke to groups outside the state to share their experience and expertise.

---

consciousness-raising efforts of the CAAC (4 and 12). We can speculate that some education and consciousness raising must have occurred in the many events held by CAAC for such purposes, in their lobbying efforts, media exposure, or other educational work, but there is not enough evidence (for example, opinion surveys for the state) to evaluate whether or not such outcomes did in fact occur. Five outcomes (listed at the bottom of the table) appear to be unrelated to goals.

In summary, we can assert that Connecticut divestment proponents seem to have been partially successful in

TABLE 4-13. An Evaluation of Goals and Outcomes in Connecticut

Goals	Outcomes		
	Achieved	Partially Achieved	Unachieved
1	29, 30		
2	33		
3	2, 3, 4, 5, 6, 7, 8, 10, 11 12, 15, 18, 19 20, 21, 27, 28 29, 30, 31, 36		
4		36?	
5		(unknown)	
6		1	14
7		9, 10, 11	
8		1	14
9		(see Chapters 2 and 6)	24
10		(unknown)	
11	1, 9, 10, 11 17, 31, 34, 35	25	22, 23, 24
12		36?	

Outcomes unrelated to goals: 13, 16, 26, 32, 33

achieving what they set out to accomplish. We turn now to an examination of divestment campaigns in Michigan and in the last chapter to a comparison of the two cases.

NOTES

1. All Connecticut General Assembly Committees are joint committees between the House and Senate.
2. These colleges and universities have divestment policies: Connecticut College, Trinity College, Wesleyan University, and Yale University.
3. The list was the only published goals available among the literature and newsletters of the CAAC. It appeared in the CAAC April 1980 newsletter.

5

The Michigan Case Study

In recent years the Michigan Legislature has been inundated with legislation on South Africa. In all, nineteen pieces of legislation have been introduced since 1978 by four different principal sponsors. Two of these measures were resolutions and both achieved passage. Across the seventeen bills, there has been considerable repetition of substance. Two have become law, one in 1980 and one in 1982. A wide spectrum of institutions and financial transactions have been targeted by the bills—public employee pension funds, educational institutions' investments, and state bank deposits. In no other state have activists and legislators attempted to achieve so broad a set of governmental anti-apartheid actions. This chapter will discuss and analyze the history of this legislation, the implementation of one of the acts that has passed, the variables impeding or facilitating passage of the bills, and the impact of the campaigns pressing for the legislation.

LEGISLATIVE HISTORY AND IMPLEMENTATION

The principal impetus for initiating anti-apartheid legislative campaigns in Michigan has come from university-based activist organizations. Since the early 1970s many colleges and universities across the state have experienced divestment campaigns directed primarily at the educational institutions themselves but often spilling over to affect other

targets as well.[1] Although most campus activities intensified in reaction to the Soweto riots (1976) and the death
of Steve Biko (1977), groups at several colleges and universities have maintained a focus on South Africa for over a
decade. These environments continue to provide a base of
organization for anti-apartheid campaigns.

Early Anti-Apartheid Activism

The most significant of these campus-based anti-apartheid
organizations is the Southern Africa Liberation Committee
(SALC) at Michigan State University (MSU) in East Lansing. It has promoted more campaigns than any other
group, been the most persistent group in pressing for state
legislation, lasted the longest, and benefited from a very
strategic location near the state capital. Since 1974 it has
moved its efforts from one arena to another as its campaigns met with some measure of success. Beginning
primarily with an educational emphasis, the group started a
long-term commitment to anti-apartheid activities that would
target the East Lansing City Council, the Michigan State
University Board of Trustees, and the Michigan legislature.
    SALC was founded by persons who had participated in
and helped organize anti-war activities during the Vietnam
conflict. They decided in the early 1970s to turn their
energies to southern Africa work. Led by a campus minister, Warren (Bud) Day, and a political science graduate
student, Carol Thompson,[2] the group spent most of its time
in its early days providing educational opportunities for
students and others and supporting campaigns conducted by
national anti-apartheid organizations. In addition, the
group began to provide direct aid (for example, clothing,
information) to resistance movements in southern Africa.
    In early 1976, the SALC began to look for local insti-
tutions that could be targeted for sanctions and divestment
activities. Members believed that divestment was an important means to continue their educational efforts on South
Africa while also addressing the issue of the role of multinational corporations in both South Africa and the U.S.
Having close contact with national anti-apartheid organizations and with activists in other parts of the country,
SALC members were aware of the strategies used in 1975
targeting city councils in Gary, Indiana, and Washington,
D.C. The group decided to try to convince the East
Lansing City Council to adopt a similar policy of purchasing
goods and services from companies not involved in South
Africa.

Day and Thompson laid much of the foundation for these efforts, but both moved out of town in the fall of 1976 before the campaign got into full swing. A friend of theirs, William Derman, had just returned from working on corporate responsibility issues for the Toronto Committee on Southern African, and he began to assume some major leadership responsibility for the city council campaign. Derman is an anthropologist at Michigan State (MSU) with an African area specialty. Fortunately for SALC, other shifts in academicians' locations brought David Wiley and Marylee Crofts, two Africanists with many years' experience on southern African issues, to town in February 1977. Wiley, a sociologist, took the position of Associate Director of the MSU Center for African Studies, and Crofts, an educator, became the Outreach Coordinator of the Center. Thus at a crucial time of leadership change and at the point that SALC turned its attention to the East Lansing City Council, it fortuitously benefited from the influx of talent and experience from three persons with high commitments to and great expertise in anti-apartheid work.

Although organizationally separate from SALC, the Center for African Studies, founded in 1960, provided an important part of the context for SALC work. The center is one of the largest of its kind in the country, and over one hundred people at MSU work on African studies. The center has served to focus attention on the issue of black rule for the continent, and it brings frequent African and Africanist visitors to campus. Wiley subsequently became its director.

SALC participants had good reason to believe that the East Lansing City Council would be receptive to its request for selective purchasing. Unlike the university administration and Board of Trustees, the council had yielded to pressures from the anti-war movement and passed resolutions condemning U.S. military involvement in Vietnam. Taking positions on foreign policy issues was nothing new for the body. If SALC could achieve a victory with the city council, members believed they could use that experience to convince the university and the state to divest.

SALC provided educational materials to council members and requested a public hearing on the issue. The group's initial approach, modeled on that of Washington, D.C., and Gary, Indiana, was to pressure for a boycott of nine specific companies that had the largest investments in South Africa. After support for the issue was demonstrated by SALC participants lobbying council members and attending weekly council meetings in large numbers, a public hearing was scheduled for March 30.

SALC took charge of organizing and publicizing the hearing. The group invited representatives of corporations as well as national and local anti-apartheid leaders to make presentations. IBM sent a person to speak and film. Panax, a now defunct corporation previously headed by John McGoff, also sent representatives, and an American Lawyer, Donald de Kieffer, attended with two others on behalf of the South African embassy. Speakers in support of the resolution included Tim Smith from the Corporate Information Center (later to become the Interfaith Center on Corporate Responsibility—ICCR), Warren Day (returned) representing the American Friends Service Committee, representatives from Amnesty International, former African Peace Corps workers, African student groups, local churches and community groups, and the high school student council. Individual faculty members from the university also spoke in favor of the proposed resolution. According to press reports, over two hundred people attended the hearing.

The council did not pass its resolution until August 3, 1977. In the intervening four months, SALC members collected signatures on petitions in support of the issue and solicited favorable letters from community leaders. University students had recently been declared franchised in their school locale if they were residents there, and SALC believed that the city council would be interested in appealing to this new constituency. There were legal objections to naming specific companies so the activists negotiated a reformulation of the resolution which declared that the council would seek suppliers who do not have investments, licenses, or operations in the Republic of South Africa. The entire resolution is shown in Appendix B.

The opposition was also active during this interim period. De Kieffer and representatives of the Panax Company made some attempt to mobilize opinion against the resolution. John McGoff, an American later to become prominent in South Africa's Information Department scandal, tried unsuccessfully to speak on a program with de Kieffer in order to present the South African point of view. The program was canceled due to protests from a number of people on campus. There was also a great deal of publicity on the issue. In 1976 and 1977 no fewer than 18 news articles and editorials appeared in the Lansing *Star,* a local leftist newspaper, and the *State News,* the largest circulation daily campus newspaper in the country. The *State News* editorials supported selective purchasing.

Although it is likely that trade-offs on other issues helped convince some council members to support the measure, SALC members were pleased when the resolution passed 5 to 0. Bids for city business have been rejected on the basis of a company's South African involvement, and at SALC's request, council members communicated the action they had taken to Michigan senators and members of Congress in a letter requesting that these representatives join in the effort to bring about U.S. sanctions against South Africa.

As SALC was busy convincing the city council to adopt its selective purchasing policy, activists in the Washtenaw County Coalition Against Apartheid (WCCAA) in Ann Arbor were pressing for divestment at the University of Michigan. A series of educational events and public forums were organized by the WCCAA in mid-1977, and a number of student organizations, with the endorsement of the campus newspaper, addressed the UM Board of Regents on 20 May to call for divestment. After a great deal of publicity on the issue and a long campaign by WCCAA, the Board voted in March 1978 to divest of "stock in any firm that fails to . . . abide by the school's bank policy [no new loans to the South African government except where detrimental to apartheid] or adhere satisfactorily to the Sullivan principles" (Myers et al. 1980, 366).

This policy was a great disappointment to WCCAA members, who continued to press for complete withdrawal of investments in companies doing business in South Africa. A student referendum was held on campus in April on the question of divestment, and students voted 3,109 to 1,169 in favor of total withdrawal (*Ann Arbor News*, 24 April 1978). Student demonstrators protesting U.S. investments in South Africa also disrupted a commencement address by then Vice President Mondale. Out of frustration over the Board of Regents' unwillingness to agree to total divestment, the WCCAA group approached their state legislative representative, Perry Bullard, asking him to introduce a bill prohibiting all state universities' funds from being invested in South Africa. Bullard responded favorably to the activists' request. His legislation will be discussed shortly.

In the meantime, observing the 1976 and 1977 anti-apartheid events in East Lansing, Ann Arbor, and at other universities in addition to anti-apartheid campus activities nationwide, and having suffered through recent student demonstrations over production of a film on campus indirectly supporting the Shah's regime in Iran, the MSU Board of Trustees Investment Committee moved to preempt divestment pressures at MSU, which they believed to be inevitable. The Board decided to hold a public hearing on the issue. One black trustee, Aubrey Radcliffe, gave particularly important leadership in having the university examine the issue. The date of the hearing was scheduled during a break between the 1978 Winter and Spring terms when few students would be on campus. Hearing news of this development, SALC publicized it in letters and advertisements in the university newspaper, and members requested that the meeting be postponed. The trustees agreed to reschedule it for March 30.

At the hearings, the trustees listened to arguments from a wide spectrum of viewpoints: persons from SALC advocating total divestment (including Africanists from the African Studies Center); persons taking positions in favor of a Sullivan Principles approach; some favoring maintenance of the status quo; and one MSU professor, Lean Weaver, who suggested that the South Africa regime was becoming more liberal in its policies toward Africans. SALC also supplied the Trustee's Investment Committee with a "South Africa Facts" folder on apartheid and divestment. Remarkably, after hearing the debate on 30 March, on 31 March 1978, the MSU Board of Trustees voted to begin, as of 1 December 1978, a program of "prudent divestment" of all holdings in companies doing business in South Africa. They referred their new policy to a university committee to establish procedures for divestment and also voted to withdraw deposits from banks granting or renewing loans to South Africa.

With this resolution, however, SALC's work on university divestment had just began. Reflecting ambivalence among some trustees and some within the administration on the board's recent action, several university committees went through an extended process of hearings and deliberations, all well attended by SALC members who testified on appropriate occasions. The issue was widely debated on campus and in the local press. SALC organized demonstrations and solicited letters of support from campus organizations and the *State News* to press for early resolution of the issue and a speedy report of divestment guidelines. Conflicts over legal liability arose, and reluctance to implement the policy on the part of MSU investment counselors had to be overcome. Opposition to the board's policy was also voiced by some faculty members, and Dow Chemical threatened to cease making financial contributions to MSU if the policy were implemented.

SALC attempted to facilitate implementation by obtaining expert opinions demonstrating the feasibility of divestment from outside investment analysts and from attorneys. In addition, Derman and Wiley, as academics with expertise on

Southern Africa, wrote extensive papers detailing the effects of U.S. investments on the South African economy, the ineffectiveness of the Sullivan Principles, and the conditions under which Africans work. This information was sent to the trustees for their consideration. Two SALC members who had joined the group after attending the March 1977 city council hearing and who subsequently became significant in the leadership of the organization were Frank and Pat Beeman. At this point they began to monitor every meeting on campus related to the divestment issue. Having been active in civil rights issues for many years, their specific interest in southern Africa came through a family connection to a church worker in Namibia. Frank is a professor who has been at MSU for over 35 years.

In July 1978 in a separate action, the Investment Committee recommended a resolution that the board adopted requesting the "federal administration to take immediate action to deny tax advantages to all corporations doing business in South Africa. . . ." They asked that this resolution be sent to the President, chairs of the House and Senate Foreign Relations Committees, Secretary of State, Michigan members of Congress, the Michigan legislature, the South African government, and the U.S. ambassador to the U.N. In December the board adopted a resolution activating its earlier divestment policy, and in March 1979 it gave specific divestment guidelines to its investment firm, Scudder, Stevens and Clark. By December 1979, MSU's divestment process was completed with sales of stock worth $7.2 million in 13 companies (including some non-South Africa related stock) out of a total portfolio of $16.6 million. Due to market conditions, the portfolio reorganization had netted the university almost one million dollars. Activists in Michigan were delighted with their second victory.

The MSU case, involving the first large public university to divest, was so extensively publicized through international anti-apartheid networks that the Tanzanian ambassador to the United States wrote MSU President Edger Harden congratulating him on the board's action. Anti-apartheid groups all over the country continue to cite this case in their various campaigns as evidence that divestment can be profitable.

During the university campaign, SALC had sidetracked an earlier intention to pursue state divestment through the legislature. Members discussed the possibility of state legislation on divestment with the East Lansing representative, Lynn Jondahl, who became a legislative supporter of divestment. Therefore, by this time university activists from both MSU and the University of Michigan had pressed their representatives to use the legislature for the anti-apartheid cause. Table 5-1 outlines a chronology of the many anti-apartheid events across the state that reinforced each other and begin to give momentum to state legislative campaigns.

The first piece of legislation introduced in Michigan was not a result of these particular university groups' pressures, however. A 1978 House Concurrent Resolution was sponsored by Jackie Vaughn, a black Democratic state representative from Detroit who subsequently became a state senator. The resolution requested the Congress and President of the United States "to impose immediate sanctions against the South African government in response to that country's disregard for human rights and dignity." Vaughn was aware of anti-apartheid activities around the country at the time and served a district in a city where support groups for several southern Africa resistance movements were active. His resolution served as another symbol legitimizing the cause of the groups in East Lansing and Ann Arbor who sought further state actions.

Vaughn's resolution passed in February 1978, and in May of that same year, Bullard, in response to constituents' requests, introduced the first divestment bill. It was to amend Michigan's Elliot Larsen Civil Rights Act to prohibit investment by educational institutions in "a corporation, partnership, or association which encourages or condones through its actions or inactions, legally required discrimination against an individual on the basis of race, religion, color, national origin, or sex." By the time the activists' desires to end university investment in South Africa got translated into legislation, the scope of institutions targeted and the behavior prohibited had broadened considerably. With Bullard's bill, all educational institutions (public and private) and a wide range of potentially discriminatory investments would be affected.

The legislation was referred to and voted out of the Civil Rights Committee, but it never reached a vote on the House floor. Bullard preferred to reintroduce it the next year without having experienced a defeat (which seemed inevitable) the first time around. Beginning with this bill, Representative Bullard and his staff became the driving force within the legislature behind all attempts at divestment.

Bullard had been a representative from Ann Arbor with a fairly safe seat since 1973. Across these years he has gained influence and staff support in the legislature as a result of having chaired three committees: Civil Rights, Labor, and Judiciary. Each of these committee assignments brought with it one or more staff persons, so that his office now has an accumulation of six staff persons working on his behalf, one of whom has principal responsibility for guiding divestment legislation through the house.

Bullard took on the divestment cause with great enthusiasm. He describes himself as a strong organizational Democrat who believes in party discipline, but he has often been willing to facilitate legislative causes that others were unlikely to touch. For example, early in his governmental career, he sponsored bills to decriminalize marijuana and prostitution. He has also introduced a state freedom of information act and a bill to grant solar and wind energy tax credits. He is proud of having been the principal mover behind the bills on South Africa because they fit well into his overall political philosophy. He is a democratic socialist, formerly a member of the Democratic Socialist Organizing Committee national advisory committee. Bullard acquired these political leanings through witnessing the Vietnam war first hand. He volunteered to serve in Vietnam and came out of that experience radically changed. Associating himself with those who oppose "wars on the edge of the empire"—U.S. governmental support for and military intervention on behalf of repressive regimes—he believes that U.S. corporations' financial ties to South Africa might one day lead to our military involvement in the area. Thus he gladly sponsors divestment legislation and other bills that he hopes will help educate the public about U.S. domination abroad but which actually accomplish what he believes are only "small reforms and minor adjustments" in the overall U.S. political and economic system.

With encouragement from activists around the state, support from a few legislative colleagues, and more information about divestment campaigns around the country, Bullard took a more comprehensive approach to divestment legislation in 1979. He introduced ten bills, with the first being an almost identical repeat of the 1978 measure on educational institutions and the other nine designed to prohibit specific pension funds[3] from being invested in any business "which practices or condones through its actions or inactions, discrimination against an individual on the basis of race, religion, color, national origin or sex." To eliminate overlap in some of the bills and in order to narrow the investment prohibitions specifically to South Africa, Bullard soon introduced four substitutes. These four disallowed investments by educational institutions and pensions funds in organizations doing business in South

TABLE 5-1. Partial Chronology of Anti-Apartheid Events in Michigan

Year	Event
1974-75	SALC becomes visibly active on southern Africa issues
1977	March 30: East Lansing city council public hearing on the selective purchasing resolution
	May 20: Student organizations address the University of Michigan Board of Regents and call for divestment by the university
	August 3: East Lansing City Council passes the selective purchasing resolution
1978	February: Michigan legislature passes Concurrent Resolution No. 462 requesting Congress to impose sanctions on South Africa
	March 17: University of Michigan Board of Regents adopts a partial divestment policy (modified in 1979)
	March 30: Michigan State University Board of Trustees holds hearings on divestment
	March: 31: MSU trustees pass a resolution of intent to divest completely of the university's investment holdings in South Africa-related companies
	April 18: East Lansing mayor and city council members send letter to Michigan senators and members of Congress urging them to press for sanctions against South Africa
	May 8: Bullard introduces the educational institution funds divestment bill
	December 8: MSU trustees pass a resolution implementing their previous divestment policy
1979	July 13: Bullard introduces HBs 4831-4840, the second educational institutions divestment bill and the first pension fund divestment legislation
	September 21: University of Michigan regents vote to amend and elaborate their partial divestment policy
	November 9, 27, and December 4: House Civil Rights Committee hearings on HBs 4831-4840 in Kalamazoo, Detroit, and Lansing

TABLE 5-1. Continued

Year	Event
1980	Prior to March: Smith introduces a bill to prohibit the deposit of surplus state funds in South Africa-related banks
	March 4: House Civil Rights Committee hearings on the several divestment bills
	March 18: House Civil Rights Committee approves the educational institution funds and banking legislation
	April 3: House passes House Resolution No. 449 commemorating the South African Freedom Conference at Wayne State University
	April 15: Legislators sponsor reception in the Capitol for representatives of southern Africa liberation movements, ANC, SWAPO, and the Zimbabwean Patriotic Front
	May 20: House passes the banking bill
	June 4: Joint hearings on divestment legislation by the House Civil Rights Committee, Senior Citizens and Retirement Committee, Subcommittee on Retirement of the Appropriations Committee, and the Department of the Treasury
	June 4: Senate Judiciary Committee approves the banking bill
	September: Trial and acquittal of 11 anti-apartheid protesters at Western Michigan University
	November 19: Eastern Michigan University Board of Regents votes to divest its holdings of South Africa-related stock beginning with $2.5 million divested from Manufacturers Hanover Trust Co. of New York
	November 21: Senate passes the banking bill
	November 25: House passes Senate version of HB 5446
	December 17: Governor Milliken signs the banking bill and it becomes Public Act No. 325
1981	March 4: Smith introduces pension fund divestment bill, and it is assigned to the Senior Citizens and Retirement Committee

TABLE 5-1. Continued

Year	Event
1981	March 24: Governor Milliken hosts public ceremony for signing Public Act 325 of 1980 with nine Nigerian state and federal legislators present
	April 2: Bullard reintroduces the educational institutions fund divestment legislation
	August 21: Activists from across the state hold a meeting with legislative sponsors to map strategies for promoting the divestment legislation
	November 17: House Civil Rights Committee hearings on the education bill
	December 15: Legislators host breakfast honoring representatives of ANC and SWAPO, southern Africa liberation movements; the representatives are in Michigan to speak at a conference at the University of Michigan on sports sanctions against South Africa
1982	January 26: House Civil Rights Committee approves education bill
	May 13: House passes the education bill amended to include Soviet Union-related companies as proscribed investments
	November: Senate Judiciary Committee approves the education bill
	December 13: Senate passes the education bill
	December 31: Governor Milliken signs the educational institution funds bill and it becomes Public Act No. 512
1983	April: Smith reintroduces the pension fund bill; the University of Michigan passes a partial divestment resolution and decides to challenge PA 512 in court
	November: House Senior Citizens and Retirement Committee holds hearings on the pension fund bill

Africa. Some of the impetus for substituting the original ten bills came from criticism that they were too broad and incapable of implementation because they referred to a wide range of discriminatory investments.

Bullard assigned Barbara Eldersveld, one of his legislative aides, the task of working on the divestment legislation. In autumn 1979, she and activists from Ann Arbor and East Lansing, joined by another anti-apartheid group from Western Michigan University (WMU) Kalamazoo, began a major effort to gain endorsements and a public show of support among a broad spectrum of groups and individuals.

In its efforts to promote the legislation, SALC began showing films about South Africa on campus at MSU about every two weeks. Every time a film was shown (with audiences varying from three to 60) literature on the divestment bills would be distributed and people would be asked to contact their representatives and urge passage of the legislation. SALC members also built five separate large portable educational displays of posters and other information dramatizing apartheid and U.S. investments. These displays were carried to various public events (festivals, art shows, meetings, and so on) and/or periodically placed in the first floor of the capitol building near a main entrance.

Eldersveld and the several activist groups across the state began tapping their networks of friends and colleagues at work and in voluntary organizations to solicit letters and resolutions in support of state divestment efforts. Eldersveld also coordinated the organization of three Civil Rights Committee public hearings on all the substitute bills in separate parts of the state: one in Lansing, one in Detroit, and one in Kalamazoo. Those presenting testimony included Africanists from the universities, ministers from local congregations as well as councils of churches, civic leaders, and representatives of student organizations.

Before the Civil Rights Committee acted on the 1979 bills, Bullard made new substitutions in early 1980. The language of the legislation pertaining to educational institutions was refined further but the substance remained unchanged. All bills regarding pension fund investments were replaced by a new, single, comprehensive measure.[4] In addition, Bullard's staff developed a new bill having to do with the deposit of surplus state funds. These are all of the operating funds of the state and amount to millions of dollars. This new piece of legislation was introduced to prohibit the deposit of such monies in banks making loans to the South African government, a national corporation of the South African government, or to a U.S. firm operating in South Africa.

To get a broader base of support for the divestment bill and in order to make black legislator's endorsement of the effort visible, Bullard asked Virgil Smith, a black lawyer and state representative from Detroit since 1977, to be the principal sponsor for the banking bill. Smith had long been acquainted with and critical of South Africa's apartheid policies and enthusiastically agreed to take on the bill. Soon thereafter he became the Legislative Black Caucus chair, an office which proved useful later in getting the bill passed.

The winter and spring of 1980 were packed with activities surrounding both the state divestment measures and anti-apartheid events underway at two universities, Western Michigan University (WMU) and Wayne State University in Detroit. In Kalamazoo, nine students, a faculty member, and a campus minister were preparing for their trial on charges of having disrupted a lawful meeting of the Board of Trustees. These eleven had staged a sit-in when the trustees refused to listen to divestment demands from a group of 125 demonstrators. The jury acquitted those arrested after they argued that the sit-in was their only available means for expressing their views on WMU's involvement in racism (Nessen 1984). At the capitol, Eldersveld organized film shows on South Africa and put together information packets with background materials and newsclippings on South Africa and anti-apartheid activities. Several legislators pushing for divestment hosted a reception in April for representatives of southern Africa resistance movements visiting the state, including members of SWAPO, ANC, ZANU-Patriotic Front, and ZAPU-Patriotic Front. For this occasion the House of Representatives passed a resolution commemorating the South African Freedom Conference at Wayne State that was responsible for bringing these representatives to Michigan. The conference was put together by a broad-based *ad hoc* Coalition for Southern African Freedom made up of state representatives, Detroit City Council members, academicians, labor union representatives, and members of Congress from the Detroit area. It and the related activities at the capitol helped further legitimize and publicize the activists' pressures for withdrawal of state funds from businesses involved in South Africa. In the meantime, endorsements and letters of support for the bills were sent from groups and individuals across the state. A list of endorsers (through 1984) is shown in Table 5–2.

Using information supplied by SALC members, Eldersveld brought in several outside experts to testify before the Civil Rights Committee and to lobby House members. Among the experts were a staff person for the Southern Africa Program of the American Friends Service Committee,

TABLE 5-2.   Divestment Legislation Endorsers: Dates and Bills

_____

Campus Groups and Individuals

Associated Students of Michigan State University; 1982--education bill
PIRGM-MSU, Public Interest Research Group in Michigan; no date, general
    endorsement of divestment; 1982--education and pension bills
Michigan Student Assembly, University of Michigan; 1979--all bills
Michigan Higher Education Student Association; 1979--general endorsement
Graduate Employees Organization, University of Michigan, Local 3550 of the
    American Federation of Teachers; 1980--all bills
Student Government, Eastern Michigan University; 1980--education and
    pension bills
Dr. David Gordon, Political Science Department, University of Michigan;
    1981--all bills
Dr. Joel Samoff, former professor in the Political Science Department,
    University of Michigan; 1979--all bills
Gayle H. Partmann, Coordinator, African Studies Program, Oakland
    University, Rochester, Michigan; 1979--all bills

Church Groups and Individuals

Coalition for Peace and Justice, Catholic Diocese of Lansing;
    1978--education bill
Bishop Thomas J. Gumbleton, Auxiliary Bishop of Detroit, Catholic Church;
    1980--general endorsement
Church and Society Committee, Episcopal Diocese of Michigan;
    1980--education and pension bills
Senate of Priests, Catholic Diocese of Lansing; 1978--education bill
Groundwork staff (Catholic intercongregational center for Michigan justice
    and peace activities), Lansing; 1980--education and pension bills
United Ministries in Higher Education at Michigan State University;
    1980--all bills
Don Van Hoeven, Campus Minister, Western Michigan University; 1980--general
    endorsement
Committee on Missions of the Covenant Association United Church of Christ,
    Jackson, Michigan; 1980--education and pension bills
Rev. Frederick L. Houghton, St. Paul's Episcopal Church, Brighton,
    Michigan; 1979--all bills
Catherine Wagner, Assistant Director, Archdiocese of Detroit;
    1980--education and pension bills
Sister Mary Rebecca Lorenz, Sisters of Mercy, Detroit; 1981--education bill
Rev. Philip E. Henderson, United Presbyterian Church, Lansing;
    1981--education bill
Duane Vore, Michigan Council of Churches, Lansing; 1979-81--all bills
Rev. Donald Coleman, Campus Minister, University of Michigan; 1979--all
    bills
Michigan Council of Churches

175

TABLE 5-2. Continued

Labor Groups and Individuals

Irving Bluestone, Vice President United Automobile Workers, Detroit;
    1980--general endorsement
United Automobile Workers; 1982--education bill
Communication Workers of America, District 4, Lansing
Michigan Coalition of Labor Union Women; 1980--general endorsement
Metropolitan Detroit Coalition of Black Trade Unionist; 1983--pension bill
Michigan AFSCME Council 25; 1983--pension bill
Michigan State Employees Association; 1983--pension bill

Other Groups and Individuals

Peace Education Center Policy Committee; 1979--all bills
Greater Lansing Area Chapter of the United Nations Association; 1980--all
    bills
Metropolitan Kalamazoo Chapter of the NAACP; 1980--all bills
Women's Conference of Concerns, Detroit; 1980--all bills
Allan Cooper, Common Cause; 1979--all bills
Institute for Global Education; 1982--education and pension bills
Michigan Council of Senior Citizens; 1984--pension bill
Detroit Association of Black Organizations, Inc.; 1983--pension bill

---

a South African journalist in exile working for the ACOA, and an investments analyst who argued that the state could make prudent and profitable investments that excluded South Africa-related companies. Bullard's office insured that news conferences were held and press releases sent out every time anti-apartheid visitors appeared in the state.

The Civil Rights Committee held two more hearings on all three bills in March. Opposition to the bills began to surface in these hearings. The State Department of Treasury opposed the divestment concept altogether. In a written analysis, the department offered detailed criticism of the banking bill. It noted that state agencies and departments throughout the state use local banks as convenient and safe depositories for daily receipts. Delayed depositing of monies, decreased control, increased risk, and potential loss of some interests were all listed as possible consequences of having to go greater distances to deposit funds (if a local bank were disqualified under the legislation). The department asserted that

> this bill would create unnecessary costs to the Department of Treasury and the banks resulting

from the filing and handling of the required affidavits. It is already cumbersome for banks to qualify as depositories of state funds. Banks must post collateral with the State Treasurer for the full amounts of such deposits. Act 88 of the Public Acts of 1979 added the requirement of banks to file reports with the commissioner of the Financial Institutions Bureau showing they are in compliance with anti-redlining requirements. Further hindrances imposed by this bill could convince banks that the requirements for acquiring state funds are not worth the benefits to them, and choose not to qualify for our deposits. This could be very detrimental to the State and its taxpayers by limiting the number of banks available as state depositories. (Michigan Department of Treasury, May 1980)

With regard to the intention of the legislation to help in ending apartheid, the department's analysis concluded that "those companies which adhere to the Sullivan Principles would appear to provide a positive impact in helping to put an end to apartheid."

A State Department of Commerce representative also testified in opposition to the banking bill. He argues that it could not be practically implemented and that the state government should not be involved in attempting sanctions activity against South Africa. Not all of the relevant state agencies opposed the legislation, however. The Department of Civil Rights endorsed the educational institutions' investments bill and supported the concept put forth in the other two. The State Board of Education originally supported the idea of the first version of the education bill but objected to its breadth. Since the version under consideration pertained only to South Africa, the board lent its support to the measure.

From the private sector, the Michigan Manufacturers' Association (MMA) sent a lobbyist to speak generally in opposition to all three pieces of legislation. Lobbyists from General Motors and Ford visited Bullard to try to convince him to stop sponsoring the legislation. The banking community, however, was less willing to be identified visibly as an opponent. Michigan Bankers' Association (MBA) lobbyist, Don Heikkinen, and Robert Duff from the National Bank of Detroit both noted their concerns about the banking bill at the hearings. They wanted more time to study the implications of the measure, suggested that it lacked clarity, and asserted that it would be impossible to implement in its current form. But, they were also willing to spend time with the bill's proponents to refine it and make it more acceptable to bankers.

The MBA is a multipurpose organization providing group insurance, educational seminars, legal advice, and a lobby at the state legislature for Michigan banks. All but two banks in the state (over 360) belong to the association. It has a staff of twelve persons, three of whom are registered lobbyists. Heikkinen is a senior vice president and staff counsel for the organization, and he took principal responsibility for negotiating with legislative proponents on changes the MBA wanted in the bill. He felt that legislators' desires to condemn apartheid were laudable, but he also believed that the state should not be involved in attempting to prohibit investments in South Africa. In his view, the legislation would add one more area of unnecessary governmental regulation to the banking business. He felt that by prohibiting deposits of state funds in banks that lend to corporations doing business in South Africa, the state was only indirectly targeting corporations, the real culprit, while punishing banks, secondary actors. And, he maintained, this indirect targeting would have no impact on corporations' investment policies. Therefore, he believed that if the state was going to be involved in sanctions or divestment activity (which it should not be), it should go after the businesses like GM, Chrysler, and Ford that make the investments and not cause problems for other organizations only peripherally involved, like in-state banks. Furthermore, if the state passed such legislation, it would have no place to deposit its funds since almost all the larger Michigan banks had some sort of business dealings with the U.S. operations of companies that invest in South Africa. Smaller banks already had difficulty qualifying to be depositories because a constitutional provision that does not allow state deposits in financial institutions to exceed 50 percent of the institutions's net worth. However, Heikkinen believed that the banking bill had enough momentum to pass in some form, and he decided not to oppose it outright. He wanted to try "to clean it up as best we could." There was a public relations liability attached to coming out against a bill designed to combat racism, and he did not want to create an image problem for Michigan banks.

Another part of the provisions of the banking bill was that the state could not make deposits in banks that lend directly to the government of South Africa or to one of its parastatals. According to information disseminated by the Campaign to Oppose Bank Loans to South Africa, based at the time in New York City, five Michigan banks had participated in loans to the South African government.[5] The Treasury Department reported that only one of these banks, the City National Bank of Detroit, was at the time a depository for state monies.[6] Both the MBA and representatives of the bank itself claimed that they knew of no such loans to South Africa, but in any case were willing to agree to the part of the legislation that prohibited them from making direct loans.

Through negotiation between Heikkinen, a number of the proponents, and Treasury Department representatives, the bill was rewritten to forbid deposits of state funds in banks that loan to the South African government, a national corporation of the South African government, or to subsidiaries of U.S. firms operating in South Africa. This meant that banks in Michigan could continue to lend to U.S. corporations such as GM and be allowed to receive deposits of state funds; but they would not be able to loan any money to public or private businesses located in South Africa such as GM's subsidiary there. Since there is no evidence of Michigan banks ever having loaned directly to a South African subsidiary of a U.S. corporation, Heikkinen was willing to remain unopposed to the measure in this form. The Treasury Department then removed its opposition apparently for two reasons: officials there also believed the rewritten measure would not disqualify any bank as depositories, and the legislative Black Caucus applied pressure to Loren Monroe, the black State Treasurer, to support the bill. With this second source of opposition gone, a major obstacle to the bill's passage was overcome.

Passage and Implementation of the Banking Bill

At this point, Bullard and Smith decided to press for approval of the banking bill before trying to get the education bill passed. The pension bill would be the last one attempted because it had received the greatest initial amount of negative reaction. They correctly assessed the degree of difficulty in passing each of the three bills and strategically ordered them so as to get an early victory that would contribute momentum for passage of the other two.

After lobbying by activists, the House of Representatives passed the banking bill by a vote of 58 to 40 on 20 May 1980, and it was sent to the Senate. Whereas Eldersveld and Bullard had shared with Smith the principal responsibility for guiding the bill through the House, at this point Smith took over the task of facilitating its passage in the Senate. Basil Brown, a black Democrat, was chair of the Judiciary Committee where the bill was being heard. Smith pressured Brown to achieve a quick, positive endorsement by the Judiciary Committee; but Brown, unaware of the previous painstaking negotiations between the MBA, Treasury, and proponents, allowed the measure to be amended so as to restore it to its original provisions— prohibiting deposits of state funds in banks that lend to corporations operating in South Africa. After being convinced that the measure would never pass the Senate in this form, Brown agreed to amend it on the floor of the Senate to match the House version, and he also agreed to help Smith press for its approval.

Smith and Brown both were involved simultaneously with state court reorganization legislation that had won them some unexpected conservative allies and friends in the Senate. They called on those allies to help secure the banking bill's passage. When it got to the Senate floor, however, there was an attempt to amend it to include an additional prohibition of state funds in banks that lend to businesses based in countries that violate the UN Universal Declaration of Human Rights. The amendment would have broadened the scope of the bill so far that support would be impossible, even by its proponents, but it failed (12 to 18) even though some senators argued that the legislature should not single out South Africa for condemnation.

With Brown's amendments to bring the Senate version in line with the House version, the legislation passed on 21 November 1980, by a vote of 22 to 7. Because the wording was still not precisely that of the House version, the bill went back to the House to receive final confirmation on 25 November. Once again a conservative member, Alan Cropsey, attempted an amendment, this time to include the Soviet Union in addition to South Africa. This amendment failed narrowly (46 to 47). The bill was finally adopted by a wide margin of 68 to 28, and with the governor's signature became Public Act 325 of 1980, shown in Appendix B.

This was not the first time nor the last that Representative Cropsey tried to amend the divestment legislation. Alan Cropsey is a religious fundamentalist, Republican, a graduate of Bob Jones University. He has opposed all of the divestment legislation. He is the only legislator who has made a point of tracking and consistently trying to amend or defeat these measures. He would prefer that the legislature not involve itself at all in foreign policy issues, but if a statement was going to be made or regulations passed on South Africa's violations of human rights, he wanted to give the same treatment to other abusive governments, especially Communist ones. That U.S. businesses have any dealings with the USSR distresses him, and he is convinced that the Soviet Union will overtake the United States with technology and machinery sold to that government by U.S. companies. With regard to South Africa, although he thinks apartheid policies need to be "relaxed considerably," he is not sure that blacks there are ready for self-government, that is, "existing under white rule for a while longer might not be so bad." He does not view himself as a racist but concedes that others might see him that way. He is the only opponent to the legislation interviewed who was not worried about openly challenging the legislation and being labeled a racist.

Back in March 1980, when all three bills were before the Civil Rights Committee, Cropsey attempted to amend the educational institution investments bill by proposing that, in addition to South Africa as a prohibited investment, all the countries (104) listed by Freedom House as 1980 violators of human rights also be included in the legislation. In addition, he wanted to attach the Universal Declaration of Human Rights as the definition of human rights. His amendment failed in committee (2 to 8). The same day that the banking bill was adopted by the committee, the education and pension fund bills also received committee approval.

Although, as was stated earlier, Bullard and Smith decided as a matter of tactics to pursue the passage of the banking bill first, they did not abandon the other two measures. In June 1980, after the House's first passage of the banking bill but before the Senate passage, a joint hearing on the others was held by the House Civil Rights Committee, the House Senior Citizens and Retirement Committee, the Retirement Subcommittee of the Appropriations Committee, and the Department of the Treasury. Again the investments analyst, Robert Schwartz, was invited to testify. Schwartz specializes as a financial counselor in socially responsible investments. He builds portfolios to avoid investments the client considers socially irresponsible (such as companies in South Africa, anti-union companies, polluters, violators of OSHA rules, and others. Even though by this time the MSU divestment experience had proven that under the right conditions divestment could be accomplished without financial loss, proponents felt that expert testimony from a person such as Schwartz could only help their cause. Therefore, SALC provided the funds to bring him from New York, and Eldersveld set up the hearing. In addition, Eldersveld solicited an opinion from a California law firm specializing in investment and financial planning,

Turner and Jovanovich, about the feasibility of divestment. The latter confirmed Schwartz's testimony. Both argued that it is feasible to construct a portfolio that restricts investments to corporations not invested in South Africa without sacrificing diversification, safety, or potential growth. Again, the hearing provided an opportunity for opposition to be voiced and this time it came from Johannes G. Pienaar, midwest director of the South Africa Foundation. Mr. Pienaar has spent a great deal of time in Michigan opposing anti-apartheid work, as will be seen later in this chapter.

Throughout the remainder of 1980, activists and legislators stayed busy securing the passage of the banking bill, and they were unable simultaneously to move forward with the other two. They were pleased with the victory on the first one, however, and were confident that its passage would aid in promoting the other two. Meanwhile, another Michigan university, Eastern Michigan University, adopted a policy of withdrawing its funds from corporations doing business in South Africa.

Divestment activities around the state and at the legislature slowed somewhat in 1981 after a very busy year and several activists victories in 1980. One major event occurred, however, in March, when there was a public ceremony for Governor Milliken to sign the banking bill. His signature had been given officially in December 1980, but the SALC activists and the legislators wanted to have an additional public rite. The occasion came when nine Nigerian state and federal legislators were visiting in Michigan. Since the government of Nigeria has been a major supporter of anti-apartheid activities in the UN, Bullard and the activists felt that it would be appropriate for the visitors to witness the Michigan state government's anti-apartheid work. The Nigerians were taken to the capitol, and in a public show of support for sanctions activity against South Africa, they watched Governor Milliken sign the banking bill. Speaking on behalf of the group to the governor and the press, Prince Israel Moronfoye, then Speaker of the House of Assembly in the Nigerian state of Kwara, congratulated the people of Michigan on having the farsightedness to enact such legislation.

According to this measure, now Public Act 325, after 4 July 1982, the state was to have no deposits in banks that make loans to the South African government, one of its national corporations, or a subsidiary or affiliate of a U.S. firm located in South Africa. The Financial Institutions Bureau (FIB) of the Department of Commerce is in charge of implementation, and its staff sent out a letter to the chief executive officers of banks serving as depositories of state funds notifying them of the new law. The letter attached an affidavit form requiring the bank to state that it has not made any loans of the kind prohibited by PA 325. In an attempt to help banks comply, in April the bureau supplied a list of U.S. corporations operating in South Africa from the U.S. Department of Commerce. The FIB also suggested that the bank executives consult their legal counsel for assistance in complying with the law. The banks only have to file one affidavit declaring themselves in compliance.

There is no annual filing requirements; that is, the bureau assumes that the original affidavit is valid until the bank files another reflecting a change in its status regarding such loans. At least 250 banks filed affidavits that they make no loans directly to the South African government, South African national corporations, or U.S. corporations' subsidiaries located in South Africa. The effect of the compromise amendment in the law is to leave unchanged the list of banks that qualify as depositories of state funds. One impact, however, is that banks serving as depositories must promise not to make loans to South Africa in the future if they want to remain as depositories.

Passage of and Challenge to
the Educational Institution Fund Bill

In the summer, following the spring reintroduction of the pension fund and educational institution investments bills, Bullard, Smith and activists from across the state continued to press for passage of the remaining legislation. More hearings were held by the Civil Rights Committee in November 1981 and January 1982. This time only the education bill was on the agenda because the pension bill had been assigned to another committee, the Senior Citizens and Retirement Committee. Only proponents appear to have been present at these hearings. In November, four representatives of religious or university groups testified in favor of the divestment measure, and in January, SALC brought in another outside expert, Gail Hovey, then the Research Director for the American Committee on Africa in New York, to lobby and testify on behalf of the legislation.

Although Cropsey's attempted amendment to the education bill in 1980 was apparently the only vocal opposition, the measure had raised concerns in some less visible quarters and faced some difficulties. Anticipating more opposition to this legislation, Bullard wrote it so as to pertain to divestment of "stock or other equity interest" rather than divestment of both stocks and bonds. He wanted to establish further the principle of noninvestment in South Africa and believed that this compromise would help accomplish this overarching goal.

Another issue that had to be faced was the scope of institutions affected by the bill. As introduced by Bullard, the legislation would affect the investment policies of both private and public educational institutions serving any age level of student (primary, secondary, or higher education). Some opposed its application to private institutions because it would mean too much governmental interference in the affairs of private educational institutions that receive no public funds and raise questions about separation of church and state. The Association of Independent Colleges and Universities had made its objections known, and a Republican representative moved to amend the bill so as to limit its scope to public educational institutions. Such an amendment was acceptable to Bullard, and it passed the committee unanimously. The legislation as a whole was then adopted without opposition by the committee.

This bill got its impetus from and has always been discussed in terms of the investment policies of universities. In Michigan there are 41 public institutions of higher education, that is, two-year and four-year universities and colleges. Information about their endowments is shown in Table 5–3. What percentage of their money is invested in corporations with South African operations is unknown. Since two of these schools had at the time already adopted total divestment policies (MSU and Eastern Michigan University), 39 would be affected by the legislation, including the University of Michigan, which has a partial divestment policy. What, if any, affect this measure would have on public educational institutions other than those in higher education is not clear and does not seem to have generated any discussion.

A further objection argued mainly by representatives from the University of Michigan, a Bullard constituent, was that the measure intruded on the constitutionally established authority of the university to control and direct all expenditures of the institution's funds. Bullard's staff believed that this argument was unfounded. The independence of universities in terms of their academic freedom, the crucial arena in which courts have required noninterference by the legislature, would not be challenged by the legislation. And, through other provisions in civil rights legislation, the state had already established its ability to prohibit

TABLE 5-3. Endowments of Michigan Institutions of Higher Education (in thousands of dollars)

Control	1977	1978	1979
Publicly Controlled	$157,980	$153,997	$168,397
Privately Controlled	96,225	101,444	119,198
All Institutions (total)	$254,205	$255,441	$287,595

Note: In 1980, the University of Michigan alone accounted for $126,627,000 of the publicly controlled endowments.
Source: U.S. Department of Education, August 1980 and 1982.

discrimination by universities. This act would be simply an extension of such nondiscrimination demands.

On the request of a legislative opponent to the bill, the state Attorney General issued a ruling that ironically did not agree with the opponents' claims. The Attorney General stated that the legislation was well within the constitutional authority of the legislature to regulate all public investment funds, including university endowments. Officials of the University of Michigan, however, did not accept this interpretation or that of Bullard's staff. They resented this extension of state control and let it be known that they would fight the legislation in court if necessary.

No substantial objections to the education bill were made by any state agencies. The Department of Treasury was the only agency with an inclination to oppose the act, but since the department had no jurisdiction over the matter, it issued no statement on it. As has already been noted, the Department of Education by this time supported the measure (although not actively) and the Civil Rights Department had approved of it from the beginning. Since there was a provision in the legislation that the Civil Rights Department compile a register of businesses operating in South Africa (from information obtained from the U.S. Department of Commerce), this department expected to incur enforcement costs of about $35,000 per year if the measure passed. Roy Castillo, the legislative liaison for the department, said that the agency staff had supported the bill enthusiastically, believing there was a moral responsibility to do so. With quite large recent budget and staff cuts due to the economic difficulties facing the state, however, he had doubts that they would be able to enforce it properly if it became law.

After the legislation received Civil Rights Committee approval in January 1982, it met the first of four major obstacles on the House floor in February. When the bill received its second reading,[7] a legislator moved to place a tie-bar on the bill; that is, he amended the legislation to require that it not take effect unless the pension bill were also enacted into law. This would kill the legislation, since there was little chance the pension bill would pass in that legislative session. Indeed, activists had no plans to press for its passage at that time. The amendment was carried by a vote of 56 to 36.

The second opposition amendment came on the same day when another representative attempted to insert a provision requiring that educational institutions not accept funds from businesses that operate in South Africa. This amendment was defeated by a margin of 50 to 42. The third attempt to kill the legislation by burdening it with unacceptable provisions was a familiar amendment from Alan Cropsey, which would prohibit educational institutions "from encouraging or condoning imperialistic communism, religious discrimination, ethnic discrimination or terrorism by knowingly making or maintaining . . . an investment in an organization operating in the Union of Soviet Socialists Republics" (Michigan House Journal, 1982). Before the amendment came to a vote another representative moved postponement.

Knowing that his bill would face further difficulty from an apparently well-organized opposition, Bullard attempted to strike a compromise with Cropsey. The two representatives met and agreed that Cropsey would remove some of his inflammatory language in the amendment and Bullard would not oppose it. In return, Bullard would make a motion to remove the tie-bar and Cropsey would support this effort. Thus, Cropsey's amendment was passed as follows: "an educational institution shall not encourage or condone religious discrimination or ethnic discrimination by knowingly making or maintaining after 1 February 1983, an investment in an organization operating in the Union of Soviet Socialist Republics" (Michigan House Journal, 1982). The tie-bar was removed (with a vote of 6 to 39) but the measure faced still another amendment attempt. Another representative reintroduced the previously defeated motion to prohibit institutions from accepting money from businesses operating in South Africa. The motion failed again, 44 to 55. The legislation was then passed by the House by an overwhelming vote of 75 to 25 on 13 May 1982. The deal that Bullard had struck with Cropsey worked to help secure passage.

Now the Senate was faced with a bill requiring educational institutions to divest from businesses operating in South Africa *and* the USSR—a radical alteration of the legislation proponents desired. Bullard's staff were confident that a serious attempt to remove Cropsey's amendment would be made in the Senate, but in the end it remained in the measure when it became law. The Senate took seven months to consider the bill. Like the banking bill in the previous campaign, it was referred to the Senate Judiciary Committee chaired by Basil Brown. Senator Brown did not speed the process, and his committee did not act on it until November, although members then voted for its passage 5 to 1. During these months a significant amount of opposition arose from the University of Michigan, major corporations in the state, especially Ford and General Motors, and the South African Consulate.

The University of Michigan's policy of partial divestment from corporations not subscribing to the Sullivan code and its objections to legislative intrusions into the autonomy of the university were both longstanding and well known positions. House passage, however, stimulated university officials to become more active against the bill. They argued in addition that the university would be likely to lose money from investment and from a decline in corporate gifts at a time when it was already facing cutbacks in state funding; that the legislature was acting hypocritically by targeting universities before divesting the pension funds under its direct control; and that divestment from corporations with major operations in Michigan was self-defeating to the state's attempt to recover from economic hardship.

The corporation lobbyists were also anxious to get the bill defeated, and together with the University of Michigan, they proposed that Senate opponents amend the measure to correspond with the university's partial divestment policy, including the Sullivan Principles. Ford and GM are Sullivan signatories and they usually get good ratings in the Arthur D. Little reports. Such an amendment would legitimize their Sullivan efforts.

The South African Consulate sent Senators a 12-page document detailing why the bill should not be adopted. The letter commended Sullivan for his approach, used the progressive force argument for why companies should stay in South Africa, and discussed the fudiciary responsibility of endowment fund trustees.

A number of groups from across the state, including a revived Washtenaw County Coalition Against Apartheid, mobilized to write letters and lobby to secure passage. Student groups from MSU, WMU, and UM were among those who spent a great deal of time contacting the legislature. Eldersveld and Bullard sent senators several lengthy communications stating why the Sullivan Principles amendment was unacceptable. In the end, the amendment was not proposed, and the bill passed 20 to 13 on 15 December.

Proponents were worried that Governor Milliken would succumb to pressure not to sign the measure or to veto it. Two precedents for such a reaction had occurred when Connecticut Governor O'Neal and former Massachusetts Governor King vetoed divestment bills. Milliken's term was over at the end of the year, and it was necessary to get his signature before he left office. Eldersveld and the anti-apartheid groups across the state mounted another drive to persuade him to endorse the legislation. He received numerous letters from within Michigan, including one from the legislative Black Caucus, and also from national anti-apartheid organizations. On 31 December 1982, he signed the bill and it became Public Act 512 (see Appendix B).

SALC and others who worked in the campaign held a celebration in February in honor of their victory. They had received a telegram of congratulations from the British Anti-Apartheid Movement, prominent coverage in the South African and Zimbabwean press, and personal congratulations from Nigerian governmental officials and Zimbabwe's Prime Minister Robert Mugabe when a Michigan trade mission went to those two countries. But their celebratory atmosphere was dampened somewhat by news of a possible legal challenge from the University of Michigan. Once again they began a letter writing campaign from Michigan residents, national organizations, and Congressman Howard Wolpe to the University's president and Board of Regents. However, most of the pressure on these decision makers to divest and not to challenge the law in court came from their own campus.

The Advisory Committee on Financial Affairs of the faculty Senate Assembly supported the administration and regents who opposed divestment, but the members were in a small minority. When they presented their report to the entire Senate Assembly, it was rejected and the Assembly voted 40 to 3 in favor of total divestment. This action followed after more than 50 faculty members signed a lengthy open letter to the regents urging divestment, and after 150 students rallied in favor of selling the securities. The student government subsequently threatened to pull its $35,000 from the university's investment pool. Local Ann

Arbor newspaper editorials and others around the state were mixed, but the state Democratic Party and officials of the United Auto Workers came out in favor of the university's complying with the law.

The regents met in February but did not make a decision on the issue until April. At the February meeting, Dennis Brutus, an exiled black South African poet who successfully fought efforts by the U.S. Immigration Service to deport him in 1982, addressed the regents and urged them to divest. The April meeting was greeted by a vigil of 35 people organized by WCCAA. In their three days of deliberation, the decision makers heard from their legal counsel in closed session, and then with other one hundred onlookers, they listened to 18 pro-divestment students, faculty, and others. No one testified in favor of keeping South Africa-related investment. The progress of the meetings were widely reported in the local media.

Two issues were at stake: divestment and the legal challenge. Some at the university who agreed with the administration's objections to the state's intrusion on university autonomy and authority nevertheless wanted full divestment. Others who wanted divestment thought that a legal challenge would be a waste of time and money, and still others believed the state had a right to tell the university to act as they wished it had when first confronted with the issue in 1978.

Through a resolution offered by Gerald Dunn, the regents decided 6 to 2 to withdraw their stock holdings from corporations doing business in South Africa except for those headquartered or with a substantial number of employees in Michigan and those securities specifically restricted from sale by the donor. They also ordered that the process be as financially prudent as possible. The exceptions were made so that the university could maintain legal standing to challenge the law in court, which the regents decided 5 to 3 to do.

The resolution affected about 90 percent of the University's South Africa-related stock holdings in 45 companies, and administrators expected the divestment process to be complete by the end of 1984. The University retained its substantial investment in bonds purchased from corporations with South African subsidiaries because, like other university administrations in the state, officials interpreted the law as only pertaining to stocks. Another university, Wayne State University (WSU), passed a divestment policy in March although the president was also worried about the issue of autonomy. He said that WSU would divest anyway because it was the moral thing to do.

The issue of whether or not universities must also sell bonds in South Africa-related companies may be significant in the future. The Department of Civil Rights is charged with implementation of the law, and its interpretation is that bonds are affected. As shown earlier, the law defined investment as "shares of stock or other equity investment," and Bullard's intent was not to include bonds. Meanwhile, the department has not proceeded with a review of all state universities' endowments because the University of Michigan's legal challenge has not been resolved. In a suit filed in the summer of 1983, the university argued that the law is unconstitutional on four points. Through the Attorney General's office, the state defends the law as constitutional and counters each of the university's arguments.

1. The University claims that PA 512 infringes on its autonomy granted by the state constitution that says in Article 8 that "the control and direction of the University's funds are vested exclusively in the Regents of the University . . ." who are directly elected by and accountable to the citizens of Michigan; that is, the university is independent of the control of the legislature and all other agents of the state.

The Attorney General's counter argument is that the university must obey laws such as the Michigan Civil Rights Act, which PA 512 amends, that pertain to everyone in the state. The university has tried on previous occasions to be exempted from such general laws, for example the one allowing public employees to organize unions and the one regarding workers' compensation; and repeatedly the courts have ruled that although the university does have autonomuous operation from the state, it must, like every other citizen, abide by laws intended to apply to all people in the state.

2. The university argues that PA 512 violates the Michigan constitutional provision known as *title object*. This provision holds that the object of any act has to be fairly announced in the act. PA 512 is in violation, the university maintains, because it pertains to the civil rights of South African and Soviet citizens and thus embodies more than the one object expressed in the title. The Michigan Civil Rights Act should not contain articles that have to do with other nations' citizenry. Furthermore, the divestment provision alters the original purpose of the Civil Rights Act and without expressly and openly doing so in fact alters another law, the 1976 Uniform Investments of Institutions Funds Act.

The Attorney General rebuts that PA 512 is appropriately within the scope of the Civil Rights Act because it does affect the civil rights of Michigan citizens. The university's investments in South Africa support the apartheid regime, the state maintains, and they put potential black students in a difficult position. Because black students know of the university's support for apartheid, they will be discouraged from attending the school.

3 and 4. The last two complaints by the university are that the act interferes with interstate commerce and thus violates the interstate commerce clause of the Constitution of the United States, and that it interferes with supremacy of the federal government in foreign policy.

The Attorney General argues that the university only has standing to sue to protect its *own* constitutional prerogatives, not those of the federal government. Therefore, the state claims, the university has no basis on which to make the last two complaints because they are none of its business.

The Attorney General, represented by the Assistant Attorney General James Riley, has taken on the case with a great deal of enthusiasm and determination to defend the state as well as possible. To add to the state's defense, Bullard and Smith have jointly filed an *amicus curiae* brief. A second such brief has been filed by the Black Student Union of the University of Michigan, the National Lawyer's Guild of Michigan (Detroit and Ann Arbor branches), and the National Conference of Black Lawyers (Detroit branch). As of September 1984, the case had not been resolved.

This is the second state in which such a suit has been filed although ironically in the other case in Oregon (as discussed in Chapter 1), the Board of Regents are fighting the ruling of the state Attorney General for the *right* to divest. Divestment proponents and opponents all over the country are very interested in the outcome in both states because future university-related campaigns in many other places may be affected by the precedents set in these cases.

The Pension Divestment Bill

Although Bullard and Smith deliberately postponed their attempts to get the pension bill passed, the legislation did receive attention. The strategy of building momentum for its approval by first securing passage of the banking and educational institutions bills was not lost on opponents to these measures, and they began to lay the foundation to stop its passage. A major source of opposition is in the Treasury Department. The former state treasurer, Loren Monroe, one of the highest ranking black state officials stated that pension funds investments should be based on safety, return, and social responsibility, and he claimed to be generally supportive of the concept of socially responsible investment. In May 1980, however, he issued a statement against the pension fund bill saying: "The indignities faced by Blacks in South Africa are many, but I also know that as state treasurer it is wrong, illogical and irresponsible to divest stock holdings in order to soothe the consciences of persons who feel that a hollow, sacrificial gesture with other people's money will end the inhumanity of whites against Blacks in South Africa" (*Michigan Chronicle*, 3 May 1980). He also noted that prominent U.S. blacks have opposed divestment. In addition, the state's Investment Advisory Committee announced its objections, and Monroe's staff wrote a legislative analysis under his signature that strongly opposed the pension bill.

The treasury staff maintain that all of their training as portfolio managers makes them view any attempt to limit their flexibility in investment decisions with alarm. They see their primary responsibility to be that of making safe and profitable investments for the state of Michigan, and to do this they want to make decisions on financial criteria alone. From their perspective, divestment severely restricts the flexibility of the state's investment program because it would limit the number and kinds of investment opportunities available. They believe it interjects a harmful set of investment criteria, and thus threatens their ability to carry out prudent management. Furthermore, they maintain that pension fund divestment cannot be compared legitimately to the profitable divestment process that took place at MSU, because the state has a significantly larger portfolio and operates under much more stringent legal investment regulations than does the university. If investment performance were reduced, this could result in an increase in employer contribution to the public employee retirement system, that is, more tax dollars. In addition, they believe that divestment by institutional investors would have no impact on the corporations doing business in South Africa because their investments are made in the secondary market, not in new issuances of stock. Therefore, divestment would have no impact on South Africa either, they argue. These staff members also suggest that holding a company's stock may be a good way to get entree to influence its South Africa policies.

A third major treasury argument against the pension fund bill is that it is counterproductive to the efforts of the Executive Office and the legislature to revive Michigan's economy, since the bill would prohibit the state from holding stock in important Michigan based companies. Table 5–4 lists corporations headquartered in Michigan that have South African subsidiaries.

In order to state their opposition to apartheid while opposing the pension bill, the Treasury Department staff suggested an amendment to the bill almost identical to the amendment placed on the banking bill. This proposed provision would prohibit pension funds from being invested in companies making "a loan to the Republic of South Africa, a national corporation of the Republic of South Africa, or a direct investment in a subsidiary or affiliate of a United States firm operating in the Republic of South Africa. . . . A subsidiary or affiliate shall not be construed to mean a subsidiary or affiliate or parent that is located in the United States" (Michigan Department of Treasury, 25 November 1981). This proposed amendment would have meant that no pension monies would be divested if such legislation passed, precisely what the department staff would like to have happen.

Another opponent, the portfolio manager for MERS, a pension fund managed outside the Treasury Department, took a position on the pension fund divestment bill very similar to that of the treasury staff, and he, too, communicated his opposition and the opposition of his board of directors to Bullard.

In 1983, when a new governor, Democractic Governor Blanchard came into office, he brought a new treasurer, Robert Bowman, who has a somewhat different perspective on the issue. After many previous requests for such information, the Treasury Department finally issued an analysis of the bill showing that more than $2 billion, or about 25 percent, of the portfolios for the six retirement systems the department manages[8] would be affected by the pension bill. An additional $88 million in MERS investments would also be divested under the act. This was the largest amount of money yet to be challenged by divestment legislation anywhere in the country.

With such enormous sums at stake and with the bill's provision that divestment occur within a year, Bowman reacted quite negatively. The department's Director of Investments, William Amerman, continued his public opposition as well. However, Smith and Bullard began a series of conversations with Bowman, and after Smith agreed to

TABLE 5-4. Michigan Businesses with Investments in South Africa

Company	Activity	Product sold to/in South Africa	Sullivan Signatory
Asgrow Seed, Kalamazoo	Manufacturing/Sales	Seeds	No
Bundy Corp., Detroit	Sales	Tubing	Yes
Burroughs Corp., Detroit	Sales	Business machines and computers	Yes
Clark Int'l., Buchanan	Manufacturing/Sales	Earth moving and mining equipment	No
Dow Chemical Co., Midland	Sales	Chemicals and pharmaceuticals	No
Dow Corning Co., Midland	Sales	Silicone products	No
Federal-Mogul Corp., Detroit	Sales	Automotive parts	Yes
Ford Motor Co., Dearborn	Manufacturing/Sales	Automobiles	Yes
General Motors Corp., Detroit	Manufacturing/Sales	Motor vehicles, earth moving and locomotive equipment, power and industrial products	Yes
Kellogg Co., Battle Creek	Manufacturing/Sales	Food products	Yes
Leco Corp., St. Joseph	Sales	Steeling sampling devices and electronic instruments	No
National-Standard Co., Niles	Manufacturing/Sales	Wire	No
Upjohn Co., Kalamazoo	Manufacturing/Sales	Pharmaceuticals	Yes
Valeron Corp., Royal Oak	Manufacturing/Sales	Engineering tooling	No

Source: American Consultate General, Johannesburg, 1979 List of American Firms, Subsidiaries, and Affiliates in South Africa; 1981 Fifth Report on the Signatory Companies to the Sullivan Principles

amend the proposal, Bowman withdrew his strong objections and became willing to negotiate a meaningful compromise.

In a substitute for the original bill, Smith made two substantial amendments (see Appendix B). The first was on the timing of implementation, and it was to have one-fifth of the funds divested per year in the five years beginning 1 January 1985. The second had to do with the funds affected, and it limited the scope of the bill to two retirement systems instead of seven. Included were the State Employee Retirement System and the Public School Employee Retirement System. Left out were five systems including the Legislative Retirement Fund, whose exclusion leaves Smith and Bullard open to charges of hypocrisy.

The Senior Citizens and Retirement Committee held hearings on the legislation on 16 November 1983. Smith explained his substitute, and Bullard argued in its favor. Bowman testified and reiterated his original objections; but he also said that the state needed to make the strongest possible statement against apartheid. He admitted that the substitute was an improvement and indicated he was willing to work further with proponents to seek a solution.

Another opponent to testify was William D. Broderick, member of the governmental relations staff at Ford. He maintained that, unlike the efforts of corporations abiding by the Sullivan Principles, divestment would do nothing to improve the lives of black South Africans. Citing various studies from other states, he also argued that the legislation would adversely affect pension funds' earnings. His last point was that Michigan's investment climate would be hurt by the bill. Other corporations with active opposition were GM and Dow Chemical.

The chair of the committee, Democratic Representative Francis Spaniola, claims to be generally sympathetic to the divestment cause but very cautious about setting up nonfinancial criteria for investments. Without his support, the bill will probably never get out of committee. Spaniola has discussed the bill at length with people in the Treasury Department and has a great deal of sympathy for their position because he, too, believes that the safety and profitability must be held above any other investment criteria. As chair of the committee, he feels that a responsibility to ensure a prudent approach to investments is a public trust placed in him by the state's retired employees.

Spaniola gets occasional visits from lobbyists concerned about the bill, one of whom is Gert J. Grobler, a representative from the South African Consul General in Chicago. Grobler has come by his office about twice a year since the bill originally was introduced (1979) to encourage Spaniola's opposition. Grobler has supplied him with information against divestment, including a report of the Connecticut governor's veto of divestment legislation.

Another active source of opposition to this measure is from an association of the retirees themselves. The Retirement Coordinating Council is a coalition of public employee organizations with one of its major functions being that of a lobby on behalf of public service retirees. The RCC has sent out occasional "Red Alerts" to members across the state warning that their funds are in jeopardy due to the introduction of the pension bill. Both Smith and Bullard have received mail as a result of these letter-writing campaigns. Treasury Department officials and staff in the Bureau of Retirement Systems are in close touch with the RCC about their united opposition to the legislation.

As usual, proponents, too, had been very active on the bill. In 1983, the activists from across the state started calling their coalition MichDivest, and they began to get more endorsements from three groups whose support had been lacking on the previous efforts: public employee labor unions, black organizations, and retired people. In the November hearings, representatives from Michigan AFSCME Council 25 and the Michigan State Employees Association gave strong positive testimony. In addition, Spaniola received letters in favor of the bill from the Coalition of Black Trade Unionists in Michigan, the Detroit Association of Black Organizations, and the Michigan Council of Senior Citizens.

Again Bullard's office had arranged for expert testimony from an investment analyst. This time the testimony came from a black New York firm, Daniels and Bell, represented by Carl Penn. David Wiley from SALC also spoke on behalf of proponents, and he, along with others, was able to add a new inducement to the legislature. As an Africanist he argued that divestment was good for business because it raised the state's status in the eyes of African trading partners.

The state has trade offices in Brussels and Tokyo, and in recent years it has been turning attention to developing trade with Africa. The Department of Commerce began a program in 1982 that eventually hired an African director and a British firm and another African businessman as consultants. The state funded the effort at $250,000, and Governor Blanchard began promoting the program. A seminar on trade with Africa was held in January 1983 with participation by 60 Michigan companies, and a trade mission was sent to several African countries in October of the same year.

Wiley, Governor Blanchard, and Okechukwu Aguwa, director of the program, all report that potential and actual African trading partners are very pleased with the state's divestment laws. They are appreciated as a sharp positive contrast to U.S. foreign policy toward Africa. The Commerce Department and others believe that the state has a competitive edge on others seeking increased trade with Africa because of its image of being progressive and concerned about racism worldwide. Since opponents to the pension divestment bill have argued that it would harm major Michigan businesses, this evidence was important for proponents of the legislation.

Other support came when Governor Dukakis of Massachusetts wrote Governor Blanchard to report on the success of divestment in Massachusetts both in taking an important anti-apartheid stand and in maintaining the safety and security of the pension funds. Congressman Howard Wolpe also wrote to Representative Spaniola urging his committee to take positive action on the pension bill.

The legislation is still in committee, however, despite the backing divestment has had. Not enough support has been gathered, and major obstacles still stand in the way of passage. Smith and Bullard are committed to working out an acceptable compromise with Bowman. One suggestion is that some of the portfolio funds be divested as an experiment of sorts on what effects, if any, occur in risk and profitability.

Whether or not the right compromise and sufficient support can be found to get the bill through the legislature remains to be seen. Our next task here is to analyze the process by which the other two bills passed, to discover why these outcomes occurred.

WHY THESE OUTCOMES

Once again we will employ the Table 3-1 list of variables to aid the analysis of why divestment legislation achieved partial success in Michigan. The Michigan legislature has considered a number of divestment bills, and this discussion will attempt to generalize across the several campaigns launched to push them through the legislature, the two most significant campaigns being those for the passage of the banking bill and for the educational institutions bill. Differences between campaigns will be noted when they appear to be significant in affecting the outcomes.

Goals, Theory of Action, Target, Time, and Context

One of the inner environment variables significant in the activists' divestment efforts is the matter of what proponents hope to achieve, or their goals. Table 5–5 displays proponents' goals categorized by the time needed for their achievement. As in the analysis of the Connecticut campaigns, long-term is considered to be three or more years, medium-term is one to two years, and short-term is less than a year. This list of goals comes from interviews with activists in SALC and legislative proponents as well as from SALC meeting minutes or other SALC documents.[9] The goals are not specific to the legislative campaigns conducted by the activists. Many could pertain to the totality of their anti-apartheid work, but their use here is specifically for an analysis of the legislative divestment efforts. Again, as with the Connecticut case study, they are identified as for the proponents, the state, or the wider national anti-apartheid movement.

The activists in Michigan reflect an ideological cleavage in their long-term goals that is more pronounced than is a similar division among the Connecticut proponents discussed in the previous chapter. Some activists see apartheid as an issue that is particularly useful in raising fundamental questions about the nature of economic organization, the necessity of understanding capitalism as an inherently unjust system, and the underpinnings that capitalism provides for racism. These sentiments are reflected in goal 19. Others prefer to downplay, or in some cases even ignore, the issues related to a broader focus on capitalism and concentrate instead on an analysis and ultimate targeting of the specific systems of racial injustice in southern Africa. Goal 17 is a capsule statement of these concerns. The East Lansing activists have discussed this cleavage among themselves in some detail, and they all have fairly clear understandings of where each person stands. Some of the activists who identify their efforts most closely with having the principal focus on southern Africa do not have large differences with those in the former category in their analyses of the significance of capitalism in perpetuating injustice in southern Africa or worldwide.

Their differences seem to emanate from two sources: a difference in opinion about tactics and strategies for anti-apartheid activism generally, and an experiential distinction between those who have lived and worked in southern Africa and those who have not. The debates over long-term strategies and tactics have focused on two significantly different types of campaigns: (1) those that are highly visible to the public with good results in exposure and education on nonelites to the issues but only moderate payoffs in terms of changed institutional policies (for example, demonstrations, mass mobilizations, teach-ins or study groups, targeting a series of local—that is, community/city, not state—institutions); versus (2) campaigns varying in public visibility, less focused on nonelites and educational efforts, but highly effective in terms of institutional policy changes (for example, lobbying behind the scenes, targeting legislatures and larger institutional investors). Those whose principal focus is southern Africa and who have first-hand experience in southern Africa sympathize more with the second category of strategies. Those whose main goals are anti-capitalist in character generally fall into the first category. These ideological cleavages are not for the most part disruptive of SALC's work because the group has agreed to disagree on the long-range issues while concentrating on achieving the short-term goals. Tensions have arisen occasionally when these philosophical orientations were pertinent to the formulation of short-term goals, but the group attempted not to let such tensions alienate members.

One of the ways of preventing alienation and disruption of the work was to make the decision on short-term goals on the basis of who wanted to, and had the time, to work on particular campaigns. That is, if any member(s) wanted to pursue a particular campaign (for example, passing the banking bill) and if they could convince others in the SALC group to help them, they could launch their campaign with the blessings but less active support of other SALC members who preferred to try a different strategy. One activist describes the working style as "truly a participatory democracy in that those who stick around all the time and do the work also *de facto* set the policies." The outcome of this non-directive approach to their work is an orientation of the bulk of SALC's efforts in recent years around legislative campaigns.

In the context of the discussion of goals in Chapter III, the degree of change required by the specific goals related to the state legislature is fairly comprehensive. That is, the proponents desire that the state end its economic associations with South Africa in several arenas—banking, pension investments, and educational institutions' investments. These goals require more change than would be necessary if, for example, the Connecticut proponents' goals were achieved; and, as social movement literature points out, the greater the degree of change sought, the greater the difficulty in achieving it.

TABLE 5-5. Michigan Proponents' Campaign Goals

Short-term

   1. For proponents to take a principled stand against Michigan
institutions profiting from racism by investing in corporations or
depositing funds in banks doing business in South Africa.
   2. For proponents to send a message to corporation executives that
they will continue to suffer moral pressure to withdraw from South Africa.
   3. For proponents to demonstrate solidarity with blacks and others in
southern Africa resisting apartheid.
   4. For proponents to send a message to the South African government
that segments of the American people are committed to the isolation of
South Africa from Western countries' economic and military support.
   5. For proponents to demonstrate disagreement with U.S. governmental
foreign policy toward South Africa.
   6. For proponents to pursue the freedoms and responsibilities as
American citizens to promote and preserve justice in the United States and
abroad.

Medium-term

   7. For proponents and the state to remove the state of Michigan's
direct support and participation in the perpetuation of apartheid.
   8. For the state to take a principled stand against apartheid and
United States corporate investment in South Africa.
   9. For proponents and the state to get corporations and banks to
rethink their policies and expend energies doing so.
   10. For the combined actions of the national anti-apartheid movement to
strengthen the hand of progressives in the corporations to pressure their
own companies to change labor practices and particular selling practices,
and to pressure South Africa.
   11. For the combined actions of the national anti-apartheid movement to
prevent new investment in South Africa.
   12. For the state to demonstrate disagreement with U.S. governmental
foreign policy toward South Africa.

   The theory of action represented by these goals is not
significantly different from the general anti-apartheid
movement's theory of action or that derived from the Connecticut activists' goals. Some of the difference between
the ways in which the proponents in these two states went
about trying to achieve their goals will be discussed in the
last chapter, but at this point, the same general evaluation
given previously can be applied to the Michigan proponent's

TABLE 5-5. Continued

---

13. For the combined actions of the national anti-apartheid movement to place constraints on U.S. foreign policy makers to prevent further U.S. government support for and cooperation with the South African government.

14. For the combined actions of the national anti-apartheid movement to legitimate the call for sanctions and noncooperation with South Africa among U.S. policy elites at all levels of government.

15. For the combined actions of the national anti-apartheid movement to place constraints on the South African government in carrying out apartheid policies.

16. For the state to demonstrate solidarity with the struggle of blacks and others in South Africa resisting apartheid.

Long-term

17. For proponents and the state to aid fundamental change in South Africa to bring about an end to apartheid.

18. For proponents and the state to contribute to worldwide anti-apartheid efforts to completely isolate South Africa economically.

19. For proponents to politicize the people in Michigan to have anti-corporate and anti-capitalist attitudes and behavior.

20. For proponents to educate people in Michigan about racism, South Africa, the U.S. corporate role in supporting racism in South Africa, and the struggles for liberation against white minority rule in southern Africa.

21. For the combined actions of the national anti-apartheid movement to educate U.S. policy elites in legislative arenas at all levels of government about racism, South Africa, the U.S. corporate role in supporting racism in South Africa, and the struggles for liberation against white minority rule in southern Africa.

22. For the combined actions of the national anti-apartheid movement to convince U.S. policy elites at all levels that actively working for black majority rule in South Africa (through nonsupport of the minority government) is in the long-term interest of the U.S. government and all people (including whites) in South Africa.

---

theory of action. That is, it is a combination of a rational and realistic appraisal of how to reach a desired political outcome combined with idealism and faith that a positive contribution is being made to the ending of apartheid. As in the previous analyses, however, the early parts of the theory of action are the more dependable and rational ones. The farther along in the theory one gets, the more faith required; the predictive capabilities of scholars and activists are not so highly developed as to foretell exactly what will be responsible for the changing of the apartheid system. Thus activists are necessarily motivated in part by faith that they are on the right track.

Two outer environment variables, the time line and the arena targeted, have been for the most part assets in the campaign. Bullard introduced the first divestment bill in 1978, with additional divestment legislation introduced in subsequent sessions. The proponents have had, therefore, a significant amount of time to organize support for their campaigns. As the pension fund measure awaits passage, however, the opposition has taken advantage of the opportunity to organize against it, and time may begin to work against the proponents. They have gathered resources and learned skills important to their legislative efforts across these four years, but there are some indicators that opponents have, too. These factors of opposition and campaign strength will be discussed later, but at this point we should note that, all things being equal, the quicker that passage of the remaining bill can be pressed, the better the changes for success.

As was the case in Connecticut, the legislative arena proved to be a responsive target for the activists. For example, an identifiable core of legislators (varying from 21 to 25) have cosponsored the education bill with Bullard since 1978. Other helpful contextual factors are that during 1978–82, the Democratic Party had majorities in both houses, although the governor was a Republican during this time. In the legislature in 1981–82, there were 13 blacks out of 110 representatives in the House and three black Senators out or 38. Again, as in Connecticut, the State Treasurer was black, but this racial identity did not really materialize into a campaign asset. In 1983, a Democratic governor who appreciates the state's anti-apartheid laws came into office. This looked like an even better campaign context. However, facing a $1.7 billion deficit, with the help of the legislature he raised taxes. This led to an attempt to recall Blanchard that failed, but in the process, two Democratic senators from districts where Blanchard did not have popular support were recalled. In 1984, they were replaced by Republicans, and the Senate is now Republican controlled. This makes the political context for the pending pension bill worse.

The Michigan legislature is a logical place for divestment campaigns in that, as has been described earlier in this chapter, other institutions in the state have been similarly targeted. In addition, as members of Congress, former Representatives Charles Diggs and Representative

Howard Wolpe, currently chair of the Subcommittee on Africa of the House Committee on Foreign Affairs, have both been in the forefront of national legislative anti-apartheid work.

Although some of these factors would seem to make Michigan a conducive environment for passage of divestment legislation, there are other contextual variables that work against that possibility. One is the significant presence of large corporations in Michigan like Ford, GM, and Dow Chemical, who have major investments in South Africa. As shown earlier, Table 5-5 lists the corporations headquartered in Michigan with subsidiaries in South Africa. With the severe economic problems that Michigan has faced in recent years (that is, high unemployment and the near failure of the Chrysler corporation) some lawmakers have been skeptical of divestment for fear that it might hurt some of Michigan's largest employers. In fact, SALC activists believe it to be remarkable that the banking and educational institutions funds bills received so much legislative support in times of such economic hardship and retrenchment. Therefore, when considering a wide range of contextual factors, the state of Michigan can be seen to be a mixed environment in which to seek support for divestment legislation.

Strength, Strategies, and Tactics

An important asset for the proponents and a part of the strength of their campaigns was the number and kind of endorsements they received from groups and individuals around the state. Table 5-2 lists those who formally endorsed the divestment or banking bills. The table shows that, especially prior to 1982, most of the backing for the bills came from church-related or university-related organizations or individuals, although there is support from labor and community groups as well. The preponderance of support comes from university and church groups because those are the people that the activists in the state know best. A significant number of representatives of this list showed up at the eight Civil Rights Committee hearings held on the various pieces of legislation from 1978-82, and the endorsers were often called on by proponents to contact their legislators to encourage their support.

Divestment proponents spent a great deal of time and energy cultivating these endorsements, and their efforts to do this have already been discussed to some degree. Activists worked to acquire support in several ways:

(1) continual educational efforts involving speaking at various organizations' meetings, film showings at MSU averaging two to three times a month across three years, literature and educational packet distribution, large mobile displays placed at public gatherings and receptions and speaking engagements for outside experts; (2) use of personal and professional organizational networks and contacts to solicit divestment support among friends and acquaintances who play leadership roles in these organizations; and (3) frequent mention of campaign progress in these organizations' newsletters. The activists did not maintain their own newsletter but Eldersveld frequently mailed out updates, hearing notices, clippings, and news releases to supporters.

Throughout these campaigns there have been activist groups across the state working in support of the legislation, but outside of the labor support that Eldersveld achieved, SALC is responsible for gaining most of the endorsements. Legislators, staff in the state bureaucracies, and members of the business community are aware of widespread support for divestment and report that it has created a favorable climate for the legislation—a climate that assumes that the legislature will act favorably on some form of the legislation, and that to be against the bill is to run the risk of being labeled racist.

Despite the success in gaining a significant number of supporters, however, the list of endorsements has some shortcomings. One is a notable lack of clearly identifiable black organizational backing for the bills, especially before 1982. If campaign backers want to create a climate of opinion surrounding the legislature so that divestment is seen as the only valid anti-racist action to take, black endorsement and active support is essential, Without it, the campaigns lack an important and powerful source of legitimacy that can add a crucial dynamic. Another significant sector missing from the list is retired workers' groups, unions, or others whose pension funds are the target of the pension fund divestment bill. The divestment activists began cultivating such endorsements in recent years, but without support from these quarters proponents can be accused of taking risks with others' money, and worse still, will encounter these groups as active opponents. A third group whose support was actively but not very successfully cultivated is that of labor. Labor unions are powerful organizations in Michigan, and although the UAW and others endorsed the divestment legislation, labor unions have not been active in terms of mobilizing workers to contact legislators or even having their lobbyists campaign for the bills.

Certainly the campaigns could have gained important strength and greater momentum with further support from these groups.

So far, the activists' efforts have had substantial legislative support, however. They always received strong approval from the House Civil Rights Committee, and as was stated earlier, the education bill has had no fewer than 21 cosponsors since it was first introduced in 1978. The Black Caucus, with Smith as its chair, endorsed all the divestment legislation, and Smith's leadership was significant in assuring passage of the banking bill in the Senate. The Black Caucus is not, however, in the forefront of persistently pressing for the measures, most likely due to other major concerns occupying members' time in a period of severe economic hardship for many of their constituents. Support for the bills has not always been casted as a crucial test of legislators' contribution to anti-racist struggles. The lack of heavy pressure from the caucus and the opposition of the former treasurer is partially responsible for this tone in the debate. Although in general the legislative support has been both substantial and consistent for these two bills, proponents will have difficulty sustaining that level of support for the pension bill, as will be explained later in the discussion of opposition.

The most important legislative ally and the principal mover behind the bills, Perry Bullard, has been a vital part of securing passage of the banking and educational institution funds bills. Without his backing, his careful attention to tactics, and the energetic involvement of his staff, especially Eldersveld, in tracking and promoting the measures, the banking and education bills probably would have encountered much more difficulty. Even though Representative Smith was the main sponsor of the banking bill, Bullard and Eldersveld can be credited with a major portion of the work that achieved its House passage.

In promoting state divestment, there was somewhat of a division of labor between the activists (outside the legislature) and Bullard and Eldersveld (inside the legislature). Activists, especially members of SALC, provided mobilization of support for the bills, expertise on southern Africa, and plenty of contacts around the country who can serve as added expertise. Bullard and Eldersveld functioned to take headcounts of legislative support, to strategize on timing for floor votes, to solicit testimony, intensive lobbying, or phone and mail campaigns from activists and other supporters, and to negotiate on amendments. This means that work on and control over the campaigns are shared by the activists and the legislative sponsors.

Bullard's work on the bill would be reduced substantially, however, if he did not have a staff person (out of six) who, at crucial points in the campaigns, could spend at least half time on these measures. Eldersveld's time was an important contribution to the success of the campaigns, and it relieved the activists of many administrative burdens. Also, Eldersveld's contribution was more than just that of time. Several people inside and outside the legislature remarked on her high commitment to securing passage of the bills even though she knew little about South Africa or divestment when she started on the campaigns. One legislator stated that she nurtured the divestment bills as "much more than a job; she took them on as a burning cause that needed to be handled well." In the division of labor described earlier, however, she has relied heavily on the activists to back her up when she needed advice and information.

The two activists groups that have been most prominent in pushing the legislation are the Washtenaw County Coalition Against Apartheid (WCCAA) and SALC, although other groups have been significant allies at points. SALC is the most consistent and reliable organization, but it, too, has experienced a decline in membership and active participation in the last few years. Remarkably, since 1974, SALC has been able to sustain itself and its anti-apartheid work through leadership transitions. Without SALC members' ongoing efforts, divestment would not be a live issue in the Michigan legislature. One of SALC's best assets is the personal commitment and perseverance of a core group of members. This core group is now about five people, although 10 to 15 others consider themselves members of SALC and sporadically attend meetings. Four of the core members have strong personal connections with persons in southern Africa or with South Africa exiles and have been working on anti-apartheid or anti-racist efforts other than divestment campaigns for many years. They see their contribution to anti-apartheid work as ongoing and as lifelong. One of its current manifestations is the legislative measures, but these people devote major amounts of time to anti-apartheid work in other arenas, too. In addition to this very strong commitment to racial justice in southern Africa, the core group members also have a high personal commitment to each other as friends and colleagues who have fought important battles together across several years. The occasional ideological tensions discussed earlier have never deeply divided the group. They stay active on the campaigns despite the burden of time required because of their southern African friends and because of each other.

Two members who seem to bear a heavier burden than anyone else are the Beemans. They stay in close touch with Bullard's staff, monitor every meeting or hearing connected with the bills, keep SALC records, oversee the film program and literature table, move the portable displays from one public gathering to the next, and keep the other SALC members informed on current events. The Beemans have been crucial in holding the organization together.

One resource that the campaigns have not had but have not needed is money. SALC's budget has been about $1,500 a year raised primarily through members' contributions, literature sales, and grants for films and speakers from the MSU student government. They also have never had a staff person of their own although Eldersveld functioned in a staff capacity for the campaigns. In addition, SALC has no office but is a member organization of the Peace Education Center, a coalition of activists groups in East Lansing. Through the Peace Center, SALC members get access to office machines, file cabinets, and other necessary equipment. There is a staff person for the Peace Center, and at times she has served as a communication node for SALC members as well as outside supporters. Thus the campaigns have been run with few resources, little office space, and no full-time staff.

An important source of strength in the campaigns is their high level of expertise and sound research. Since the legislative divestment efforts have been based primarily in universities with Africanists participating in the various activist groups,[10] the campaigns never lacked for up to date information and thoughtful analysis on southern Africa, the potential impact of sanctions and the current strategies of the anti-apartheid movement in the United States and worldwide. Furthermore, these people knew where to get outside experts both to validate their arguments and to supply expertise they could not provide.

Some of the anti-apartheid activists/experts that have visited to speak and press for divestment are: Dumisani Kumalo, a South African journalist mentioned in connection with the Connecticut campaign and currently working with the ACOA; Gail Hovey, formerly the Research Director of ACOA; Tim Smith, the head of the ICCR; and Prexy Nesbitt, former research secretary of the World Council of Churches Program to Combat Racism. In addition, representatives of the resistance movements involved in guerilla war in southern Africa have been hosted in Michigan and have spoken to legislators. Proponents report that these members of the ANC and SWAPO have been especially important in securing black legislators' active backing of the bills.

Members of SALC and Eldersveld have attempted to build their case by calling on financial experts to provide information about the feasibility and prudence of divestment. These experts documented the financial success of portfolios that use social responsibility criteria and supplied important evidence on the potential profitability of divestment. Although they performed no analysis on the specific impact of divestment on Michigan funds, the four experts used by proponents agreed that a portfolio excluding South Africa-related companies need not sacrifice diversification, safety, or potential growth. For still more evidence in this matter, activists pointed to the profits made by MSU in the portfolio reorganization that accompanied its divestment.

The extent of South Africa-related stock held by the various Michigan institutions affected by the anti-apartheid legislation was never fully researched until the Treasury Department did an analysis in 1983. And there was no definitive analysis of the amounts involved in educational institutions' potential divestment. This is difficult and tedious research to conduct, and although several attempts were made by Eldersveld to investigate the total amount of monies at stake, proponents did not take time out from other pressing matters to accomplish the task. Their case could have been strengthened, however, if they had been able to speak authoritatively on the actual impact of the bills.

Nevertheless, the sophistication and depth of expertise that has been marshalled for these campaigns has helped to establish an asset important to campaign strength that is often very difficult for activists to achieve: legitimacy. At least two strong opponents of the divestment efforts view the proponents as "leftist intelligensia aimed at producing revolution," naming Bullard specifically as a "card carrying socialist." But other opponents, observers, and supporters give them much higher marks for credibility of argument and cleverness of strategy. Their access to impressive outside experts as well as their own qualifications as experts has been noteworthy to a number of legislators.

Another source of legitimacy for these efforts is that proponents constantly reminded legislators of the good company they would keep by passing the legislation. Lists of other institutions around the country that have divestment policies or that have advocated sanctions were circulated to legislators to assure them that they would be joining an important mainstream movement for racial justice already begun by others whom they respect. Among these others are, of course, several in Michigan: MSU, the East Lansing city council, and the legislature itself, which passed a resolution in 1978 supporting sanctions against South Africa. In addition, the recent evidence that trade with African countries will be enhanced because of divestment laws gives the pension campaign added legitimacy.

Eldersveld reported that campaign legitimacy was also aided enormously when Zimbabwe gained independence. When black majority rule came through a popular election of those who had led the guerilla movement against a white minority government, weight was added to proponents' claims that the long-term interest of the United States lay in supporting blacks' struggles for an end to apartheid in South Africa. If the U.S. government was not going to demonstrate solidarity with South African blacks in their conflict with the apartheid regime, they argue, then other institutions in the country must show support for blacks, that is, show that the State Department and others officiating over foreign policy are not representing the will of the American people. Zimbabwean independence also helped to convince some that the black governments in southern Africa are more capable of building multiracial societies based on equality than were white governments.

One area of declining strength for the state's divestment campaign is membership and leadership in SALC. Student participation may have been hampered at points by the division between experts and nonexperts in the group. SALC old-timers speculate that the occasional domination of experts in SALC meetings was intimidating and discouraging to students, causing some to drop out of the group. There may be other important explanations of the decline in student participation (such as decline in student activism generally), but there are also fewer active nonstudent members now than in previous years. Shifts in personal priorities, other demands on members' time, moves to other locations, and for some, little interest in working on legislative campaigns seem to be some of the reasons for this trend. Although the core group is likely to remain highly committed in the future, the decline of their organizational base may prove troublesome as they continue pressing for passage of the pension fund bill. There are too many tasks for too few people who are already too busy.

In summary, proponents in Michigan built strong campaigns across more than four years despite some problems along the way. This strength came from a combination of factors described here including the number of public endorsements collected by proponents; the level of personal commitment and perseverance by a core group of activists;

fairly strong backing in the legislature, including Bullard's willingness to devote significant amounts of staff time to the campaigns and endorsement by the Black Caucus; sophisticated and in-depth research and expertise on the issue; and the legitimacy built up by proponents for themselves and for the issue.

In addition to a strong campaign, at several points there were important tactical choices made that aided the campaigns a great deal. After consolidation of all the 1978–79 bills into three measures specifically targeted at South Africa (instead of the general issue of human rights), a useful overarching strategy was to push for passage of only one piece of legislation at a time and to start with what seemed to be the easiest measure, the banking bill. This served to focus proponents' energies and prevented the development of firm unity among opponents in banking, other businesses, the State Treasury, and retirees groups. In addition, the passage of the banking bill has been used to build legitimacy and momentum for the educational institution funds bill.

Another tactic that proved helpful in recruiting further legislative support and lending credibility to the anti-racist character of the bills was Bullard's recruitment of Smith to sponsor the banking bill and the pension bill. Furthermore, Bullard and Smith proved themselves capable of negotiating amendment compromises that neutralized the opposition. This was done with both the Michigan Bankers' Association and with Representative Cropsey and may be possible with Treasurer Bowman. Both legislators also demonstrated good tactics by attempting to have their bills brought onto the floor of the House or the Senate at a time when chances for passage were good and by attempting to get favorable committee assignments in both houses.

Lastly, a significant strategy was the orchestration of help outside the legislature. When Bullard or Eldersveld indicated that hearings or floor votes were approaching, activists, especially SALC, would rally supporters, provide good witnesses to testify, and lobby intensively. This proved to be a productive division of labor that demonstrates a symbiotic relationship between the activists and the legislators/legislative staff.

Reaction and Opposition

As was stated earlier, although there have been significant pockets of opposition, coalitions among opponents developed late in the campaign on the educational institutions bill and never at all with the banking bill. This has meant that the greatest amount of pressure on the legislature has come primarily from one direction, those favoring passage. One might expect significant opposition from the business community but so far relatively little has materialized. Even the MBA did not demonstrate entrenched opposition to the banking bill. Believing that it would inevitably pass, the MBA lobbyist chose instead to seek an amendment that would dampen its impact. At first many business opponents believed that they would be seen as racist or pro-apartheid if they vigorously resisted this package of legislation. When opposition statements were made they were carefully worded. For example, the Michigan Manufacturer's Association formally opposed the bills on the grounds that they raised difficult legal and constitutional problems regarding jurisdiction in foreign policy. Lobbyists from large corporations such as Ford and GM were active in opposing the education bill in its final stages and, together with others such as Dow Chemical, they will be significant obstacles to passage of the pension fund bill.

Active opposition from the executive branch has been limited to the Treasury Department. In contrast, both the Civil Rights and Education Departments have supported the legislation—the Civil Rights Department all three bills and the Education Department the education measure. Even the Commerce Department appears to support the pension fund bill. Treasury did not take a position on the education bill because the staff did not believe it to be in their jurisdiction, but their opposition to the banking bill remained significant until two events occurred—the amendment negotiated to limit the scope of the legislation, and pressure on the treasurer to support the measure from the legislative Black Caucus. The staff are not likely to be convinced easily to say yes to the pension fund bill unless Bowman strikes an agreeable compromise. There is a higher probability that they will help mobilize strong forces against it, especially if some agreement is not reached. They are in contact with the Retirement Coordinating Council that early on urged defeat of the bill and generated the beginnings of an opposition campaign among their constituents. Treasury staff have also maintained close consultation with the Senior Citizens and Retirement Committee of the House and its chair, Spaniola. The committee is not likely to approve the bill with strong opposition from both the retirees and Treasury.

Other significant legislative opposition to the banking and education measures came from conservative Republican legislators like Alan Cropsey, who on principle reject the legislation for several reasons. They believe that the state ought not be involved in making laws on foreign policy issues; they assert that South Africa should not be singled out as a violator of human rights because they think the bigger threat to human rights is Communism; and they generally do not believe the state should be attempting to place moral restrictions on businesses. Theses legislators tried several tactics to defeat the banking and education bills, which usually came in the form of amendments that would be so obnoxious to supporters that, if passed, the supporters would abandon their efforts. There were a core of opponents consistently voting against these bills, especially in the House.

Some legislators report that on the whole, seeing little significant vocal and organized opposition, many of their colleagues were willing to "give" these bills to "the liberals and the blacks." That is, these legislators would not obstruct legislation to which they had no principled objections if the passage was an important achievement for the sponsors and if there was not a great deal of pressure to oppose it. Now that two of the three bills have passed, many legislators may feel that they and the state have done enough on this issue and that Bullard and Smith have used up their credit in this regard. This would make passage of the pension bill more difficult, and the proponents' original strategy of taking the measures one by one may begin to backfire.

Among other groups, the University of Michigan, together with the car companies, had opposed the education bill. Although the university now is challenging the law in court, it did not organize a significant visible counter campaign early enough to defeat the bill in the legislature. With regard to the pension fund bill, the long-standing opposition of the nongovernmental Retirement Coordinating Committee is highly visible and capable of mobilizing large numbers of retirees against the measure. Proponents have given presentations on divestment to members of the RCC, but unless the committee can be convinced not to oppose the measure, they could be a significant obstacle to passage.

In other arenas of opposition, Michigan has been targeted by people outside the state who want to take momentum away from divestment campaigns all over the country. The most obvious of these are South Africans themselves. Their public appearances probably do not represent the entirety of their efforts in lobbying and speaking against the legislation, but these appearances alone are substantial and noteworthy. Not all of South African activity in Mich-

igan has been targeted at the divestment bills in the legislature, however. The long-term activity appears to be
directed at accomplishing several goals: educating community leaders and elites that South Africa is an important ally
of the West; generally building a favorable image of South
Africa through inundating the media and school system with
public relations materials for instructional and other purposes; combating the divestment movement generally in any
way possible; winning friends among Michigan community
leaders through a variety of means, including cooperation
with tourist agencies to subsidize friendly tours to South
Africa; and campaigning against Representative Howard
Wolpe so that he will not be returned to Congress to continue anti-apartheid work there.

To accomplish these goals the South African Consulate
in Chicago, the embassy in Washington, and the South
African Foundation have employed a wide range of tactics.
As described earlier, two men have been sent to testify at
hearings. De Kieffer, an American lawyer retained by the
embassy, and at one point a member of the Reagan administration, testified in the East Lansing City Council hearing
in March 1978, and Pienaar from the South Africa Foundation testified in the joint hearings in the House in June
1980. In addition, legislators have received mailings of
materials promoting South Africa, and a lobbyist, Grobler,
from the Chicago consulate, visits Spaniola to discuss the
legislation, especially the pension bill, about twice a year.

To create better relations between the United States
and South Africa, Leon Weaver, a retired professor of
criminal justice at MSU, has given numerous pro-South
Africa testimonies in various arenas, sought to arrange
travel tours to South Africa, and arranged for South Africans to speak in various forums in the state. There apparently are small, formal friendship associations for South
Africa in Grand Rapids and other Michigan cities out of
which Americans and South Africans give speeches and
presentations to clubs, schools and any other willing audiences. South Africa Foundation, embassy and consulate
representatives have spoken in Kalamazoo, Battle Creek,
Grand Rapids, and Lansing, mainly to Rotary and Kiwanis
Clubs.

Two of the more extravagant and bold South African
attempts to win influence have been the use of John McGoff
to buy media in the United States, and the campaign to
unseat Howard Wolpe. In the first incident, as described
in Chapter II, McGoff, a publisher and resident of Williams-
town, Michigan, was utilized by the South Africa Department of Information to try to buy U.S. newspapers. At

one point he owned a printing firm in South Africa, but he no longer travels there because he has been accused of pocketing over $6 million of South African government funds that were intended for purchasing newspapers. In the past McGoff was involved in promoting South Africa in Michigan in various arenas including universities, the East Lansing city council, and in private settings. He also arranged low-cost tours for Michigan influentials to visit South Africa. His commercial operation, Global Communications, Inc., controlled several newspapers in the state and was a major partner in International-Television News (UPI-ITN) in London.

A less well-documented South African project was to unseat Howard Wolpe. Wolpe is now the chair of the African Subcommittee of the U.S. House Committee on Foreign Affairs and has visited South Africa in this capacity. He has been the most frequent and consistent governmental critic of current U.S. policies of constructive engagement in South Africa, and he is one of the most active congressional subcommittee chairs on international issues. He has been attacked extensively by the *Namibia News Gazette,* a South African newspaper published about six times a year in Washington by the U.S.-South West Africa Trade and Cultural Council, Inc., with wide distribution to academics, politicians, business people, and others. Pienaar gave speeches in Michigan attacking Wolpe during his campaign for reelection, and there were purported to be well-known friends of South Africa including McGoff and his family managing and helping to finance the campaign of Wolpe's opponent, Richard Milliman. Milliman was at one time the editor of a McGoff newspaper in a small town (Washington Office on Africa, Autumn 1982).

South Africa's extensive activities in Michigan are in part likely to be the results of having both close friends and determined opponents in that state. People in Michigan on both sides have gained national prominence in either the pro-apartheid or anti-apartheid forces. That the pro-apartheid forces have not been highly organized against all the divestment legislation in Michigan is interesting, but some of them clearly have attempted to establish a climate of opinion against all sanctions efforts across the state. As the fight over the pension fund bill gets heated, the heavy South African presence may become even more visible. However, since there are so many state legislatures across the country considering divestment legislation, and since a major South African ally in Michigan (McGoff) received a great deal of negative publicity, South African divestment opponents may not have the resources to continue to devote so much attention to Michigan.

Another significant arena of reaction that can harm or help the Michigan campaigns is the media. The issue of divestment in various arenas sporadically has captured the attention of newspapers in the state, especially those in Lansing and Ann Arbor and the campus newspapers at MSU and the University of Michigan. For example, in 1976 and 1977, no fewer than 16 articles or editorials appeared on the East Lansing city council's consideration of the selective purchasing resolution. Of these, 11 articles appeared in the MSU paper, the *State News*. From 1978 to May 1984, no fewer than 100 articles or editorials appeared in newspapers across the state on the legislative divestment campaigns. Five of these articles were of national significance.[11] Twenty-nine of the 100 articles appeared in campus newspapers, whereas the remainder were found in prominent Michigan papers such as the *State Journal,* the *Detroit Free Press,* and the *Michigan Chronicle* or in smaller town papers such as the *Ann Arbor News, Kalamazoo Gazette* and *Muskegon Examiner.* The articles and editorials mentioned here as illustration are probably not all of the newsprint items generated by the campaigns. These articles and editorials demonstrate that the legislative divestment campaigns were getting attention, but we cannot surmise from this evidence alone how extensive the media attention was or whether it helped or harmed the campaigns. Bullard's staff were confident of the positive contribution media coverage could make because they were diligent in notifying newspapers and radio stations of any events (for example, hearings, guest speakers) related to the divestment legislation; but SALC members were quite displeased at some of the coverage, especially that on television.

The factors contributing to the success of the Michigan divestment legislative campaigns are summarized in Table 5–6. They are: a climate of opinion in favor of the legislation created by strong campaigns with high degrees of credibility and legitimacy organized by persistent and committed activists and legislative supporters; important compromises in the provisions of the banking and education bills; tactical decisions regarding serial passage of the bills; withdrawal of the little opposition that existed for the banking bill and insufficient opposition to the education bill; and legislative willingness to accept proponents' pressures to pass these two bills, and legislative unwillingness to be charged with insensitivity to racial-justice issues. The campaigns achieved their success despite fairly radical goals with regard to the comprehensiveness of divestment

TABLE 5-6. Summary of Variables Significant in the Passage of Divestment Legislation in Michigan

---

Inner Environment

1. Goals: comprehensive and requiring a great deal of change
2. Tactics and Strategies:
   a. extensive and expert testimony
   b. pushing for passage of the bills one at a time, beginning with the easiest to pass and ending with the most difficult
   c. negotiations with potential opponents on amendments
   d. persistent lobbying as well as phone and mail contact with legislators
3. Strength:
   a. A significant number of endorsements and supporters inside and outside the legislature
      (1) continual educational efforts
      (2) use of personal and professional networks and contacts
      (3) use of support organizations' newsletters for updates on campaign progress; mailings of educational packets and pamphlets
      (4) assignment by Bullard of significant staff time to the promotion of the legislation
      (5) consistent support among a substantial core group of legislators, including the black caucus
      (6) Bullard's leadership in steering the measures through the legislature
      (7) experts on southern Africa and divestment in leadership in the activist organizations
      (8) single issue focus of the campaign
      (9) legitimacy established and maintained for the activists and for the campaigns
   b. highly committed, expert, and skilled campaign leadership

Outer Environment

4. Reaction and Opposition:
   a. Legislature: receptive to being convinced to pass banking and education bills; more resistance likely to the pension bill
   b. Department of Treasury: active opposition to pension bill; unopposed to banking bill as amended (after initial opposition); no activity on education bill
   c. Department of Civil Rights: supportive of all three measures
   d. Department of Commerce: inactive opposition to divestment concept; charged with implementing the banking bill
   e. Department of Education: supportive of educational bill
   f. Business: bankers willing to compromise; others expressing opposition but exhibiting relatively little activity
   g. Media: some attention

216

TABLE 5-6. Continued

---

      h. South African Embassy, Consulate, and Foundation: significant
          and visible opposition expressed through lobbying and testimony
      i. Retirement organizations: mobilizing opposition to the pension
          bill
5. Target: large and accessible
6. Time: an accumulation of four years' work; heaviest thrust of
    activities was two years after the first bill's introduction
7. Mixed (some positive or supportive factors, some negative)
    political environment in the state

---

sought in three arenas and a mixed political environment in the state. Certainly the proponents' activities alone were not sufficient to secure the outcomes they desire; but without them, or even with the legislators and activists acting separately, the two measures that received approval would not have passed. Whether or not the same combination of factors will succeed in achieving a receptive hearing for and passage of the pension bill remains to be seen. The length of time the state has been considering the issue, together with other factors, may begin to work against the last divestment measure.

What remains for this analysis, however, is to discuss the impact of the campaign outcomes.

IMPACT AND EFFECTIVENESS

As in the Connecticut case study all of the detectable intended and unintended consequences of these campaigns will be examined in a goals-based evaluation.

The goals and theory of action have already been discussed and assessed for their significance in the campaigns' effectiveness. Important at this point is a calculation of what the campaign consequences were. Table 5-7 lists the outcomes and categorized them according to their principal recipients. Table 5-8 contrasts these outcomes with proponents' goals—the achieved, partially achieved, and unachieved goals. The table also lists unintended consequences.

An examination of Table 5-8 demonstrates that at least seven of the twenty-two activists' goals have been fully achieved resulting in some important degree of success for the Michigan campaigns. Proponents have effectively: taken

TABLE 5-7. Partial List of Outcomes in Michigan

For the State Government of Michigan

Legislature

1. The educational institution funds bill with the USSR amendment passed both houses in 1982 and became law.
2. The amended banking bill passed both houses in 1980 and became law.
3. The legislature took a principled stand by passing the banking bill and the educational institution funds bill.
4. Legislators have hosted, interacted with, and publicly commended representatives of the southern Africa resistance movements (for example, the ANC and SWAPO).
5. At least one legislator, Spaniola, has been visited by South African lobbyists; several legislators have received promotional materials from South African interests.
6. Smith and Bullard have filed an amicus curiae brief on behalf of the Attorney General in the suit brought by the University of Michigan.

Executive

7. Different departments advocated different positions on the divestment bills.
8. The Department of Treasury staff have spent time analyzing the implications of the banking and pension bills; also contributed to the negotiated amendment to the banking bill; may negotiate compromises on the pension bill.
9. The Department of Commerce Financial Institutions Bureau staff have spent time (a) notifying depository banks of the requirements of Public Act No. 325, (b) soliciting affadavits re their compliance, and (c) obtaining information from the U.S. Department of Commerce re U.S. corporations' subsidiaries or affiliates located in South Africa.
10. The Department of Commerce and Governor Blanchard are using the divestment laws as indicators of the state's sensitivity to racial injustice worldwide in their promotion of trade between Michigan and African nations.
11. Department of Civil Rights staff have spent time monitoring and supporting the legislation.
12. Governor Milliken signed Public Act No. 325 into law and hosted a public signing ceremony with Nigerian officials present; after some delay he also signed Public Act 512 into law.
13. The Attorney General is spending significant time and resources defending the state against a suit by the University of Michigan on Public Act 512.
14. State Treasurer Bowman abstained in a vote on a resolution by the National Association of State Treasurers recommending a Sullivan Principles approach to pension fund divestment.

TABLE 5-7.   Continued

_____

For Business

15. Depository banks were required to submit affadavits re their compliance with PA 325; banks' staff time and money were spent to comply with the law.
16. As far as is known, no banks were disqualified as depositories.
17. The Michigan Bankers Association lobbyist negotiated the amendment to the banking bill.
18. Staff from the National Bank of Detroit spent some time on the banking bill considering its implications, testifying, and negotiating the amendment.
19. Business lobbyists, especially from car manufacturers, have spent time opposing all the measures.
20. All the state universities except the University of Michigan have sold all their stocks in corporations with subsidiaries in South Africa.

For the U.S. Government

21. The U.S. State Department, Department of Commerce, and the Africa subcommittees' staff in the House and the Senate are aware of the state's actions.
22. State Department officials spoke out against the Michigan educational institutions divestment bill suggesting that the legislature institute a Sullivan Principle-style measure instead.
23. Congressman Howard Wolpe encouraged Governor Milliken to sign the educational institution funds bill and encouraged the University of Michigan to divest all its South Africa-related securities.

For South Africa

24. The South African Embassy and UN Mission are aware of the state's actions.
25. Representatives of the South American government and the South Africa Foundation have spent time testifying and lobbying against the bills in the legislature; they have sent legislators and others pro-South Africa materials.
26. Representatives of the resistance movements (that is, ANC and SWAPO) have spent time giving speeches and lobbying in support of the bills; they have indicated their approval of the state's actions.
27. The South African press has reported on Michigan divestment actions.

For the National Anti-Apartheid Movement

28. Smith and Bullard shared information on the Michigan legislative divestment campaigns with other anti-apartheid activists at a June 1981 conference in New York City and an April 1983 conference in Boston.

TABLE 5-7. Continued

---

29. Smith made a presentation at the National Conference of Black Legislators in Baltimore, October 1981, to alert black legislators around the nation to the issue.

30. Legitimacy for the movement is gained due to sanctions policies being adopted by two city councils, serveral universities, and the state legislature in Michigan.

31. There is an accumulation of experience on how to conduct legislative divestment campaigns.

32. Local and national groups across the country have taken a great deal of interest in the Michigan campaigns.

For the Michigan Divestment Proponents

33. From 1977 to 1984, SALC and other anti-apartheid groups have spearheaded campaigns in three arenas: (1) universities; (2) East Lansing and Grand Rapids City Councils; and (3) the state legislature.

34. The activists are perceived to be pressing for a principled cause.

35. The activists gained a large number of endorsements and support for their campaigns.

36. Through the entire process the activists have gained credibility and legitimacy for their organizations, their leaders, and their issue.

37. The Prime Minister of Zimbabwe and the British Anti-Apartheid Movement sent congratulations to the activists on passage of the educational institution funds bill.

38. The Zimbabwean press reported on passage of the educational institution funds bill.

Other

39. A Nigerian governmental delegation expressed approval of the state's passage of the banking bill and urged Michigan officials to continue their anti-apartheid efforts.

---

a principled stand against racism, apartheid, and U.S. corporate involvement in apartheid (goal 1); demonstrated solidarity with those from Southern Africa in resistance to apartheid (goal 3); sent a message to the South African government of their commitment to sanctions (goal 4); demonstrated disagreement with U.S. governmental foreign policy (goal 5); achieved a principled stand against apartheid and against U.S. foreign policy toward South Africa by the state (goals 8 and 12); and, together with the state, made a contribution to sanctions efforts to the

TABLE 5-8. An Evaluation of Goals and Outcomes in Michigan

| Goals | Outcomes | | |
	Achieved	Partially Achieved	Unachieved
1	33, 34		
2		15, 17, 18, 19, 20	
3	26, 37, 38	1, 2, 3	
4	24, 25, 27		
5	21, 22		
6		- - - - -	
7		1, 2, 9, 12, 13	
8	3		
9		(see Chapters 2 and 6)	
10		(see Chapters 2 and 6)	
11		(see Chapters 2 and 6)	
12	21, 22		
13		(see Chapters 2 and 6)	
14		10, 30 (and see Chapters 2 and 6)	
15		(unknown)	
16		3, 4, 12	
17		(unknown)	
18	1, 2, 3, 4, 6, 9, 11, 12, 13, 23, 28, 29, 30, 31, 32, 33, 34, 35, 36, 37, 38, 39		
19		35?	
20		35?	
21 & 22		(see Chapters 2 and 6)	

Outcomes unrelated to goals: 5, 7, 8, 14, 16

worldwide anti-apartheid movement (goal 18). Five of the goals have been partially achieved, whereas the achievement of another six is difficult to assess in isolation from an examination of the national anti-apartheid divestment movement. The degree of success in meeting three of the goals is unknown.

The proponents are assessed as having only partially succeeded in sending a message to corporate executives that their investments in South Africa are perceived to be immoral (goal 2) because it is not clear to what extent the policymakers in Michigan businesses invested in South

Africa have been forced to pay attention to the issue. Their lobbyists and other staff have had to contend with the issue, and if the pension bill gains enough support for passage, corporate executives will become significantly more aware that a moral statement is being made. Until that time, however, it is possible that some policymakers are not fully cognizant of the attempts to apply moral pressure against them.

The goal of expressing solidarity with those from southern Africa in resistance to apartheid (goal 3) is listed both as achieved—because of three outcomes—and partially achieved because of three others. Because representatives of resistance movements, Prime Minister Mugabe and the Zimbabwean press have expressed their approval and appreciation for the proponents' legislative accomplishments, the goal is considered fulfilled in one respect. But because the state has not yet passed all the legislation in the form that proponents most desired, it is considered as yet only partially achieve. For this latter reason, goal 7, getting the legislation passed, and goal 16, having the state demonstrate solidarity with those from southern Africa in resistance to apartheid, are also considered partially accomplished.

Through their campaigns, several proponents wanted to politicize people in Michigan to have anti-corporate and anti-capitalist views. Certainly more people are aware of U.S. corporations' involvement in South Africa as a result of the campaigns, but *how many* more is unclear because no data exists to assess this. And, although the awareness level may have been increased, this does not mean that it will be accompanied by anti-corporate or anti-capitalist points of view. Because the campaigns have been quite narrowly focused on South Africa, because they have not been mass campaigns, and because this goal has not been significant for most campaign participants, it is likely that this goal of politicization (or even widespread education) has probably not achieved any notable measure of success.

The impact of these campaigns on the investment policies of U.S. corporations and on policy making in the U.S. and South African governments (goals 9, 10, 11, 13, 14, 15, 17, 21, and 22) have been discussed to some extent in chapter II and will be discussed again in the next chapter. In summary, however, we can state that, despite some difficulties in their years of campaigning for divestment legislation, the Michigan proponents have succeeded in accomplishing a significant amount of what they set out to do. More of their impact and a comparison between their efforts and those of the divestment proponents in Connecticut will be examined next in the concluding chapter of this study.

NOTES

1. The colleges and universities that have had divestment campaigns are: Kalamazoo, University of Michigan, Michigan State University, Western Michigan University, Eastern Michigan University, Wayne State University, Central Michigan University and Oakland University (Rochester). The ones with divestment policies are: University of Michigan, MSU, and Eastern Michigan University.

2. Warren Day is now the representative for Oxfam in Harare, Zimbabwe, and Carol Thompson is an Associate Professor of Political Science at the University of Southern California. Day and some of the others who became active in SALC had participated in the work of the Southern Africa Committee of the University Christian Movement. The University Christian Movement was a part of the first bank campaign described in Chapter I.

3. Pension funds affected would be those of municipal employees, judges, probate judges, Michigan legislators, state employees, public school employees, and fire and police workers.

4. There is some disagreement as to which funds would be covered by the substitute bill 4838 and subsequent pension bills (4315). A House Legislative Analysis claims that retirement funds included under the 1980 version of 4838 would be those for state police, state employees, public school employees, probate judges, and judges (notably leaving out the state legislators). Officials in the Treasury Department and the Retirement Bureau in the Department of Management and Budget assume that all public employee retirement systems are affected at state, country, and local levels.

5. These banks are: Bank of Lansing, First Citizens Bank of Troy, City National Bank of Detroit, National Bank of Rochester, and Union National Bank and Trust of Grand Rapids (Michigan House Legislative Analysis 1980).

6. A Corporate Data Exchange study (Klein 1978) also lists the City National Bank as extending $50 million in credit to the South African Ministry of Finance from 1972 to 1975.

7. All bills receive three readings in the Michigan legislature before they are allowed to pass. At each of the first two readings the bill must be passed temporarily to reach the next reading.

8. The funds for which Treasury has fudiciary re-

sponsibility are: The Legislative Retirement Fund, Michigan State Police Pension Fund, State Employees Retirement Funds, Probate Judges Retirement Fund, Judges Retirement Fund, and Public School Retirement Funds.

9. A shortcoming of this goals list is that it does not include expressions of goals by activists in Michigan anti-apartheid organizations other than SALC. Attempts to interview activists in these other organizations were not successful.

10. Africanists participating in the anti-apartheid campaigns in universities other than MSU are: Len Suransky, Political Science, University of Michigan; Joel Samoff, formerly Political Science, University of Michigan; Gayle H. Partmann, African Studies, Oakland University; James D. Graham, History, Oakland University; Vincent Khapoya, History, Oakland University. Other academics: Don Cooney, Social Work, Western Michigan University.

11. There were articles in the following: three in the *New York Times;* two carried by UPI; five carried by Associated Press; and one in the *Chronicle of Higher Education.*

6

Conclusions

This study began in part as an attempt to describe system-atically and to discern the significance of the anti-apartheid movement in the United States. We will continue that effort through comparing the case studies presented in the previ-ous two chapters and by discussing some general reflections on divestment campaigns, the anti-apartheid movement, and the process of evaluating activism. The two case studies were structured to address two central questions: How are campaign outcomes achieved? and, What impact do they have? These same questions will provide the basic struc-ture for the comparison between cases in this chapter as well.

COMPARISON OF THE CAMPAIGN PROCESSES

Goals and Theory of Action

If we compare what the proponents wanted to achieve in both states, we see important differences and similarities. The two divestment groups wanted publicly to demonstrate their own opposition to apartheid and their prosanctions stance, and they also wanted their state governments to establish divestment policies. By pressing for and achiev-ing such policies, proponents believe that they are making a significant contribution to worldwide sanctions efforts. Their contribution provides further public legitimation of demands for the economic isolation of apartheid.

The goals diverge, however, over what precise steps the proponents want the state to take. In some respects in Michigan the aims were much more ambitious, in that legislation was introduced to cover three separate arenas of the state's economic ties to South Africa: bank loans and deposits of state funds; the investment portfolios of university endowments; and the investment portfolios of pension funds. Proponents began with the easiest of these legislative goals and have yet to press with full mobilization for the most difficult. In contrast, the Connecticut proponents had a singular legislative goal, although it, too, was a difficult one: total divestment of state pension funds. Therefore, both campaigns sought to achieve fairly dramatic changes in policies; but with this important difference in goals, the two sets of divestment campaigns are problematic to compare in terms of their achievements.

Another important dissimilarity in the goals of the two groups is the degree to which the groups wanted to raise public consciousness about the structure and behavior of corporations and the linkages between corporate collusion with racism in South Africa and the United States. Having an important base in labor union activities, the Connecticut activists were more clear in their public expressions of anti-corporate sentiment than were the Michigan activists. In fact, those in Michigan who are most concerned that SALC campaigns reflect an anti-corporate perspective are less active than others in the legislative campaign. The group now is much more focused than it was in earlier years on the issue of racial oppression in South Africa and not on the issue of the relationship between capitalism and racism generally. Interesting to note, however, is that the principal legislative sponsors in both cases are somewhat out of step with the ideological expressions of the activist leaders. Dyson in Connecticut is not publicly identified as a socialist or as being anti-corporate in his beliefs, whereas Bullard is. As was stated in both case studies, the question of ideological identification has been a bit contentious in both sets of campaigns with each group resolving it in a different fashion. The Connecticut group suppressed the question for pragmatic reasons. The Michigan group allowed those who wanted to work on any particular campaign to do so, and those who did not want to work were not required to do so in order to remain members of SALC. This laissez faire style meant that those who gave the most energies to the legislative campaigns were the same ones who were not interested in promoting anti-corporate beliefs and attitudes.

The theories of action, and extension of goals, also

have interesting variation in the two cases. Connecticut activists believe more strongly than do the Michigan proponents that there is a relationship between their efforts and an outcome of black majority rule in South Africa. They have a great deal of faith in the theory of action outlined in the Connecticut case study. That is, they see themselves contributing to world-wide sanctions activities that, if successful, will aid in ending apartheid and in bringing about a nonracial political system that reflects the will of the majority. The Michigan activists express more skepticism about their work. Most are reluctant to predict that sanctions or corporate withdrawal would eventuate in majority rule. They are convinced, however, that U.S. and other Western corporate investments, trade, and loans buttress apartheid and must be removed. As one activist put it, they know that economic ties help sustain white minority rule. Therefore, the ties must be severed. They are not sure that breaking the relationship or imposing sanctions will bring about black majority rule, but they are confident that maintaining the relationship as it is cannot help, and indeed obstructs, majority rule. Thus, some of the Michigan activists express their theory of action in terms of removing obstacles to change rather than contributing a significant international factor to cause change.

In the aggregate, the goals sought were quite ambitious, especially with regard to changes desired in public policy. According to social movement and interest group literature, goals attempting substantial change are often harder to achieve. Therefore, partial achievement of their goals is for both groups a significant accomplishment, In both states there was an interactive element, as suggested by Freeman (1975) and others, between the reforms achieved and the fairly radical goals sought. The activists did not really get the substance of the legislation they originally wanted, that is, that the states undertake full divestment. Nevertheless, by keeping the vision and possibility of full divestment constantly in mind, the activists achieved reformist positions that went far beyond token gestures to substantial changes in public policy.

Tactics, Strategy, Strength, and Opposition

A significant difference in tactics and strategies of the two sets of campaigns is the amount of publicity sought and the amount of public education attempted. For example, in order to get endorsements, the Connecticut activists did a great deal of public speaking at other organizations' meetings, hosted receptions for out of state visitors, and organized cultural and educational events for large numbers of people. They also promoted their campaign in weekly columns of a newspaper targeted at black audiences, wrote occasional editorials for other newspapers, held rallies at the capitol, and requested interviews with newspaper reporters. Their intention was to be highly visible.

The Michigan group was much more low key. Although they got about the same number of endorsements as the Connecticut group did (Tables 4–2 and 5–2), the endorsement list consists mainly of persons rather than organizations. This reflects a difference in style, in that Michigan activists wanted simply to demonstrate to legislators that important community leaders across the state supported their efforts. The Connecticut group wanted to show the same thing as well as have the organizations themselves become aware and active on the issue. Thus Connecticut activists took their educational goals more seriously and spent a great deal of time pursuing them. However, it is doubtful that the endorsement of an organization rather than a leader would make a great deal of difference to legislators in either state. That is, legislators knew in both cases that there was a climate of opinion favoring divestment within certain politically aware constituencies, and they had to respond to it.

Despite the difference in degree of publicity and public endorsement sought and achieved, the Connecticut campaign was not a mobilization campaign in the sense that large numbers of people were brought into the political process. And, in neither state was a massive mobilization of popular support necessary for the adoption of the legislation. Indeed, as suggested by those who study interest groups (Cohen 1973; Kegley and Wittkopf 1982, 262), had a massive and highly visible mobilization occurred early in the process, it may have alarmed opponents and alerted them to the need to pay more attention to the bills and to the creation of counterproposals to divestment. This may indicate a significant difference in tactics needed for interest groups versus those needed by social movements, with high visibility more desirable for the latter since larger numbers of adherents are involved. In the two cases here, the CAAC would have liked to be the core organization that stimulated a wider social movement in the state, whereas the Michigan activists intended their work to be that of a lobby particularly in their legislative activity.

The trade-off in not having mobilization campaigns within the context of a social movement is that educational efforts reach fewer people. Leaders of community organizations and governmental officials in the two states may be well aware of the apartheid and divestment issues as a result of the activists' campaigns, and that is a significant achievement. But there is not likely to have been a substantial increase of awareness and education among the public in general. In this regard, the campaigns resembled lobbies more than social movements, and the activists have probably not achieved their educational goals to the degree that they desire.

Again like lobbies, the campaigns in Michigan and Connecticut were led and run by small groups of about six people. However, unlike most lobbies and contrary to conventional wisdom in interest group literature (Hughes 1978, 184, 211) very little money was needed for conducting the campaigns. They were financially inexpensive but very costly in terms of proponents' commitment of time. In both cases the activists afforded the time and energy required because of their high personal commitment to the issue. Personal commitment and persistence are a set of variables understudied with regard to group effectiveness in interest group and social movement scholarship.

An important difference between the Connecticut and Michigan experiences was in who among the proponents managed the ongoing decisions regarding campaign strategy and tactics—for example, decisions about when and how to press for floor votes, the acceptability of language for amendments, the organization of testimony at hearings. In Michigan these kinds of decisions were made primarily by Bullard and Eldersveld within the legislature but in consultation with activists, whereas in Connecticut strategy was basically directed by the activists with some consultation of legislative allies. Thus the activists in Connecticut retained more control over the campaigns than did those in Michigan. This is not to say that Connecticut activists did not have well-established and fruitful working relations with legislative sponsors, but they were less dependent than were their Michigan counterparts on these sponsors for making crucial decisions about the management of the campaign.

This difference is due in part to the fact that the legislative sponsors in Connecticut do not have any aides or professional staff. There is no one in Connecticut anti-apartheid circles with a position comparable to that of Eldersveld's in the Michigan legislature. Hoffman and Buchanan function in Connecticut in the role that Eldersveld fulfilled, and if they did not, the legislators themselves would not be able to pick up the slack in the work. Michigan legislators are full-time lawmakers and each one has at least a secretary for support staff. Many have aides, too, and as was discussed in Chapter 5, Bullard alone has six full-time staff members. Legislators in Connecticut are part-time lawmakers, and only committee chairpersons have secretaries and/or aides. Most of these support staff also work part-time.

Another difference in the legislative environments for the two sets of campaigns is the degree of participation by the Black Caucus in actively pressing for the divestment measures. In Connecticut prominent members of the Black Caucus were the bills' principal movers but in Michigan they were not. Smith played a key role in getting the banking bill through the Senate and the caucus has been supportive of the legislation; but Bullard, with the caucus' blessings, has taken the lead in pressing for divestment in Michigan. Interestingly, both states have had black treasurers—in Michigan an appointed one, former Treasurer Monroe, and in Connecticut an elected one, Parker. Although Parker cannot be characterized as enthusiastic about divestment, he did not publicly oppose the full divestment legislation and was responsive to proponents' pressures, especially pressures from the Black Caucus. In contrast, Monroe publicly criticized pension fund divestment and has given leadership to an attempt by Treasury Department staff to undermine the pension fund bill. He did, however, support the banking bill once it was amended and described himself as a supporter of socially responsible investment. What is clear from both cases is that black public officials are not automatically in favor of anti-apartheid activists' divestment efforts.

The two cases share some other outer environmental factors in common. They are both in northern industrial states with previous experiences of fairly high concentrations of anti-apartheid activism in other institutions. And, they both have major investments by corporations with substantial operations in South Africa. The latter factor so far has proven to be more of a hindrance to divestment in Connecticut than in Michigan, but that is probably because the pension fund bill has not yet been the focus of attention in the Michigan legislature. The matter of geographic location has been a significant pattern in all the state and local campaigns. Most of the states that have passed binding divestment legislation are northern states. Few states in the Southeast have had legislation introduced but some in the West and Southwest are among those entertaining divestment bills. Other than Washington, D.C., Atlanta is the only city in the Southeast to have either considered or passed divestment legislation. The anti-apartheid movement generally has never been strong in the Southeast. Its greatest areas of concentration have always been in the Northeast and on the West Coast.

The degree to which the state political environment will tolerate the entertainment of such campaigns is a factor that may prove to be important to passage of divestment legislation, but is not adequately addressed by the research here or by other scholarship dealing with social movements and interest groups. It may be the case that lawmakers, government officials, and the general public in states such as Michigan and Connecticut are more willing on the whole to listen to arguments for divestment because they are accustomed to pressure from a wide range of political perspectives. Perhaps they have greater experience with and less objection to "liberal" or "leftist" causes than persons in other states. For example, would the same mix of factors that made for success in either Connecticut or Michigan work in Alabama, Texas, or Utah? This is a question that could be answered best by a full range of case studies on the divestment campaigns in all the states where legislation has been introduced.

Despite Michigan's distance from the Northeast, the location of most national anti-apartheid organizations, the campaigns there have benefited from the willingness of national organizations, especially ACOA, to be of assistance in providing expertise and information. This is the function of reticulation put forth in the Gerlach and Hine (1970) framework. Both sets of campaigns used literature developed by ACOA and had ACOA staff as well as other prominent anti-apartheid figures lobby and testify in the legislatures and make presentations in other arenas in the states. Both groups of proponents are appreciative of the aid they have received from national organizations, but the activists in Michigan have been critical of these organizations for not giving more attention and publicity to state and city campaigns earlier in their development. The Michigan activists do not believe national organizations have a responsibility for initiating state or city efforts, but they would like to see more concentrated efforts at giving these campaigns support services and high visibility so that other anti-apartheid activists across the country can apply the experiences gathered so far to their own situations. The national organizations began to do this in 1981.

Although the activists in both Connecticut and Michigan were quite resourceful in bringing research and expert testimony to support their divestment efforts, their opponents, especially those in Michigan, were not so quick to draw on such useful tools. The activists in both states always held an advantage over their opposition in being more knowledgeable about the issues involved. The business community in Connecticut eventually used outside expertise to their advantage, an important instance being during the sessions to convince the governor to veto the 1981 full divestment bill. Business leaders pointed to the recently released Rockefeller Study Commission advocacy of both the Sullivan Principles and no divestment as a precedent for the state to follow. But even in the Task Force negotiations where the business representatives had their staffs helping them to come up with policy options, Hoffman, who had no access to such support services, proved herself expert, capable of thorough analysis of the issues, and a formidable negotiator over details and technicalities.

Both groups achieved an element of strength that Cohen (1959) and others emphasize as necessary for success by voluntary organizations, and that is legitimacy and credibility. An important difference in the two states' campaigns is that some of the activists in Michigan are academics whose area of expertise is southern Africa. The Connecticut activists did not have the benefit of such advanced formal training. The Michigan activists are also well-established professionals in their community, whereas the Connecticut activists are younger and, with one exception, less well known for their professional status than their connections to other activist groups and leftist causes. This meant that the Connecticut group had more work to do to establish their credibility and legitimacy with regard to expertise about the issue. Interestingly, however, they did more research (that proved very useful to their campaign) on the actual impact of divestment on state funds than did the Michigan activists.

There were other important differences in strategy as well. Although both groups recruited a number of endorsements, the Connecticut activists sought and got support from two types of groups that were not among the early endorsers of the Michigan divestment efforts: labor unions and black organizations. Having the backing of the unions whose pension funds were at stake was quite helpful in the Connecticut campaigns, and although the Michigan activists have recruited some of this kind of support in the last year, weakness in this area is likely to be an important detriment to passage of the Michigan pension fund bill. Black organizations' endorsements in Connecticut added enormous weight to the activists' pressures for the state to take an active stand against racism. Without more support from black groups in Michigan, activists pushing for pension divestment in the future will be vulnerable to the charge, even from black leaders like Loren Monroe, that they are trying to make "a hollow, sacrificial gesture with other people's money" (*Michigan Chronicle,* 3 May 1980). On the other hand, the Michigan activists used church-related networks quite effectively in their campaigns, whereas the Connecticut activists appear to have less church-related support or involvement.

Part of the strength of both sets of campaigns was the creation of a political climate in which, for those attentive to the issue, the only clear anti-racist option for state policy was total disengagement from South Africa. Activists were able to cast the debate so that a moral issue was at stake, and to be against the legislation was to risk a public association with racism. Because of their careful coalition-building across racial lines both inside and outside the legislature, the Connecticut' activists did a more effective job of creating this type of political climate and defining the issue as a moral stand against racism; but both groups of proponents were able to stretch the spectrum of seriously considered policy options to the point that many decision makers did not view complete divestment as an extraordinary measure; that is, total divestment became an acceptable policy outcome. Then, when compromise was necessary, proponents could fall back on less stringent divestment options that, although disappointing in some respects, were important legislative accomplishments of economic disengagement from South Africa.

That decision makers both inside and outside of government felt vulnerable to being labeled racist, or as having an association with racism, is surely a relatively new phenomena in American politics and is not the result of these particular anti-apartheid campaigns. However, the activists were responsible for invoking this vulnerability. They used to their advantage the perceived political liability of leaders and state institutions being seen as supporters of apartheid. The activists were able to do this in a time of economic hardship and greater visibility of conservative political forces nationwide, and in such a climate the outcomes to some degree are surprising and even remarkable.

Surprising also is that opposition forces, and especially business groups, were not more united and clever in discovering and proposing policy options that would promote a nonracist image of themselves and still prevent divestment legislation from passing. In both states, the opposition was fairly fragmented, especially in the beginning, and there appear to be several explanations for this. One is that business opponents seem initially to have miscalculated the potential for passing bills and allowed themselves to remain preoccupied with other pressing issues. Another is that there was no united business voice in either state. Bankers and industrialists were at times at odds, as were those representing big business versus those representing small business.

The only highly visible opponents, especially in the legislatures, were those on the fringes of the far right, and the more moderate opposition was not in a hurry to be identified with these people. With time, however, in both cases the opposition became better organized and more aware of counterproposals palatable to a wide range of people involved in decision making but undermining of activists' efforts. For the most part, therefore, legislators did not have to cope with polarized opinions on the issue, and according to assertions made by Cohen (1973), fewer contending forces leave decision makers with more room for maneuverability.

The slow and disjointed response of opposition in these campaigns may be due in part to the issue having a primarily international focus. Apartheid is not as well known or perhaps not as well understood by the public as domestic issues such as access to abortion or the Equal Rights Amendment are. In addition, the number of groups or individuals who perceived that the legislation would impact them directly was generally quite small. For companies, there was at stake a moral judgment on their operations and the public reactions liability of being seen as bad corporate citizens; but they were not likely to suffer substantial financial harm. Opponents also believe that, because the legislation pertained to an international issue, the legislature would not pay it a great deal of attention. Activists were thus able to move divestment bills through the legislative process without raising the ire that a domestic, more well known and contentious issue might attract. Important to note again, however, is that the Connecticut activists made sure they had no active opposition from the retirees who had reason to be concerned about the direct financial impact of divestment on their well-being. The CAAC even succeeded in enlisting the retirees' endorsement in addition to support from public employee unions.

Another similarity in the two states' processes is that they were both incremental—in Michigan by design and in Connecticut by accident. The Michigan legislative sponsors had in mind a strategy of building momentum from the easiest bill to pass to the most difficult, but at the same time they have given opponents more opportunity to get better organized to defeat or significantly compromise the pension fund bill. This illustrates an observation made in

Chapter 3 that the relationship between time and chances of success may be curvilinear so that after a certain point, increases in the amount of time decision makers spend considering an issue may work against its proponents. In Connecticut, up until the point of the veto, the incremental strategy seemed to work in the activists' favor. They took a suboptimal outcome of the passage of the first bill, the one containing the Sullivan Principles, and showed why it was unacceptable. They convinced enough people of its unacceptability to win what they believed to be an optimal outcome, a total divestment bill. It may have been that the passage of the Sullivan Principles bill actually helped the next year's campaign because it introduced the issue and put the state on record as willing to take a stand on the issue. After the veto, however, activists faced a tough battle to forge an acceptable outcome in the face of enormous pressures to compromise a great deal. Because of their clarity about the limits of their willingness to compromise, in the end the activists achieved in the Task Force recommendations a product that took the business community far beyond where it expected to go.

In both cases, in summary, there seem to be three general sets of factors accounting for the degree of success achieved in the divestment campaigns. The first is the thorough, persistent, and intense work done by the proponents to create a political climate in and around the legislature so that total divestment was taken to be a serious policy option. In both cases, activists demonstrated strong capabilities for convincing legislators and enough politically relevant people outside the legislature that divestment was the morally preferable alternative for state action. The campaigns were seen to have some important degree of support, to reflect some of the best expertise available on the issue, and to have a great deal of legitimacy. Thus the highly committed and intense involvement of a relatively few people who were able to create credibility for themselves and their cause is in large part responsible for these campaigns' success.

The second major factor in explaining success is that the opposition was slow to respond and get organized well enough to counteract the divestment campaigns. In addition, activists anticipated many of the arguments their opponents might raise and established counter arguments well in advance. The activists were much quicker and more thorough in establishing that morality, expert opinion, and a high degree of consensus among those who pay attention to the issue were on their side. In the face of visible and persistent pressure from proponents and with disorganized, and at time reticent, pressure from opponents, legislators yielded to proponents' demands.

That the issue was an issue of race is the third major factor that explains the success of the campaigns. One of the reasons that some opponents were reticent is that they did not want to risk being labeled racist. Many legislators were also wary of such an association. However, when opponents began a concerted and careful effort to articulate a different perspective on the issue—that a conscientious person could be against divestment and racism at the same time—the race factor became less powerful. Nevertheless, for a long time in both sets of campaigns, legislators and opponents believed themselves to be vulnerable to being seen as racists if they openly and actively opposed divestment. In that the question of race is somewhat peculiar to this issue, activists attempting campaigns on other international issues may face more obstacles in counteracting their opponents that did these anti-apartheid groups.

With both a great deal in common and with significant differences, the two groups of divestment proponents in Connecticut and Michigan have achieved much of what they set out to do in both states. We move now from a comparison of how they achieved what they did to a discussion of the significance of these campaigns.

COMPARISON OF OUTCOMES AND IMPACT

In both Michigan and Connecticut divestment proponents succeeded in getting legislation adopted that curbs each state's economic ties to South Africa. Although significant compromises in the measures were required to get them passed, these laws stand as some of the toughest and most far-reaching sanctions-related legislation in the country. And, they stand as further evidence that state legislatures are willing to make laws with important foreign policy implications that are counter to official national policy.

As one might expect, there are interesting similarities and differences between outcomes of the two sets of campaigns. One of the most obvious differences is the legislative outcomes. Two pieces of legislation having to do with state bank deposits and university endowments have passed in Michigan, whereas the final law passed in Connecticut restricts investments of pension funds. Activists in both states worked about the same number of years (1978–82) to achieve passage of these bills. A second difference is that the Michigan legislature has probably had more exposure to the issue of apartheid than has the Connecticut legislature because it has passed legislation on South Africa other than the divestment bills. In addition Bullard sponsored several educational events on the issue for his colleagues, and he, together with other legislators, has hosted receptions for visitors from South Africa. Representatives of the South African government or South Africa Foundation apparently have paid more attention to the divestment process in the Michigan legislature. Or, at least their presence in Michigan is more easily detected than in Connecticut. As was explained in the Michigan case study, however, the South African government and its friends have had a strong interest in Michigan anti-apartheid activities for some time.

In the executive offices in the two states, officials have been required to spend significant amounts of time on the divestment issue. Because of the veto in Connecticut, the governor there was much more involved in debates around the issue than was the Michigan governor. In addition to the governor in Michigan, however, three other departments—Treasury, Commerce, and the Civil Rights—have spent time analyzing the bills, suggesting and negotiating amendments, testifying in committee hearings, and implementing the resultant laws. Only the Treasury Department in Connecticut has allocated major amounts of staff time to the issue and to implementation. However, because the final product was the result of a task force recommendation with the task force being chaired and managed by the treasurer, it is likely that the Treasury Department in Connecticut expended a great many more resources considering divestment policy options than did any of the governmental bureaucracies in Michigan. In addition, the Connecticut treasurer commissioned outside research to analyze the options available for the state's investments. As is already evident, when the campaign to push for passage of the pension fund bill gains momentum in Michigan, executive officials there will be required to pay more attention than they have at this point to the issue.

With $75 million in securities already sold in Connecticut after only partial implementation, it appears as though the state investments bill will impact substantially more funds than the banking bill and university endowment bills in Michigan combined. However, if a comprehensive pension divestment bill eventually passes in Michigan, that state will have the most far-reaching set of divestment laws in the country. Not only will there be large sums of money affected ($2 billion in pension funds alone) but also three separate types of funds will be governed in part by divestment criteria.

Within the business community, corporations with connections to South Africa from both states and beyond are well aware of these new divestment policies. Representatives from some of these corporations and/or persons hired to lobby on their behalf have contacted legislators and other government officials in an attempt to change or prevent passage of some of the legislation. Business representatives in Connecticut also took an active part in shaping the Governor's Task Force recommendations and in promoting the type of compromise reached there to decision makers in other arenas outside the state. In order to do business with either state (that is, to qualify as a bank depository in Michigan or as an allowable investment in Connecticut), banks and corporations have had to complete questionnaires and affidavits explaining their connections, if any, to South Africa. This means that company managers necessarily have allowed the divestment issue to impinge on their decisions with regard to how to run their businesses. Bankers in Michigan must promise not to loan money to the South African government or corporations located there, whereas in Connecticut corporations must demonstrate their compliance with a complex set of criteria set down by the state. As one example of the impact on corporate policies, General Electric cited the Connecticut legislation as the basis for some of its decisions regarding business in South Africa. If the educational institutions' divestment bill survives the court challenge in Michigan, more impact on business may be seen there, especially because of the precedent this may set for other states.

The Sullivan Principles as a code of conduct for corporations have not yet arisen as a significant issue in Michigan, but in Connecticut they became a serious compromise for which businesses and governmental officials pressed. In many occasions activists and legislative proponents had to argue forcefully about why the principles were an unacceptable alternative to divestment. One result of these thorough discussions about divestment and the Sullivan Principles is that some corporate executives and the treasurer are more convinced than ever that the code is a necessary, responsible, and small but sufficient business response to divestment pressures. This, from the perspective of the activists, is not progress on the issue, although in neither case did activists expect to convert business leaders to their point of view.

In other arenas outside the state, South African government officials and others who would defend apartheid, as well as leaders in the resistance movements, have been attentive to these processes in Connecticut and Michigan. Both the sympathizers and the opponents of apartheid from

South Africa have been involved in trying to affect the process in these two states because both parties strongly believe that international opinion and pressures can be important in the outcome of their struggle for control of the country. The State Department and some members of Congress also paid attention to the two sets of campaigns and attempted to influence the outcome. A State Department official spoke out against the Michigan education bill whereas Howard Wolpe and Senator Tsongas (Massachusetts) at various times encouraged divestment efforts in the state. Commerce Department officials are known to dislike state and local governments' anti-apartheid efforts and to have been critical of the full divestment bill in Connecticut.

In Connecticut and Michigan, the divestment process has been important for the internal dynamics of activist groups. The Michigan proponents have accomplished the passage of two of the pieces of legislation they want to become law and, of course, they have learned a great deal along the way. As they approach the fight over the pension bill, however, they have less organizational strength than in past years, and whether or not they will be able to sustain themselves and an operational base from which to attain passage of the most difficult piece of legislation is not clear. The Connecticut group wants to continue to press for more aggressive implementation of the 1982 law and to move further toward full divestment. In both states the activists' organizations are not highly institutionalized and are very dependent on the participation of a few people who carry a great deal of the work. Their future operation will be determined in large part by the degree to which those individuals can carry the bulk of the work and/or recruit new energetic and committed participants. Whether or not these two sets of anti-apartheid activists carry on with similar or new campaigns, however, they have already made a substantial and important contribution to the movement in the United States. In addition, their efforts have been appreciated worldwide by those attempting to end apartheid.

The question of which group of activists was most successful is a difficult one. The legislative goals sought were different for the two cases. The Michigan proponents have a more comprehensive approach to restricting the state's relationship, and they have achieved two-thirds of the legislation they wanted. But they have probably not yet overcome two-thirds of the difficulty to be encountered in such a program of action. The Connecticut proponents set out to get a very difficult piece of legislation passed and achieved a great deal, but not all, of what they wanted. Thus, although the Michigan proponents have more state laws to show for their efforts, their organizational abilities, campaign strength, and resolve in the face of determined and clever opposition has not been tested to the degree that was the case in Connecticut.

In reflecting on the process of evaluation itself, we find that in this study the goals-based evaluation provides in some respects a fairly generous standard for judging success and failure because of the ambiguity of some of the campaign goals. The goal of getting legislation passed is clear, but what is not clear is how much compromise in the language of the bills is too much. It proved easier to get bills passed once changes were made regarding the stringency of their provisions. The activists in both Michigan and Connecticut are satisfied that they have achieved passage of the toughest laws possible, given the political realities they faced. It is to their credit that the measures are as far-reaching as they are. Nevertheless, substantial compromises were made, and if the goals were to get the original legislative intent passed, the campaigns have fallen short of reaching those aims. Thus, other goals that are also somewhat ambiguous—expressing solidarity or taking a principled stand—are attained to a lesser degree than they would have been had the original legislation passed.

For the national anti-apartheid movement, divestment campaigns targeting state and local governments demonstrate that, even though there is little receptivity in national governmental bodies to the policies advocated by the anti-apartheid movement, there is high receptivity in subnational governmental bodies. These campaigns may prove to be one of the most powerful components of the movement's activities for several reasons. One is that the campaigns are decentralized and thus hard to counteract. Activists have many points of access across the fifty states and potentially could have divestment policies operation all over the country. Because there is not one institution, for example like the U.S. Congress, that can say a final yes or no to there scattered divestment policy proposals, activists may have better chances of success. In this regard, targeting state and local governments is like targeting individual colleges and universities, except that in the case of these governments, much more money is at stake. In 1984, public pension funds alone held more than $300 billion in investments (Apcar 1984). The addition of operating funds and other monies under the control of state and local governments would increase this total substantially. Targeting these institutions is also somewhat similar to targeting local church institutions across the country, but in the case of churches there are usually national organizations that can establish national policies or guidelines. Except for federal courts, there is no national authority to which opponents can appeal for help against these state and local laws. However, the decentralization may make activist efforts more difficult, too. If opponents have no national place of final appeal, neither do proponents. Sharing of information and strategy among activists, reticulation in the Gerlach and Hine (1970) framework, becomes even more important in these kinds of campaigns.

There is growing attention and opposition to divestment efforts in state and local governments, and the courts may be the place where opponents have an opportunity to stifle the momentum of the movement. Although activists have been able to counteract arguments about potential legal problems over divestment, the courts, specifically those in Michigan and Oregon now considering some of these issues, have yet to rule on them. Whatever the outcome in these cases, more legal challenges are sure to be made.

There are several legal questions raised by the exclusion of South African-related businesses from a public fund's investment portfolio. One has to do with fiduciary responsibility and prudence, which require that the trustees be held legally responsible for the safety as well as the income of the investment. Many states have laws that define in one way or another what the minimal requirements for portfolio safety are. Among those who observe and take part in the divestment debate as well as among investment managers, there is considerable disagreement regarding whether a trustee can fulfill these requirements while excluding companies doing business in South Africa from the portfolio (see Baldwin et al, 1980, 128–43; Bavaria, April 1983; Chettle 1983, 504–13; and Eager et al. 1983). Although this issue is not now before a court, it may well be the basis of legal action in the future.

Another issue of legality raised by divestment opponents, including the University of Michigan in its suit, is that of state and local governments' interference with the federal government's sole right to regulate commerce with other nations and make foreign policy (see Chettle 1983, 515–26; National Lawyers Guild 1981; and Wisconsin Attorney General 1978). Divestment proponents have argued that state officials have the authority to determine how state finances are to be managed, even to the extent of keeping them out of companies involved in South Africa. But opponents reply that such management extends far beyond a state's reasonable concern for the welfare and dignity of its own citizens into the federal government's preserve of formulating policy toward other nations. The ruling of the Michigan courts on this point will have major ramifications for the future activities of the anti-apartheid movement.

Whatever the legal implications are, state and local governments clearly are willing to get involved in making judgments about foreign policy issues. Some state governments have been demonstrating for a number of years that they understand the significance of world interdependence. For example, they establish trade offices or missions abroad or send teams of representatives to other countries to attract foreign investment to their areas. The divestment measures show, however, that they will get involved in foreign policy even when there is little or no clear and direct material benefit to be had. By doing so, they give greater legitimacy to pressures for the U.S. government to institute non-cooperation with South Africa, and they provide an alternate outlet for the expression of anti-apartheid policies.

As shown in Chapter 1, along with increasing opposition there are also an increasing number of fairly successful divestment campaign experiences across the country. Activists in these campaigns often attempt to share information about campaign strategy with others in the movement. This is done with the aid of national organizations, especially ACOA, publishing case studies of how divestment legislation was achieved and some of its impact. Nonetheless, because of the limited resources of both local and national activists and because of the highly decentralized nature of this activity, groups across the country are still having to forge their way through campaigns in some significant isolation from one another.

One of the most important pieces of information the activists need, but also one of the most elusive, is the financial impact of divestment. As these state and local campaigns become more prominent, the debate over their financial implications has intensified dramatically. Two types of evidence have been used by both opponents and proponents to prove their separate cases. One is the actual experience of funds that have sold securities of corporations doing business in South Africa, and the other is statistical studies comparing the performance and risk of a "sanitized" portfolio to some standard portfolio of securities. The outcomes in both cases are mixed, and thus there is room for a great deal of argument over financial consequences.

A case of successful divestment frequently cited by proponents is that of Michigan State University, which, due to market conditions at the time, gained about $1 million from its 1979 sale of South Africa-related securities. The MSU portfolio is quite small compared to state and city pension holdings, and therefore the case provides only a partially useful precedent. Several governments have now ordered fund managers to divest parts or all of their South African investments, and their experience can provide a better basis for comparison. However, in many cases the process is not yet complete, making judgment about impact difficult. Often when the process has been completed, it is still too early to discern the long-term impact on performance and risk.

The Connecticut partial divestment policy is in the process of implementation, and so far the outcome has netted the state $6.85 million from sales of securities over $75 million. Although Massachusetts Governor Dukakis declared in August 1983 that the states $2.25 billion pension funds had suffered no ill effects from divestiture of $90 million in securities, the *Wall Street Journal* reported in April 1984 that another state official said the funds had lost $11 million (Apcar 1984). The same kind of conflicting reports pertain to Philadelphia's divestment experience as well. Part of the difficulty in calculating the financial impact is that at the time that divestment laws were passed, some of these funds were already experiencing a significant decline in the market value of some securities. Therefore, to sell those particular securities at that point would be a loss. On the other hand, it is not clear that continuing to hold a security of declining value is a more responsible or less costly decision. Much more systematic and non-polemic study needs to be made of the actual and long-term impact on the various funds that have gone through a divestment process.

The other category of evidence with regard to financial impact is statistical studies done by investment analysts. Most studies have shown that across previous years a "sanitized" portfolio free of South Africa-related securities yielded higher returns than various portfolios constructed for comparison that included South African investments (usually the Standard and Poor 500). There is disagreement, however, about the degree to which the higher yields were statistically significant (Bavaria, March 1983; Connecticut Office of the Treasurer 1982, 31–53). There is also widespread consensus among studies that a portfolio prohibiting South Africa-related holdings would exclude investments in large portions of some industry groups and probably would be less diversified than one without such a restriction. Decreased diversification means increased potential risk. Four studies found the risk to be insignificant (Baldwin et al. 1980, 93–105; Bavaria, March 1983; and Connecticut Office of the Treasurer 1982, 33–41) whereas two others found the increased risk to be very important (Connecticut Office of the Treasurer 1982, 31–32; and Eagar et al. 1983). Therefore, the evidence from investment managers' studies is also inconclusive at this point.

Two surveys done of the opinions of investment managers found that most do not enthusiastically embrace the idea of managing a large portfolio without access to purchasing South Africa-related securities. Such restrictions make a portfolio more difficult to handle and more demanding of managers' time (Connecticut Office of the Treasurer 1982, 42–53; and Eager et al. 1983, 46–73). However, there are increasing numbers of firms willing to take on such tasks, especially since a greater number of clients are placing demands on them for more socially responsible investment practices.

State fund managers are among the growing and vocal opposition to this latest thrust in the economic sanctions efforts of anti-apartheid activists. In 1983, the National Association of state Investment Officers adopted a resolution opposing laws that force managers to make investment decisions based on any criteria other than the best interests of pension fund members (Apcar 1984). In the same year the National Association of State Treasurers showed some opposition to full divestment when the body approved a resolution congratulating the State of Connecticut for its Sullivan Principles approach and recommending it to other states.

Other active opposition that is getting better organized is in the business community. Some groups of companies have hired research firms to help them keep better track of legislation introduced in states and cities so that they can move more quickly to counteract it. The American Chamber of Commerce in South Africa circulated its study of the positive impact of U.S. business on South Africa to members of Congress and other opinion leaders in the country. The staff of the South Africa Foundation, not a business itself but backed by South African business interests, has been very active in holding press conferences and writing articles claiming that the state and local divestment efforts produce ill-conceived and illegal policies (see Chettle 1983 and 1984). This opposition is likely to grow, making remaining and future campaigns more difficult for activists.

Many divestment proponents hope that anti-apartheid actions by state and local governments will build momentum toward congressional action for economic sanctions. Clearly the actions taken in Connecticut, Maryland, Massachusetts, Michigan, Nebraska, and Wisconsin as well as several cities are in conflict with the U.S. government policy of constructive engagement with South Africa, and officials in the executive branch believe these measures to be counterproductive. Among many in the House of Representatives, however, there is a different point of view. The House has succeeded on several occasions in recent years in attaching restrictions on U.S. government or commercial relations with South Africa onto the Export-Import Authorization bill and the allocation of monies for the International Monetary Fund. Although only one of these restrictions has passed in the Senate to become law, their discussion presented occasions when members of Congress noted the growth in state and city divestment activity as a lead that Congress should follow. Certainly these state and city measures give legitimacy to the call for economic pressure against South Africa, but to get Congress to address the issue more fully will require a concerted campaign or series of campaigns directed specifically toward that purpose.

CONCLUSION

For over three decades the international anti-apartheid movement has tried to isolate South Africa economically because of its apartheid policies. This study has shown that a significant new thrust of sanctions-related activities among state and local governments in the United States is having an interesting and important impact across many arenas: U.S. businesses and business groups; the U.S. government as well as the subnational governments directly targeted; South African, both those supportive of and those opposed to apartheid; and the U.S. anti-apartheid movement itself. The degree of success demonstrated by both cases in this study has also shown that people can effectively use institutions locally available to address international issues.

Activists working on other global issues such as stopping the nuclear arms race could learn a great deal from the efforts of anti-apartheid activists, especially in the factors that gave strength to their campaigns. Although there may be a saturation point regarding the degree to which these subnational lawmakers are willing to act on such questions, activists working on any international problem will have to convince these officials that they have sufficient expertise, jurisdiction, and constituency pressure to make an informed and appreciated decision. To the rest of the world such decisions could be an indication of the degree of support or nonsupport there is for official U.S. foreign policy among the elected representatives of the American people. And this is precisely what divestment activists want: visible, legitimate, and responsible voices from across America objecting and providing alternatives to continued United States governmental and corporate support for apartheid.

Appendixes

A. Persons Interviewed in the Research

For the Connecticut Case Study

Activists

Peggy Buchanan, Co-chairperson, Connecticut Anti-Apartheid Committee; former treasurer of the CAAC; 2 June 1982.
*Christy Hoffman, former Co-chairperson, CAAC; 22 March 1982; 17 May 1984.

Legislators

*William Dyson, Representative, New Haven; 22 March 1982.
Marcella C. Fahey, Senate Co-chairperson, Appropriations Committee, General Assembly; 2 June 1982.
*Abraham L. Giles, Representative, Hartford; 23 March 1982.
Boyd Hines, former Connecticut state Representative; June 1982.
Cathy Landau-Painter, Legislative Aide to Ernest N. Abate, Speaker of the House; 22 March 1982.
Timothy J. Moynihan, Assistant Majority Leader, House of Representatives; 22 March 1982.
Richard F. Schneller, Senate Majority Leader; 3 June 1982.
Irving J. Stolberg, House of Representatives Co-chairperson, Finance, Revenue and Bonding Committee; 3 June 1982.

State Executive Office Staff

*Henry Parker, Treasurer, State of Connecticut; June 1982; 16 May 1984.
Barbara Reid, Investment Officer-Social Compliance, Office of the Treasurer, State of Connecticut; 16 May 1984.
Lee Van Meter, Deputy Treasurer, State of Connecticut; 22 June 1982.

Persons in Business

Joseph Crisco, Corporate Coordinator of Government Relations, United Technologies Corporation; 3 June 1982.

John Day, President, Insurance Association of Connecticut; June 1982.

David Delabetta, Director, Governmental Relations Program, Connecticut Bankers' Association; June 1982.

*Frank Donovan, Manager, Connecticut Government Affairs, General Electric Company; June 1982.

Anita Loalbo, Lobbyist and Lawyer, Connecticut Business and Industry Association; 4 June 1982.

*Dean Patenaude, Chairperson, Investment Advisory Council, State of Connecticut; Vice President, Securities Division, Connecticut Mutual Insurance; 21 June 1982.

*Isaac D. Russell, Lawyer, Day, Berry and Howard Attorneys at Law; 3 June 1982.

Peter Shapiro, Vice President and Director of Governmental Affairs, Connecticut Bank and Trust; 3 June 1982.

*Dale Van Winkle, Vice-president, United Technologies Corporation; June 1982.

Others

*Sanford Cloud, Counsel, Aetna Life and Casualty Insurance Corporation; former Connecticut state representative; 3 June 1982.

Douglas T. Cook, Assistant Director of Program, The Episcopal Diocese of Connecticut; June 1982.

*Edythe Gaines, Commissioner, Public Utilities Control; 21 June 1982.

Others with whom I attempted to have interviews but was unsuccessful

John G. Groppo, House of Representatives Majority Leader.

Michele Jacklin, Reporter, *Hartford Courant*.

Jay Jackson, Counsel to the Governor, State of Connecticut.

Bruce Kauffman, Reporter, Hartford *Advocate*.

Dick Polman, Columnist, *Hartford Courant*.

Russell T. Semelsberger, Vice President, Otis Elevator, United Technologies.

Those who refused to be interviewed

*Frank Stanley, Senior Vice President, Trust Division, Hartford National Bank.

---

*Task Force Members.

For the Michigan Case Study

Activists

Frank Beeman, Faculty, Michigan State University; SALC member; 27 January 1982.

Pat Beeman, SALC member; 27 January 1982.

Marylee Crofts, Outreach Coordinator, African Studies Center, Michigan State University; SALC member; 28 January 1982.

William Derman, Department of Anthropology, Michigan State University; SALC member; 27 January 1982.

David Dwyer, Department of Anthropology, Michigan State University; SALC member; 27 January 1982.

Linda Linteau, Student, Michigan State University; member PIRGM; 29 January 1982.

David Wiley, Director, African Studies Center, Michigan State University; SALC member; 27 January 1982; 14 May 1984.

Legislators

Perry Bullard, Representative, District 53 (Ann Arbor); 28 January 1982.

Alan L. Cropsey, Representative, District 88 (DeWitt); 27 January 1982.

Barbara Eldersveld, Legislative Aide to Representative Bullard; 29 January 1982.

David Evans, former chairperson of the House Civil Rights Committee; 28 January 1982.

Roger Kerson, Legislative Aide to Representative Bullard; 15 May 1984.

Dan Sharp, Legislative Aide to Representative Bullard; 15 May 1984.

Virgil Smith, Representative, District 10 (Detroit); 28 January 1982.

Francis (Bus) Spaniola, Chair of the Senior Citizens and Retirement Committee, House of Representatives; 20 May 1982.

Jackie Vaughn III, Senator, District 5 (Detroit); 21 May 1982.

State Executive Office Staff

Roy Castillo, Assistant Director, Department of Civil Rights; 20 May 1982.

John Fonger, Director, Municipal Employees Retirement System, Bureau of Retirement Systems; 20 May 1982.

Norvel Hansen, Deputy Director, Bureau of Retirement Systems, Michigan Public School Employees Retirement System; 20 May 1982.

Gordon Lindsey, Assistant Director in the Bureau of Finance, Department of Treasury; 20 May 1982.

Loren E. Monroe, former Treasurer, State of Michigan; 20 May 1982.

Barry Stevens, Administrator in the Stock Division, Bureau of Finance, Department of Treasury; 20 May 1982.

Curtis Townsend, former Deputy Treasurer, Department of Treasury; 20 May 1982.

Persons in Business

Richard Augenstein, Michigan Manufacturers Association; 19 May 1982.

Don Heikkinen, Senior Vice President and Staff Counsel, Michigan Bankers Association; 21 May 1982.

Bob Smith, Farhat, Smith and Hoisington; June 1982 (by phone).

Others with whom I attempted to have interviews but was unsuccessful

William D. Broderick, Director, International Governmental Affairs, Ford Motor Company.

Basil Brown, Senator, District 3 (Highland Park).

Phillip E. Runkel, Superintendent of Public Education, Department of Education.

Joel Samoff, former Faculty, University of Michigan; former Member of WCCAA.

Rachel Samoff, former Member of WCCAA.

Len Suransky, Faculty, Center for African and Afro-American Studies, University of Michigan.

Those who refused to be interviewed

William Amerman, Investment Director, Department of Treasury.

Others Involved in Apartheid Issues

Activists

Carol Collins, Coordinator, Campaign to Oppose Bank Loans to South Africa, Washington, D.C.: 16 January 1982.

Myloann Heckathorn, leader of the Stop Banking on Apartheid Campaign in Berkeley, California, New York

City; 13 June 1981.

Gail Hovey, former Research Director, American Committee on Africa, New York City, 21 January 1982; 10 May 1984.

George Houser, Director Emeritus, American Committee on Africa, New York City; 19 January 1982.

Paul Irish, Associate Director, American Committee on Africa, New York City; 21 January 1982.

Richard Kapchick, National Chairperson, The American Coordinating Committee for Equality in Sport and Society, New York City; 18 January 1982.

Dumisani Kumalo, Projects Director, American Committee on Africa, New York City; 21 January 1982.

Prexy Nesbitt, Secretary for Programme, Programme to Combat Racism, World Council of Churches in Geneva, Switzerland, Columbus, Ohio; 7 April 1980.

Jean Sindab, Executive Director, Washington Office on Africa, Washington, D.C.; 12 January 1982.

Tim Smith, Executive Director, Interfaith Center on Corporate Responsibility, New York City; 21 January 1982; 10 May 1984.

Doug Tilton, Research Associate, Washington Office on Africa, Washington, D.C.; June 1982.

U.S. Government Officials

Robert Cabelli, former Consultant, U.S. Department of State (now the Special Assistant to the Assistant Secretary for African Affairs); 19 January 1982.

Johnnie Carson, Subcommittee Staff Director, Subcommittee on Africa, Committee on Foreign Affairs, U.S. House of Representatives, Washington, D.C.; 15 January 1982.

David Dlouhey, South Africa Desk Officer, Africa Bureau, U.S. Department of State, Washington, D.C.; 11 January 1982.

Persons in Business

J. Wayne Fredricks, Executive Director, International Governmental Affairs, Ford Motor Company, New York City; 18 February 1982.

Wilfred Koplowitz, Vice President International Public Affairs, Citibank, New York City; 18 February 1982.

Robert Schwartz, Vice President, Shearson American Express, New York City; 20 January 1982.

Mark Sussman, International Affairs Analyst, Corporate Social Policy, Chemical Bank, New York City; 18 February 1982.

United Nations Officials

Abdennour Abrous, Chief of Branch, United Nations Centre
  Against Apartheid, New York CIty; 18 January 1982.
Yusuff Maitama-Sule, former Nigerian Ambassador to the
  United Nations and Chair of the United Nations Special
  Committee Against Apartheid; 14 August 1981.
Hamib Semichi, Algerian Representative to the United Na-
  tions Special Committee Against Apartheid; 14 August
  1981.

South Africans

John Chettle, Director, South African Foundation, Washing-
  ton, D.C.; 12 January 1982.
Sean Cleary, Political Counselor, South African Embassy to
  the United States, Washington, D.C.; 13 January 1982.
Leo Conradie, Deputy Permanent Secretary, South African
  Mission to the United Nations, New York City; 20 Janu-
  ary 1982.
John Makatini, African National Congress Representative to
  the United Nations; 13 August 1981.
John Matisson, Washington Correspondent, *Rand Daily Mail,*
  Washington, D.C.; 11 January 1982.
Richard Walker, New York Correspondent, *Rand Daily Mail,*
  Washington, D.C.; 11 January 1982.
Two persons currently living in South Africa who are a
  part of the resistance movement there.

Others

Desaix B. Myers III, Director, Investor Responsibility
  Research Center, Inc., Washington, D.C.; 14 January
  1982.
Ron Walters, Professor of Political Science, Howard University, Washington D.C.; 11 January 1982.

Others with whom I attempted to have interviews but was
unsuccessful

Randy Barber, Director, Pension Investment and Control
  Issues, Washington, D.C.
Goler Butcher, Professor of Law, Howard University,
  Washington, D.C. (former assistant to Representative
  Charles Diggs).
Chris Chamberlain, Aide to Senator Paul Tsongas, Washing-
  ton, D.C.
Leonard G. Miller, First Vice President, Associate General

Counsel, Shearson American Express, New York City.
Eugene Reddy, Assistant General Secretary, United Nations Centre Against Apartheid, New York City.
William Schweke, Conference on Alternative State and Local Policies, Washington, D.C.
Daniel Simpson, Director for Southern Africa Affairs, Africa Bureau, U.S. Department of State, Washington, D.C.
Marie Lee Swearer, Vice President, Corporate Responsibility, Chemical Bank, New York City.

B. Legislation from Connecticut, Massachusetts, and Michigan

The Massachusetts Divestment Law

The Commonwealth of Massachusetts
In the Year One Thousand Nine Hundred
and Eighty-two.

An Act ending the investment of public
pension funds in firms doing business in or
with South Africa.

(vi) After January 1, 1983, no public pension funds under this subsection shall remain invested in any bank or financial institution which directly or through its subsidiaries has outstanding loans to the Republic of South African or its instrumentalities, and no assets shall remain invested in the stocks, securities or other obligations of any company doing business in or with the Republic of South Africa. Any proceeds of sales required under this paragraph shall be invested as much as reasonably possible in institutions or companies which invest or conduct business operations in Massachusetts so long as such use is consistent with sound investment policy.

(vii) Notwithstanding the provisions of the preceding paragraph, if sound investment policy so requires the investment committee may vote to spread the sale of such investments over more than three years so that no less than one-third the value of said investments is sold in any one year. So long as any funds remain invested in any bank, financial institution or firm referred to in paragraph (vi), the investment committee shall annually, on or before January thirty-first, file with the clerk of the senate and the clerk of the house of representatives a report listing all South Africa-related investments held by the fund and their book market value as of the preceding December first.

Legislation Introduced by Representative Giles
in Connecticut in 1981

An Act concerning the State Investment Policy in relation to South Africa.

Be it enacted by the Senate and House of Representatives in General Assembly convened:
Section 1. (NEW) The state treasurer shall review the invested assets of all state funds to ensure that no such assets are invested in: (1) Any financial institution making loans to the republic of South Africa, a national corporation of the republic of South Africa or a subsidiary or affiliate of a United States company operating in the republic of South Africa or (2) any stock or obligations of any company doing business in or with the republic of South Africa. On or after the effective date of this act no such assets shall be invested in any such institution or any such stock or obligations and any such assets so invested on said date shall be disinvested within a reasonable period of time as determined by the state treasurer.
Sec 2. Section 3-13f of the general statues is repealed.
Sec. 3. This act shall take effect from its passage.

Resolution on South Africa
by the City Council of East Lansing

Based on the public inquiry conducted by the East Lansing City Council on March 30, 1977, and other information which has been made available to the Council, the Council resolves as follows:

1. The minority white government of South Africa should not be assisted to maintain its system of apartheid, of economic repression, and of force, terror and violence against the majority non-white people of Southern Africa. The Republic of South Africa should not be assisted to occupy the territory of Namibia or to continue as the primary supplier of war material to the illegal regime of Rhodesia.

2. The people of the United States know, because of their historical experience with systems of segregation, the disastrous and long-lasting effects of segregation upon the nation and its citizens; they therefore bear a special responsibility not to support such systems.

3. American investments, licenses or operations in South Africa have helped the minority white government to grow and to perpetuate apartheid. A number of American corporations investing in South Africa have voluntarily taken advantage of the racial system of job discrimination and low wages. Likewise, some American corporations have increased their business activities, while repression has increased and in spite of pleas from the United Nations, the Organization of African Unity, and many world leaders.

4. To implement this policy, the City of East Lansing, to the extent authorized by applicable law, shall seek competitive suppliers of goods and services who do not have investments, licenses, or operations in the Republic of South Africa. The City shall attach to all invoices and bids the following statement signed by the Mayor:

> The City Council of the City of East Lansing is gravely concerned about the system of segregation and official repression against the non-white majority in the Republic of South Africa. Our concern forces us to seek when and where possible and in accordance with applicable law, competitive suppliers of goods and services who do not have investments, licenses, or operations in the Republic of South Africa.

5. This resolution shall expire automatically upon action by the Council.

Passed 5-0 on August 3, 1977.

Michigan Public Act No. 325

The Banking Bill

An Act to amend section 5 of Act No. 105 of the Public Acts of 1855, entitled as amended "An act to regulate the disposition of the surplus funds in the state treasury: to provide for the deposit of surplus funds in certain financial institutions; to require certain reports by those institutions; to lend surplus funds pursuant to loan agreements secured by certain commercial or industrial real and personal property; to authorize an appropriation; and to prescribe the duties of certain state agencies" as added by Act No. 88 of the Public Acts of 1979,

The People of the State of Michigan enact:

Section amended; surplus funds in treasury.
Section 1. Section 5 of Act No. 105 of the Public Acts of 1855, as added by Act No. 88 of the Public Acts of 1979, being section 21.145 of the Compiled Laws of 1970, is amended to read as follows:

21.145   Financial institution as depository of state funds; eligibility; disclosure reports; list of financial institutions failing to comply; conclusive presumption of compliance; certification of compliance as condition to deposit of additional funds; prohibited conduct; affidavit; definitions. [M.S.A.3.693]

Sec. 5. (1) The state treasurer shall not deposit any surplus funds belonging to the state in a financial institution with total assets of more than $10,000,000.00 at the end of its last full fiscal year unless the financial institution complies with subsection (5), and files with the commissioner, either voluntarily or pursuant to Act No. 135 of the Public Acts of 1977, being sections 445.1601 to 445.1614 of the Michigan Compiled Laws, the disclosure reports required pursuant to section 6(1) or (2) of Act No. 135 of the Public Acts of 1977, being section 445.1606 of the Michigan Compiled Laws, and 1 of the following:
(a) The disclosure reports required pursuant to section 6(3) and (4) of Act No. 135 of the Public Acts of 1977.
(b) A copy of the information to be disclosed under section 6(4) of Act No. 135 of the Public Acts of 1977, relating to mortgage loans foreclosed, and a copy of the federal loan application register maintained by savings and loan associations pursuant to federal home loan bank board

regulation, 12 C.F.R.528.6(d), together with the following information as to each loan application:

(i) The type of loan applied for, divided into the following categories: home improvement loans; conventional mortgage loans on 1- to 4-family, owner-occupied dwellings; conventional mortgage loans on 1- to 4-family, nonowner-occupied dwellings; federal housing administration, farm home administration, or veterans administration mortgage loans; loans secured by junior liens; and loans on family dwellings for 5 or more families.

(ii) If a loan application other than for a loan secured by a mortgage on a multifamily dwelling is denied, the reason given for the denial.

(iii) The county code assigned by the commissioner.

(c) A report disclosing the information relating to loan applications contained in any other report maintained by a financial institution pursuant to federal law or regulations containing the information required to be disclosed under subdivision (b).

(2) The information required to be disclosed under subsection (1)(b) or (c) relating to the reason for denial of a loan, the owner-occupied or nonowner-occupied dwelling designation for a conventional mortgage loan, and the county code shall be provided only with respect to loan applications received after September 1, 1979.

(3) During December of each year, the commissioner shall request each financial institution in this state not required to file reports pursuant to section 6 of Act No. 135 of the Public Acts of 1977, to voluntarily file the reports as provided in subsection (1) before March 31 of the following year.

(4) Before May 1 each year, the commissioner shall publish a list of financial institutions with total assets of more than $10,000,000.00 at the end of their last full fiscal year which have failed to comply with subsection (5), or which have failed to file with the commissioner reports substantially complying with the requirements of subsection (1) for the last fiscal year of that financial institution ending not later than December 31 of the prior year. A financial institution which does not appear on that list shall conclusively be presumed to have complied with subsection (5) and to have filed the required reports for purposes of determining its eligibility to be a depository of state funds. Additional funds shall not be deposited in a financial institution which appears on the list until the commissioner certifies that the financial institution has complied with subsection (5) and has filed the required reports, or until 91 days after the end of a subsequent year for which the

required reports are filed with the commissioner, whichever occurs sooner.

(5) To be a depository of surplus funds belonging to the state, a financial institution shall not encourage or condone legally required discrimination against an individual on the basis of race or color, by knowingly making or maintaining a loan to the Republic of South Africa, a national corporation of the Republic of South Africa, or to a subsidiary or affiliate of a United States firm operating in the Republic of South Africa. A financial institution shall be considered to have complied with this subsection if the financial institution has filed with the commissioner an affidavit attesting to the fact that it has after July 4, 1982 no existing loans to the Republic of South Africa, a national corporation of the Republic of South Africa, or to a subsidiary or affiliate of a United States firm operating in the Republic of South Africa, as determined from information obtained from the United States department of commerce. As used in this subsection:

(a) "Financial institution" means a bank chartered under the laws of this state or of the United States.

(b) "National corporation" means a corporation, or a subsidiary or affiliate of a corporation, that is more than 50% owned or operated by the government of the Republic of South Africa.

(c) "Subsidiary or affiliate of a United States firm operating in the Republic of South Africa" means, as determined by the United States department of commerce, a firm incorporated under the laws of the Republic of South Africa, domiciled in the Republic of South Africa, and controlled by a United States firm. A subsidiary or affiliate shall not be construed to mean a subsidiary or affiliate that is located in the United States.

(d) "Surplus funds" means, at any given date, the excess of cash and other recognized assets, that are expected to be resolved into cash or its equivalent in the natural course of events and with a reasonable certainty, over the liabilities and necessary reserves at the same date. Surplus funds does not include the proceeds of bond and note issues which are deposited for a period of not more than 10 days in a financial institution for settlement purposes.

Approved December 17, 1980.

Michigan Public Act No. 512

The Educational Institution Funds Act

AN ACT to amend section 402 of Act No. 453 of the
Public Acts of 1976, entitled as amended "An act to define
civil rights; to prohibit discriminatory practices, policies,
and customs in the exercise of those rights based upon
religion, race, color, national origin, age, sex, height,
weight, or marital status; to preserve the confidentiality of
records regarding arrest, detention, or other disposition in
which a conviction does not result, to prescribe the powers
and duties of the civil rights commission and the department
of civil rights; to provide remedies and penalties; and to
repeal certain acts and parts of acts," being section 37.2402
of the Compiled Laws of 1970.

The People of the State of Michigan enact:

Section 1. Section 402 of Act No. 453 of the Public Acts
of 1976, being section 37.2402 of the Compiled Laws of
1970, is amended to read as follows:

Sec. 402. (1) An educational institution shall not:
(a) Discriminate against an individual in the full uti-
lization of or benefit from the institution, or the services,
activities, or programs provided by the institution because
of religion, race, color, national origin, or sex.
(b) Exclude, expel, limit, or otherwise discriminate
against an individual seeking admission as a student or an
individual enrolled as a student in the terms, conditions, or
privileges of the institution, because of religion, race,
color, national origin, or sex.
(c) For purposes of admission only, make or use a
written or oral inquiry or form of application that elicits or
attempts to elicit information concerning the religion, race,
color, national origin, age, sex, or marital status of a
person, except as permitted by rule of the commission or as
required by federal law, rule, or regulation, or pursuant to
an affirmative action program.
(d) Print or publish or cause to be printed or published a catalog, notice, or advertisement indicating a
preference, limitation, specification, or discrimination based
on the religion, race, color, national origin, or sex of an
applicant for admission to the educational institution.
(e) Announce or follow a policy of denial or limitation
through a quota or otherwise of educational opportunities of
a group or its members because of religion, race, color,

national origin, or sex.

(f) Encourage or condone legally required discrimination against an individual on the basis of race or color by knowingly making or maintaining after April 1, 1984, an investment in an organization operating in the republic of South Africa. This subdivision shall not apply to a private educational institution.

(g) Encourage or condone religious discrimination or ethnic discrimination by knowingly making or maintaining after February 1, 1983, an investment in an organization operating in the Union of Soviet Socialist Republics.

(2) The department shall compile, from information obtained from the United States department of commerce, a current register of organizations operating in the republic of South Africa and the Union of Soviet Socialist Republics. The department shall make the register available, upon request, to a person, board, or commission for a reasonable charge.

(3) As used in this section:

(a) "Investment" means money placed in shares of stock and other equity interests. Investment does not include an evidence of indebtedness arising from a transfer of direct obligations of, or obligations that are fully guaranteed as to principal and interest by, the United States or any agency thereof, that a bank is obligated to repurchase or a bank deposit made in the ordinary course of business.

(b) "Organization" means a United States firm, or a subsidiary or affiliate of a United States firm, as determined by the United States department of commerce.

Approved December 31, 1982

Michigan House Bill No. 4516
The Pension Funds Bill

A bill to amend Act No. 314 of the Public Acts of 1965, entitled as amended

"An act to authorize the investment of assets of public employee retirement systems or plans created and established by the state or any political subdivision; to provide for the payment of certain costs and investment expenses; to authorize investment in variable rate interest loans; to define and limit the investments which may be made by an investment fiduciary with the assets of a public employee retirement system; and to impose duties on an investment fiduciary,"

as amended, being sections 38.1132 to 38.1140h of the Michigan Compiled Laws, by adding section 13a.

The People of the State of Michigan enact:

Section 1. Act No. 314 of the Public Acts of 1965, as amended, being sections 38.1132 to 38.1140h of the Michigan Compiled Laws, is amended by adding section 13 a to read as follows:

Sec. 13A. Notwithstanding any other provision of this Act, a public employee retirement system shall not encourage or condone legally required discrimination against an individual on the basis of race or color, by knowingly making or maintaining after July 4, 1983, an investment of assets in an organization operating in the Republic of South Africa subject to the fiduciary dutires imposed in this Act, the proceeds of a sale of assets required under this Section shall be invested, insofar as possible, in entities or properties that do business in or are located in this state. A public employee retirement system shall be considered to have complied with this Section if the public employee retirement system has not made an investment in an organization that is listed in the Register of Organizations Operating in the Republic of South Africa, as prepared by the Department of Civil Rights Pursuant to Section 402 of the Elliott-Larsen Civil Rights Act, Act No. 453 of the Public Acts of 1976, being Section 37.2402 of the Michigan Complied Laws.

Substitute for
House Bill No. 4516

A bill to amend Act No. 314 of the Public Acts of 1965, entitled as amended

"An act to authorize the investment of assets of public employee retirement systems or plans created and established by the state or any political subdivision; to provide for the payment of certain costs and investment expenses; to authorize investment in variable rate interest loans; to define and limit the investments which may be made by an investment fiduciary with the assets of a public employee retirement system; and to impose duties on an investment fiduciary,

as amended, being sections 38.1132 to 38.1140h of the Michigan Compiled Laws, by adding section 13a.

The People of the State of Michigan enact:

Section 1. Act No. 314 of the Public Acts of 1965, as amended, being Sections 38.1132 to 38.1140h of the Michigan Compiled Laws, is amended by adding Section 13a to read as follows:

Sec. 13. (1) Notwithstanding any other provision of this Act, the State Employees' Retirement System established under the State Employee's Retirement Act, Act No. 240 of the Public Acts of 1943, being Sections 38.1 to 38.47 of the Michigan Compiled Laws, and the Public School Employees Retirement System Established under the Public School Employees Retirement Act of 1979, Act No. 300 of the Public Acts of 1980, being Sections 38.1301 to 38.1407 of the Michigan Compiled Laws, shall not encourage or condone legally required discrimination against an individual on the basis of race or color, by knowingly making after January 1, 1985, or knowingly maintaining after January 1, 1990, an investment of assets in an organization operating in the Republic of South Africa.
(2) Beginning January 1, 1985, investments required to be divested under subsection (1) shall be divested at the rate of not less than 1/5 of the total portfolio of such investments per calendar year.
(3) Subject to the fiduciary dutires imposed in this Act, the proceeds of a sale of assets required under this Section shall be invested, insofar as possible, in entities or properties that do business in or are located in this State.

(4) A retirement system referred to in subsection (1) shall be considered to have complied with subsection (1) if the retirement system does not make or maintain after the applicable dates an investment in an organization that is listed in the Register of Organizations Operating in the Republic of South Africa, as prepared by the Department of Civil Rights Pursuant to Section 402 of the Elliott-Larsen Civil Rights Act, Act No. 453 of the Public Acts of 1976, being Section 37.2402 of the Michigan Compiled Laws.

Bibliography

Adams, James L. *The Growing Church Lobby in Washington.* Grand Rapids, Mich.: Eerdmans, 1970.

Africa Fund. South Africa: Taking Stock of Divestment. Pamphlet. New York, October 1979.

———. U.S. Business in South Africa: Voices for Withdrawal. Southern Africa Perspectives Pamphlet No. 2. New York, February 1980.

———. *Annual Report.* New York, 1981.

———. Black Unions in South Africa. Pamphlet. New York, 1982.

———. Church and University Action Against Apartheid: A Summary of Withdrawals and Divestment. Pamphlet. New York, 1983.

———. *Annual Report.* New York, 1983.

———. South Africa: Questions and Answers on Divestment. Southern African Perspectives Pamphlet No. 4. New York, 1981.

———. South Africa Fact Sheet. Southern African Perspectives Pamphlet No. 1. New York, 1984.

Africa News. $28 Million in Munitions List Sales to Pretoria. Durham, N.C., 30 January 1984.

———. IMF Gets $40 Million Boost. Durham, N.C., 28 November 1983.

———. Anti-Apartheid Groups Encouraged by Spring Offensive. Pamphlet. Durham, N.C., 31 May 1981.

———. All Star Concert Spotlights Southern Africa. Durham, N.C., 13 July 1979.

Alger, Chadwick F. Local, National and Global Publics in the World: A Challenge to International Studies. International Studies Association *Notes.* Spring 1978.

———. Foreign Policies of U.S. Publics. *International Studies Quarterly* 21, No. 2(June 1977).

Alger, Chadwick F. and David Hoovler. The Feudal Structure System of International Organizations. *Proceedings* of the International Peace Research Association Conference, 145–82, Varanasi, India, February 1975.

Alinsky, Saul D. *Reveille For Radicals.* New York: Random House, 1969.

———. *Rules for Radicals: A Pragmatic Primer for*

Realistic Radicals. New York: Random House, 1972.

American Committee on Africa. South Africa: Taking Stock of Divestment. Pamphlet. New York, October 1979.

————. *Annual Report*. New York, 1977.

————. *Annual Report*. New York, 1983.

————. Make it in Massachusetts, Not in South Africa: How We Won Divestment Legislation. Pamphlet. New York, March 1983.

————. ACOA Action News. No. 11. New York.

————. ACOA Action News. No. 12. New York.

————. ACOA Action News. No. 13. New York.

————. Summary of State and Municipal Legislative Action on South Africa. Pamphlet. New York. January 1981.

————. Legislative Action Against Apartheid: A Case Study of the Connecticut Campaign. Pamphlet. New York, January 1982.

————. Public Investment and South Africa. Newsletter. No. 1. New York, January 1982.

Angell, Robert C. *Peace on the March: Transnational Participation*. New York: Van Nostrand Reinhold, 1969.

Apcar, Leonard M. Anti-Apartheid Pension Policies Criticized by Some Fund Managers. *Wall Street Journal*. 18 April 1984, 33.

Archer, Agnus. New Forms of NGO Participation in World Conferences. United Nations: UNITAR Discussion Paper, October 1976.

Ash, Roberta. *Social Movements in America*. Chicago: Markham, 1972.

Bailey, Martin, and Bernard Rivers. *Oil Sanctions Against South Africa*. United Nations Special Committee Against Apartheid, June 1978.

Baker, James E., et al. *Full Report of Public Opinion on American Attitudes Toward South Africa*. New York: Carnegie Endowment for International Peace, 1979.

Baker, Pat. The Canadian Campaign to End Bank Loans to South Africa. United Nations Centre Against Apartheid Notes and Documents, July 1979.

Ball, George. Asking for Trouble in South Africa. *Atlantic Monthly* (October 1977): 43–51.

Baldwin, Stuart A., et al. *Pension Funds and Ethical Investment: A Study of Investment Practices and Opportunities State of California Retirement System*. New York: Council on Economic Priorities, 1980.

Barber, James. Economic Sanctions as a Policy Instrument. *International Affairs* 55, No. 3(July 1979): 367–84.

Barber, James, Jesmond Blumenfeld, and Christopher R. Hill. *The West and South Africa*. London: Routledge and Kegan Paul, 1982.

Barnes, Tom. Bill to Limit Investments Clears House. *Hartford Courant,* 27 April 1982.

Bauer, Raymond A., ed. *Social Indicators.* Cambridge: MIT Press, 1966.

Bauer, Raymond A., Ithiel de Sola Pool, and Lewis Anthony Dexter. *American Business and Public Policy: The Politics of Foreign Trade.* New York: Atherton Press, 1963.

Bauer, Raymond A. *Second Order Consequences.* Cambridge: MIT Press, 1969.

Bavaria, Joan. Letter to Council member John Ray. Boston, 29 March 1983.

————. Speech to the Conference on Public Investment and South Africa. Mimeographed. Boston, 16 April 1983.

Beaubien, Michael C. The Cultural Boycott of South Africa. *Africa Today* 29, No. 4(1982): 5–16.

Berger, Peter L. *Pyramids of Sacrifice: Political Ethics and Social Change.* Garden City, N.Y.: Anchor Books, 1976.

Blaser, Arthur, and Steven Saunders. Human Rights Nongovernmental Organizations: A Study of a Social Movement. Paper presented at the Midwest Political Science Association Annual Meeting, Chicago, 1978.

Bobrow, Davis B. *International Relations: New Approaches.* New York: Free Press, 1972.

Boyer, Sandy. Divesting from Apartheid: A Summary of State and Municipal Legislative Action on South Africa. New York: American Committee on Africa, March 1983.

Brown University Approves South Africa Stock Policy. *New York Times,* 15 April 1984, Section 1, 37.

Bullard, Perry. Speech delivered at the Conference on Public Investment and South Africa, New York City, 12 June 1981.

Business International SA. *Apartheid and Business: An Analysis of the Rapidly Evolving Challenge Facing Companies with Investment in South Africa.* New York: Business International, 1980.

California. Office of the Governor. *Governor's Public Investment Task Force Interim Report.* Los Angeles, March 1981.

Cameron, William Bruce. *Modern Social Movements.* New York: Random House, 1966.

Cape Times. Union Reviews Sullivan Code. Cape Town, 19 January 1982.

Carter, Gwendolen M. *The Politics of Inequality: South Africa Since 1948.* New York: Praeger, 1958.

Carter, Gwendolen M., and Patrick O'Meara, eds. *International Politics in Southern Africa.* Bloomington:

Indiana University Press, 1982.
——. *Southern Africa: The Continuing Crisis.* 2d ed. Bloomington: Indiana University Press, 1982.

Cassell, Joan. *A Group Called Women: Sisterhood and Symbolism in the Feminist Movement.* New York: David McKay, 1977.

Chamberlain, Neil W. *The Limits of Corporate Responsibility.* New York: Basic Books, 1973.

Chatfield, Charles. *Peace Movements in America.* New York: Schocken Books, 1973.

Chettle, John H. South African Divestment: Bitter Fruits of a Well Meaning Idea. *Legislative Policy* (January/February 1984): 41–44.

——. The Law and Policy of Divestment of South African Stock. *Law and Politics in International Business* 15(1983): 445–528.

Chirot, Daniel. *Social Change in the Twentieth Century.* New York: Harcourt, Brace, Jovanovich, 1977.

Chittick, William. *State Department: Press and Pressure Groups.* New York: John Wiley, 1970.

Christenson, Philip L. United States-South African Economic Relations: Major Issues in the United States. In *The American People and South Africa,* edited by Alfred O. Hero, Jr. and John Barratt. Massachusetts: Lexington Books, 1981.

Cohen, Bernard C. *The Political Process and Foreign Policy: The Making of the Japanese Peace Settlement.* Princeton: Princeton University Press, 1957.

——. *The Influence of Non-governmental Groups on Foreign Policy Making.* Boston: World Peace Foundation, 1959.

——. *The Public's Impact on Foreign Policy.* Boston: Little, Brown, 1973.

Cohen, Laurence. South African Visitors Avoid Investments Issue. *Hartford Courant,* October 1981.

Connecticut Anti-Apartheid Committee. *Newsletters.* Hartford, 1978–82.

Connecticut General Assembly. Committee on Appropriations. *Hearings.* Hartford, 5 March 1981.

——. House of Representatives. *Journal.* Hartford, 27 May and 20 July 1981.

——. Senate. *Journal.* Hartford, 1 June 1981.

Connecticut Office of the Treasurer. *Annual Report of the Treasurer.* Hartford, 1979–82.

——. Report of the Governor's Task Force on South African Investment Policy. Hartford, 1982.

Connecticut. Public Act No. 82-324. *General Statutes.* Hartford.

————. Public Act No. 80-431. *General Statutes.*
Hartford.
Crocker, Chester. South Africa: Strategy for Change.
Foreign Affairs (Winter 1980–81): 323–51.
Danaher, Kevin. U.S. Policy Options Toward South Africa:
A Bibliographic Essay. *A Current Bibliography on
African Affairs* 13, No. 1(1980–1981): 2–25.
Davis, Jennifer. Financial Consequences of Divestment from
South Africa. Mimeographed. New York: American
Committee on Africa, November 1983.
Detroit News. June 8, 1980.
Doxey, Margaret P. The Rhodesian Sanctions Experiment.
Yearbook of World Affairs 25(1971): 142–62.
————. International Sanctions: A Framework for Analysis
with Special Reference to the UN and Southern Africa.
International Organization 26, No. 3(Summer 1972).
————. Sanctions Revisited. *International Journal* 31, No.
1(Winter 1975–76): 53–78.
————. *Economic Sanctions and International Enforce ment.*
London: Macmillan for the Royal Institute of International
Affairs, 1980.
Dunlap, David W. Pension System to Drop Stocks Over
Apartheid: City Fund's Board Acts Against South Africa.
New York Times, 4 August 1984.
Eager, David, Caroline Cummings, and Cathy Keil. *District
of Columbia Special Investment Study: South Africa
Proposal.* Louisville, Kentucky: Meidinger Asset
Planning Services, 1983.
Feld, Werner. *Nongovernmental Forces and World Politics.*
New York: Praeger, 1972.
Fellows, Mark. Bills May Prevent War. *The State News.*
East Lansing, 16 May 1980.
Feraru, Anne Thompson. Transnational Political Interest
and the Global Environment. *International Organization*
28, No. 1(Winter 1974): 31–60.
Ferguson, Clyde, and William Cotter. South Africa: What is
to Be Done? *Foreign Affairs* 56, No. 2(January 1978):
253–74.
First, Ruth, Jonathan Steele, and Christabel Gurney. *The
South African Connection: Western Investment in Apart-
heid.* Middlesex, England: Penguin Books, Ltd., 1973.
Freeman, Jo, ed. *Social Movements of the Sixties and
Seventies.* New York: Longman, 1983.
————. *The Politics of Women's Liberation.* New York:
David McKay, 1975.
————. Resource Mobilization and Strategy: A Model for
Analyzing Social Movement Organization Actions. In *The
Dynamics of Social Movements,* edited by Mayer N. Zald

and John D. McCarthy. Cambridge, Mass.: Winthrop Publishers, 1979.

Frieden, Joyce. Divestment in South Africa Profitable for MSU. *The Michigan Daily,* 27 January 1980.

Gamson, William A. *Power and Discontent.* Homewood, Ill.: Dorsey Press, 1968.

Gerhart, Gail M. *Black Power in South Africa: The Evolution of an Ideology.* Berkeley: University of California Press, 1978.

Gerlach, Luther P. Movements of Revolutionary Change: Some Structural Characteristics. In *Social Movements of the Sixties and Seventies,* edited by Jo Freeman. New York: Longman, 1983.

Gerlach, Luther P., and Virginia H. Pine. *People, Power, Change: Movements of Social Transformation.* Indianapolis: Bobbs-Merrill, 1970.

Gibson, Richard. *African Liberation Movements.* London: Oxford University Press, 1972.

Gordon, Raymond L. *Interviewing: Strategy, Techniques, and Tactics.* Homewood, Ill.: Dorsey Press, 1969.

Gunther, Marc, and Michele Jacklin. Assembly Sustains All O'Neil Votes. *Hartford Courant,* 21 July 1981.

Guerilla Acts on the Rise in South Africa, Intelligence Study Says. *Africa News* 19, Nos. 18, 19(1, 8 November 1982): 1,2.

Hance, William. The Case For and Against U.S. Disengagement from South Africa. In *Southern Africa and the United States,* edited by William Hance. New York: Columbia University Press, 1968.

Hanshew, Georgia. Resolution Urging Boycott May Be Off E. L. Agenda. *The State News.* East Lansing, 18 April 1977.

Hartford Inquirer, 1 May 1981; 15 July 1981; 1 August 1981; 15 August 1981.

Haslam, David. The Campaign Against Bank Loans for Apartheid. United Nations Centre Against Apartheid Notes and Documents, June 1981.

Hauck, David, Meg Vorhees, and Glen Goldberg. *Two Decades of Debate: The Controversy Over U.S. Companies in South Africa.* Washington, D.C.: Investor Responsibility Research Center, 1983.

Heberle, Rudolph. *Social Movements.* New York: Appleton Century Crofts, 1951.

Heil, Jim. South African Stock Divestiture By State Legislature Postponed. *The State News.* East Lansing, 18 November 1981.

————. Divestiture Bill Wins Approval of Committee. *The State News,* 27 January 1982.

Hero, Alfred O., Jr., and John Barratt. *The American People and South Africa*. Lexington, Mass.: Lexington Books, 1981.

Hilsman, Roger. *The Politics of Policy Making in Defense and Foreign Affairs*. New York: Harper and Row, 1971.

Hoffman, Christy. Speech delivered at the Conference on Public Investment and South Africa, New York City, 12 June 1981.

Howard, John R. *The Cutting Edge: Social Movements and Social Change in America*. Philadelphia: Lippincott, 1974.

Howard, William, and Timothy Smith. The U.S. Church Campaign Against South Africa. Paper presented at the International Seminar on Loans to South Africa, Zurich. 5–7 April 1981.

Horowitz, Ralph. South Africa: The Background to Sanctions. *Political Quarterly* 24, No. 2(1971): 165–76.

Houghton, D. Hobart. *The South African Economy*. New York: Oxford University Press, 1976.

House, Ernest R. *Evaluating with Validity*. Beverly Hills: Sage Publications, 1980.

Houser, George M. Ending Bank Loans to South Africa. United Nations Centre Against Apartheid Notes and Documents, June 1979.

————. The International Impact of the South African Struggle for Liberation. United Nations Centre Against Apartheid Notes and Documents, January 1982.

Hovey, Gail, James Carson, and Jennifer Davis. Economic Disengagement and South Africa: The Effectiveness and Feasibility of Implementing Sanctions and Divestment. *Law and Policy in International Business* 15, No. 2(1983).

Hubner-Dick, Gisela, and Reimund Seidelmann. Simulating Economic Sanctions and Incentives: Hypothetical Alternatives of United States Policy on South Africa. *Journal of Peace Research* 15, No. 2(1978): 153–74.

Hudson, Richard L. Publisher McGoff Settles SEC Charges of Failure to Disclose South African Tie. *Wall Street Journal,* 15 September 1983.

Hughes, Barry B. *The Domestic Context of American Foreign Policy*. San Francisco: W.H. Freeman and Co., 1978.

Interfaith Center on Corporate Responsibility. The Case Against U.S. Investment in South Africa. Brief, May 1979.

International Defence and Aid Fund for Southern Africa. *Apartheid, the Facts*. London, 1983.

International Monetary Fund. *Direction of Trade Annual.*

Washington, D.C.: IMF, 1971–84.

Investment in South Africa: One and a half way traffic. *The Economist,* 25 June 1983.

Jacklin, Michele. Multinational Companies Insist Their South African Ventures Alleviate the Evils of Apartheid. *Hartford Courant,* 16 August 1981.

———. O'Neil's Vetoes Likely to Stand. *Hartford Courant.* 20 July 1981.

———. State Pension Funds Wield No Threat to South Africa. *Hartford Courant,* 16 August 1981.

———. Senate Approves Divestment Bill. *Harford Courant,* 4 May 1982.

Janger, Allen R., and Ronald E. Berenbeim. *External Challenges to Management Decisions: A Growing International Business Problem.* New York: The Conference Board, 1981.

Jenkins, Simon. Destabilization in Southern Africa: Potgieter Counter Attacks. *The Economist* 16(1983): 19–28.

Jewell, Malcolm E., and David M. Olson. *American State Political Parties and Elections.* Homewood, Ill.: The Dorsey Press, 1978.

Johnson, David L. Sanctions and South Africa. *Harvard International Law Journal* 19, No. 3(Fall 1978): 887–930.

Kalley, Jacqueline A. Sanctions and Southern Africa: A Bibliographical Guide. *A Current Bibliography on African Affairs* 14, No. 3(1981–82).

Kapungu, Leonard T. *The United Nations and Economic Sanctions Against Rhodesia.* Lexington, Mass.: Lexington Books, 1971.

Karis, Thomas, and Gwendolen Carter. *From Protest to Challenge: A Documentary History of African Politics in South Africa, 1882–1964.* Stanford: Hoover Institution Press, 1972.

Karis, Thomas G. Revolution in the Making: Black Politics in South Africa. *Foreign Affairs* 62, No. 2(Winter 1983/84): 378–406.

Kauffman, Bruce. Hartford's $76 Million Pension Pool Doesn't Get Invested in Hartford. *Hartford Advocate,* 5 July 1978.

———. Hartford's Investment in Apartheid. *Hartford Advocate,* 4 June 1980.

———. Unloading the South Africa Connection. *Hartford Advocate,* 12 May 1982.

Kegley, Charles W., Jr., and Eugene R. Wittkopf. *American Foreign Policy: Pattern and Process.* 2d ed. New York: St. Martin's, 1982.

Keohane, Robert, and Joseph S. Nye. *Transnational*

Relations and World Politics. Cambridge: Harvard
University Press, 1972.
King, Martin Luther, Jr. Appeal for an International
Boycott of South Africa. United Nations Center Against
Apartheid, 1982.
Klein, Beate. *Corporate Data Exchange Handbook: U.S.
Bank Loans to South Africa.* New York: Corporate Data
Exchange, 1978.
Knight, Derrick. *Beyond the Pale: The Christian Political
Fringe.* Leigh, England: Caraf Publications, 1982.
Kotze, D. A. *African Politics in South Africa 1964–1974:
Parties and Issues.* New York: St. Martin's, 1975.
Lake, Anthony. *The Tar Baby Option: American Policy
Toward Southern Rhodesia.* New York: Columbia
University Press, 1976.
Lansing Star, 18 February 1977; 3 April 1977; 8 April 1977;
7-20 October 1977; 1 January 1978; 5 May 1979; 8 June
1980.
Lapchick, Richard E. *The Politics of Race and Inter-
national Sport: The Case of South Africa.* Westport,
Conn.: Greenwood Press, 1975.
————. Sports Boycotts in the International Campaign
Against Apartheid. United Nations Centre Against
Apartheid Notes and Documents, February 1977.
————. ACCESS Report on 1981 Springbok Rugby Tour.
Unpublished report, 1981.
Lauer, Robert H., ed. *Social Movements and Social
Change.* Carbondale: Southern Illinois University Press,
1976.
Laurence, John C. *Race, Propaganda and South Africa.*
London: Victor Gollancz, 1979.
Leiss, Amelia C., ed. *Apartheid and United Nations
Collective Measures: An Analysis.* New York: Carnegie
Endowment for International Peace, 1965.
Lemarchand, Rene, ed. *American Policy in Southern
Africa: The Stakes and Stance.* Washington, D.C.:
University Press of America, 1981.
Leonard, Richard. *South Africa at War: White Power and
Crises in Southern Africa.* Westport, Conn.: Lawrence
Hill, 1983.
Levering, Ralph B. *The Public and American Foreign
Policy 1918–1978.* New York: Morrow, 1978.
Lewin, Tamar. Apartheid: New Focus. *New York Times,*
19 November 1983.
Lipsky, Michael. Protest as a Political Resource. *American
Political Science Review* 62(December 1968): 1144–58.
Litvak, Laurence, et al. *South Africa: Foreign Investment
and Apartheid.* Washington, D.C.: Institute for Policy

Studies, 1978.

Lowery, Donald. Let it Be Heard: A Warning on American Investment in South Africa. *Boston Globe,* 28 September 1980.

Lynch, Hollis R. *Black American Radicals and The Liberation of Africa: The Council on African Affairs 1937–1955.* Cornell University: Africana Studies and Research Center Monograph Series, No. 5, 1978.

Magubane, Bernard M. *The Political Economy of Race and Class in South Africa.* New York: Monthly Review, 1979.

Makgetla, Neva, and Ann W. Seidman. *Outpost of Monopoly Capitalism: South Africa in the Changing Global Economy.* Westport, Conn.: Lawrence Hill, 1980.

Mansbach, R. W., Y. H. Ferguson, and D. E. Lampert. *The Web of World Politics: Nonstate Actors in the Global System.* Englewood Cliffs, N.J.: Prentice-Hall, 1976.

Marquard, Leo. *The Story of South Africa.* London: Faber, 1973.

Marvin, J. D. Sanctions Against South Africa: The Impact and the Aftermath. In *Sanctions Against South Africa,* edited by Ronald Segal. Harmondsworth, England: Penguin, 1964.

Marx, Gary T., and James L. Wood. Strands of Theory and Research in Collective Behavior. In *Annual Review of Sociology,* edited by Alex Inkeles, James Coleman, and Neil Smelser, vol. 1, 363–428, 1975.

Marx, Gary T. External Efforts to Damage or Facilitate Social Movements: Some Patterns, Explanations, Outcomes, and Complications, in *The Dynamics of Social Movements,* edited by Mayer N. Zald and John D. McCarthy. Cambridge, Mass.: Winthrop Publishers, 1979.

Matisonn, John. Is Mudge Re-Launching "Muldergate" in the U.S.? *Rand Daily Mail,* Johannesburg, 30 September 1981.

Mauss, Armand L. *Social Problems as Social Movements.* Philadelphia: Lippincott, 1975.

McCarthy, John D., and Mayer N. Zald. *The Trend of Social Movements in America: Professionalization and Resource Mobilization.* Morristown, N.J.: General Learning Press, 1973.

McConnell, Grant. *Private Power and America Democracy.* New York: Knopf, 1966.

Michigan Daily. Ann Arbor, 19 March 1980; 29 May 1980; 7 June 1980.

Michigan. Department of Treasury *Annual Report of the State Treasurer.* Lansing, Mich.: Publications and

Information Section, Department of Treasury, 1978–81.
———. Analysis of Bill Substitute of HB 5446 (H-4). Lansing, 1980.
———. Analysis of Bill No. 4315. Lansing, 25 November 1981.
Michigan. State Legislature. House of Representatives. House Legislative Analysis Section Analysis of House Bill 4831, Substitute H6 and House Bill 4838, Substitute H2. Lansing, 1980.
Michigan. State Legislature. House of Representatives. *Journal*. Lansing, 20 May 1980 and 25 November 1980.
———. *Journal*. Lansing, Mich., 17 February 1982; 3 May 1982; 6 May 1982; 13 May 1982.
Michigan. State Legislature. Senate. *Journal*. 30 June 1980; 18 November 1980; 21 November 1980; 25 November 1980.
Milbrath, Lester. *The Washington Lobbyists*. Chicago: Rand McNally, 1963.
———. Interest Groups and Foreign Policy. In *Domestic Sources of Foreign Policy*, edited by James N. Rosenau. New York: The Free Press, 1967.
Miller, Jake C. *The Black Presence in American Foreign Affairs*. Washington, D.C.: University Press of America, 1978.
Minty, Abdul D. Utilizing the System: A Nongovernmental Perspective. In *International Organization: A Conceptual Approach*, edited by Paul Taylor and A. J. R. Groom. New York: Nichols Publishing, 1978.
Mitzman, Barry. The Divestiture Demonstrations. *The Nation*, 13 May 1978.
Molotch, Harvey. Media and Movements. In *The Dynamics of Social Movements*, edited by Mayer N. Zald and John D. McCarthy. Cambridge, Mass.: Winthrop Publishers, 1979.
Myers, Desaix, III, et al. *U.S. Business in South Africa: The Economic, Political, and Moral Issues*. Bloomington: Indiana University Press, 1980.
NARMIC. *Automating Apartheid: U.S. Computer Exports to South Africa and the Arms Embargo*. Philadelphia: American Friends Service Committee, 1982.
National Lawyers Guild, Eugene Chapter. Remarks on Divestment Legislation and Language. Mimeographed. Eugene, Oregon, 6 March 1981.
Nesbitt, Prexy. Anti-Apartheid Activities in the United States of America: A Rising Tide. United Nations Centre Against Apartheid Notes and Documents, December 1977.
———. That Tens of Thousands March with Us. Toward

the Formulation of New Strategies for International Action Against Transnational Corporate Collaboration with Apartheid. Paper presented at the International Seminar on the Role of Transnational Corporations in South Africa, London, 2–4 November 1979.

———. Taking Stock: A Call for a Conference to Review Anti-Apartheid Work. *Southern Africa* (March 1980).

Nessen, Joshua. From Campus to Capetown: Student Movement Broadens its Base. *Dollars and Sense* 96(April 1984): 15–17.

New York Times. Yale Seniors Limit Use of Class Fund. 15 December 1983, Section 2, 2.

———. South Africa Draws Investors. 3 November 1982.

———. 21 July 1981; 2 June 1978

Nickel, Herman. The Case for Doing Business in South Africa. *Fortune* (19 June 1978): 60–73.

Oberschall, Anthony. *Social Conflict and Social Movements*. Englewood Cliffs, N.J.: Prentice-Hall, 1973.

Obuszewski, Max. The South African Face Lift. *ICCR Brief* 12, No. 10(1983): 3A–3D.

Ogene, F. Chidozie. *Interest Groups and the Shaping of Foreign Policy: Four Case Studies of United States African Policy*. New York: St. Martin's, 1983.

O'Meara, Dan. *Volkskapitalisme: Class, Capital and Ideology in the Development of Afrikaner Nationalism 1934–1948*. New York: Cambridge University Press, 1983.

O'Neil, William A. Letter to the Honorable Barbara B. Kennelly, Secretary State. Hartford, 1 July 1981.

Patton, Michael Quinn. *Utilization-Focused Evaluation*. Beverly Hills, Calif.: Sage, 1978.

People for Southern African Freedom. Notes on the Divestment Issue: Oregon State System of Higher Education. Mimeographed. Eugene, Oregon.

Perry, Joseph B., Jr., and M. D. Pugh. *Collective Behavior: Response to Social Stress*. New York: West Publishing, 1978.

Piven, Frances Fox, and Richard A. Cloward. *Poor People's Movements: Why They Succeed, How They Fail*. New York: Pantheon Books, 1977.

Polman, Dick. Victim of Apartheid Knows Effects of Investment. *Hartford Courant,* 18 July 1981.

———. O'Neil is Deaf to Lawmakers' Call to Divest. *Hartford Courant,* 6 April 1982.

———. Going Through the Motions Over Apartheid. *Hartford Courant,* 8 April 1982.

Porter, Richard C. Economic Sanctions: The Theory and the Evidence from Rhodesia. *Journal of Peace Science* 3,

No. 2(Fall 1978): 93–110.

———. International Trade and Investment Sanctions: Potential Impact on the South African Economy. *Journal of Conflict Resolution* 23, No. 4(December 1979): 579–612.

Rand Daily Mail, 3 July 1981.

Republic of South Africa. Department of Foreign Affairs and Information of South Africa. *Official Yearbook of the Republic of South Africa.* 10th ed. Johannesburg, South Africa: Chris Van Rensburg Publications, 1984.

Richards, Trevor. Apartheid in Sports: Business as Usual. United Nations Centre Against Apartheid Notes and Documents, August 1977.

Richter, Maurice. South African Program Postponed, Adviser Says. *The State News.* East Lansing, 6 May 1977.

Rogers, Barbara, and Brian Bolton. *Sanctions Against South Africa: Exploding the Myths.* Manchester, England: Manchester Free Press, 1981.

Rogers, Barbara. *White Wealth and Black Poverty: American Investment in Southern Africa.* Westport, Conn.: Greenwood Press, 1976.

Rosenau, James. *Public Opinion and Foreign Policy.* New York: Random House, 1961.

———. *National Leadership and Foreign Policy.* Princeton: Princeton University Press, 1963.

———. *Linkage Politics: Essays on the Convergence of National and International Systems.* New York: Free Press, 1969.

Rosenthal, Alan. *Legislative Life.* New York: Harper and Row, 1981.

Rossi, Peter H., Howard E. Freeman, and Sonia R. Wright. *Evaluation: A Systematic Approach.* Beverly Hills, Calif.: Sage Publications, 1979.

Rothmeyer, Karen. The South Africa Lobby. *The Nation,* 19 April 1980.

Roux, Edward. *Time Longer Than Rope: A History of the Black Man's Struggle for Freedom in South Africa.* Madison: University of Wisconsin Press, 1964.

Sale, Kirkpatrick. *SDS.* New York: Random House, 1973.

The Sanctions Working Group. Toward An Effective Oil Embargo of South Africa. *Monthly Review* 32, No. 7(1980): 58–62.

Saul, John S., and Stephen Gelb. *The Crisis in South Africa: Class Defense, Class Revolution.* New York: Monthly Review, 1981.

Schmidt, Elizabeth. *Decoding Corporate Camouflage: U.S. Business Support for Apartheid.* Washington, D.C.:

Institute for Policy Studies, 1980.

Segal, Ronald, ed. *Sanctions Against South Africa.* Harmondsworth, England: Penguin, 1964.

Seidman, Ann, and Neva Seidman. *South Africa and U.S. Multinational Corporations.* Westport, Conn.: Lawrence Hill, 1977.

Shepherd, George W., Jr. *Anti-Apartheid: Transnational Conflict and Western Policy in the Liberation of South Africa.* Westport, Conn.: Greenwood Press, 1977.

Simon, Herbert. *The Sciences of the Artificial.* Cambridge: MIT Press, 1969.

Simon, John G., Charles W. Powers, and Jon P. Gunnemann. *The Ethical Investor: Universities and Corporate Responsibility.* New Haven: Yale University Press, 1972.

Sjollema, Baldwin. *Isolating Apartheid.* Geneva: The World Council of Churches, 1982.

Skjelsbaek, Kjell. The Growth of International Non-governmental Organization in the Twentieth Century. In *Transnational Relations and World Politics,* edited by Keohane and Nye. Cambridge: Harvard University Press, 1972.

Skolnick, Jerome H. *The Politics of Protest.* New York: Simon and Schuster, 1969.

Smelser, Neil J. *Theory of Collective Behavior.* New York: The Free Press, 1962.

Soriano, John. Alternative Fund Set Up at Princeton. *New York Times,* 22 January 1984, Section 11, 12.

Southern Africa Project of Lawyers Committee For Civil Rights Under the Law. *Annual Report.* Washington, D.C., 1983.

Spandau, Arnt. *Economic Boycott Against South Africa: Normative and Factual Issues.* Johannesburg, South Africa: Juta and Company, Ltd, 1983.

State News, East Lansing, 30 March 1977; 31 March 1977; 12 May 1977; 5 August 1977.

Stechuk, Bob. Support State Bills Controlling South African Ties. *The Michigan Daily,* 1980.

Stefani, Patti David. U.S. Government Rebuked for Aiding Repressive Policy. *The State News.* East Lansing, 9 November 1981.

Stoltenberg, Thorvald. Nordic States and South Africa: Initiatives for Action Against Apartheid. United Nations Centre Against Apartheid Notes and Documents, March 1978.

Strack, Harry R. *Sanctions: The Case of Phodesia.* New York: Syracuse University Press, 1978.

Study Commission on U.S. Policy Toward Southern Africa.

South Africa: Time Running Out. Berkeley: University of California Press, 1981.

Sylvan, Donald A. Planning Foreign Policy Systematically: Mathematical Foreign Policy Planning. *Journal of Conflict Resolution* 23, No. 1(March 1979).

Symphony for Apartheid. *Drum* (November 1982): 78–86.

Taylor, Paul, and A. J. R. Groom. *International Organization: A Conceptual Approach*. New York: Nichols Publishing, 1978.

Teutsch, Clifford. State Unit Asks Curbs on Investment Policy. *Hartford Courant,* 21 April 1982.

Tharp, Lawrence. Citizens, Experts and Corporations to Meet at Apartheid Hearing. *Detroit Free Press,* 3 April 1977.

Thibault, Ray, and Bill Derman. ASMSU Fails Test on Africa. *The State News.* East Lansing, 15 April 1977.

Thompson, Leonard, and Andrew Prior. *South African Politics*. New Haven: Yale University Press, 1982.

Thompson, Leonard, and Jeffrey Butler. *Change in Contemporary South Africa*. Berkeley: University of California Press, 1975.

Turner, Ralph H. The Public Perception of Protest. *American Sociological Review* 34, No. 6(December 1969): 815–31.

United Nations. United Nations Trust Fund for South Africa. New York, 1981.

United Nations Centre Against Apartheid. Notes and Documents. Over Two Thousand Mayors From Fifty-Four Countries Call For Immediate Release of Nelson Mandela and other South African Political Prisoners. New York, August 1982.

———. Nordic Countries Support Action Against Apartheid in South Africa. New York, November 1976.

———. International Trade Union Action Against Apartheid: Recent Developments. New York, June 1977.

———. Actions By Nongovernmental Organizations in the Implementation of UN Resolutions on the Problem of Apartheid. New York, March 1978.

———. State and Local Legislative Action on South Africa. New York, January 1981.

———. *Newsletter.* January 1982.

United Nations Centre Against Apartheid. Appeal by Martin King, Jr. for an International Boycott of South Africa. New York, 1982.

United Nations Commission on Transnational Corporations. Studies on the Effects of the Operations and Practices of Transnational Corporations. New York, June 1983.

United Nations Economic and Social Council, Commission on

Human Rights. *The Role of the Sub-Commission in the Implementation of the Programme for the Decade for Action to Combat Racism and Racial Discrimination.* New York, 22 June 1978.

United States Consulate General. American Firms, Subsidiaries and Affiliates—South Africa. Johannesburg, 1981.

United States Department of Commerce. *Survey of Current Business.* Washington, D.C.: Government Printing Office, 1958–83.

United States Department of Education. *Financial Statistics of Institutions of Higher Education.* Prepared by the National Center for Education Statistics. Washington, D.C.: Government Printing Office, 1980.

———. *Digest of Education Statistics.* Washington, D.C.: Government Printing Office, 1982.

United States Office of the Federal Register. *Code of Federal Regulations.* Washington, D.C.: Government Printing Office, 1981.

United States Congress. Committee on Foreign Relations, Subcommittee on African Affairs. *U.S. Corporate Interest in Africa.* 95th Cong., 1st sess. Washington, D.C.: Government Printing Office, 1978.

Vandenbosch, Amry. *South Africa and the World.* Lexington: University of Kentucky Press, 1970.

Vogel, David. *Lobbying the Corporation: Citizen Challenges to Business Authority.* New York: Basic Books, 1978.

Von Bothmer, Lenelotte. Opposition to Apartheid in the Federal Republic of Germany. United Nations Centre Against Apartheid Notes and Documents, March 1981.

Wall Street Journal, 16 April 1984; 29 May 1984.

Wallensteen, Peter. Characteristics of Economic Sanctions. In *A Multi-Method Introduction of Internation Politics,* edited by William D. Coplin and Charles W. Kegley, 128–54. Chicago: Markham, 1971.

Washington Office on Africa. *Washington Notes on Africa.* Washington, D.C.: Summer 1982.

———. *Washington Notes on Africa.* Washington, D.C.: Autumn 1982

———. *Washington Notes on Africa.* Washington, D.C.: Winter 1984.

Weiss, Carol. *Evaluation Research: Methods of Assessing Program Effectiveness.* Englewood Cliffs, N.J.: Prentice-Hall, 1972.

Wilkinson, Paul. *Social Movement.* New York: Praeger, 1971.

Wilson, Monica, and Leonard Thompson. *A History of South Africa to 1870.* Boulder, Colo.: Westview Press, 1983.

Wilson, John. *Introduction to Social Movements*. New York: Basic Books, 1973.

Wisconsin Office of the Attorney General. *Opinions of the Attorney General*. Vol. 67. Madison, 1978.

Zald, Mayer, and Roberta Ash. Social Movements Organizations: Growth, Decay and Change. *Social Forces* 44(1966): 327–41.

Zald, Mayer N., and John D. McCarthy, eds. *The Dynamics of Social Movements: Resource Mobilization, Social Control, and Tactics*. Cambridge: Winthrop Publishers, 1979.

Zeigler, L. Harmon, and G. Wayne Peak. *Interest Groups in American Society*. Englewood Cliffs, N.J.: Prentice-Hall, 1964.

Index

About the Author

Janice Love is an assistant professor in the Department of Government and International Studies at the University of South Carolina, where she has taught since 1982. She received her Ph.D. from Ohio State University in 1983 and won the Political Science Department's Bryan Prize for her dissertation. Her other research interests include international political economy, political development, and women in politics.

In addition to her faculty appointment, Dr. Love serves on the Central and Executive Committees of the World Council of Churches, a nongovernmental organization headquartered in Geneva. She is the moderator (chairperson) of the Program Unit on Justice and Service, one of three WCC program units.

DATE DUE